# Tell Me So I Can Hear You

## A Developmental Approach to Feedback for Educators

---

ELEANOR DRAGO-SEVERSON
JESSICA BLUM-DeSTEFANO

Harvard Education Press
Cambridge, Massachusetts

Library of Congress Control Number 2015950420

Paperback ISBN 978-1-61250-881-8
Library Edition ISBN 978-1-61250-882-5

Published by Harvard Education Press,
an imprint of the Harvard Education Publishing Group

Harvard Education Press
8 Story Street
Cambridge, MA 02138

Cover Design: Ciano Design
The typefaces used in this book are ITC Stone Serif, ITC Stone Sans, and Filosofia

*For the many generous people who have
offered us feedback with love and care,
and for all who dedicate themselves nobly
to the support and growth of others.*

# Contents

# CHAPTER 1

## A Developmental Approach to Feedback

*Alone we can do so little; together we can do so much.*

—HELEN KELLER

Feedback is more important in education today than ever before. As high-stakes decisions in schools and districts increasingly rely on performance evaluations and other standardized measures of success, educators across the system—principals, assistant principals, coaches, teachers, district leaders, and more—are being asked to help other adults improve their practice through feedback. Indeed, there is a growing sense that feedback can and should be a powerful tool for educational change. When done well, for instance, feedback can directly inform and support improved instruction and instructional leadership. It can also help educators across roles more effectively create and sustain cultures of learning in their schools, districts, and teams. Put most simply and profoundly, feedback can help all of us grow.

Yet providing effective, meaningful, and actionable feedback can be challenging for teachers and leaders throughout the system. After all, doing so requires complex organizational, theoretical, pedagogical, and content-area expertise, and—less frequently recognized but just as important—it requires the ability to deliver and relay feedback *in ways others can actually hear and take in.*

Toward this end, this book introduces a new, developmental approach to feedback that we call *feedback for growth.* Drawing from and extending Robert Kegan's constructive-developmental theory, which outlines the process and trajectory of development in adulthood, our conceptualization of feedback for growth is grounded in the premise—borne out by research—that adulthood is not a monolithic or static life stage.[1] Adults are not "done" learning and growing simply because they've reached an age of maturity. In fact, there is great developmental diversity in terms of how adults make sense of their work, lives, and relationships. We often describe these different orientations to thinking, perceiving, understanding, and being—or ways of knowing—as the *lenses* through which adults see and interpret their worlds.

You will learn more about the different ways of knowing throughout this book, but for now it might be helpful to know that adults with different ways of knowing orient to and prioritize different things, such as meeting concrete needs, the expectations of valued others, or their own ideals and judgments. A developmental approach to feedback recognizes that adults with different ways of knowing will need different kinds of supports and challenges in order to fully hear, understand, and implement feedback as they grow and learn over time. Similarly, adults with different ways of knowing will have different styles of providing feedback—which may or may not dovetail with the developmental needs of the people on the receiving end.

To be most effective, then, feedback must take into account the different developmental capacities of *both* feedback givers and receivers. It must help us to meet each other where we are developmentally, and to nurture a deeper awareness of how we and others are making sense of the exchange. Yet, despite the great promise of a developmental perspective for enhancing feedback and communication, these ideas—and their implications—have been largely missing from the feedback literature. Accordingly, this book offers practical, developmental strategies for improving performance and building capacity in our schools and organizations through our feedback—and in our lives more generally.

With this in mind, we call our approach *feedback for growth* because it explicitly recognizes the expansion of our own and others' developmental capacities as central to the experience of good feedback. By "developmental capacities" we are referring to the cognitive, affective (emotional), intrapersonal (self-to-self), and interpersonal (self-to-other) abilities that we bring to problems of practice, relationships with others, and the larger value propositions we generate and encounter every day. These capacities—which you might also think of as our stores of internal reserves and perspectives—likewise influence how we orient to feedback; the kinds of feedback we need to grow, learn, and improve in our work; and our abilities to manage the mounting complexities of learning, teaching, leading, and living. Promisingly, when provided with the appropriate supports and challenges, we can continue to grow our developmental capacities over time—regardless of our roles and hierarchical positions—in order to more effectively see into and manage the complex challenges associated with improving education.

As we will share throughout this book, our conceptualization of feedback for growth stems from and expands our previous work about learning-oriented leadership and leadership development, and offers a close-up look at feedback as an ongoing process that can both strengthen performance and build internal capacity.[2] For example, and as we will continue to explore, a developmental approach to feedback can help you:

- better meet adults "where they are" developmentally, so that communications can best be heard and understood;
- offer more constructive, helpful, and effective feedback during evaluations and other meetings (both formal and informal) that attends to both performance and developmental capacity;
- bolster collaboration so that it is even more meaningful and productive—and so that teachers and other educators can work together more effectively and constructively (e.g., in teams, in peer-to-peer observations, and in professional learning communities [PLCs]);
- understand how your own development influences your capacities to give and receive feedback; and
- grow through the processes of giving and receiving feedback to support internal capacity building and performance (these are intimately connected), both for yourself and others.

Ultimately, by highlighting the ever-present but underrecognized developmental dimensions of feedback that operate just below the surface of almost any feedback exchange, this book expands the conversation about feedback and presents a promising roadmap for making feedback more meaningful, actionable, and growth-enhancing for all participants.

## NEW FEEDBACK IMPERATIVES

In our work with educators and leaders of all kinds, we have experienced what feels like a universal urgency around feedback. More specifically, as mounting policy initiatives and practical imperatives push this vital aspect of leadership and collaboration front and center, principals, assistant principals, district-level leaders, teacher leaders, coaches, mentors, university professors, and professional developers emphasize that they want and *need* to get better at this important work.

In particular, today's policies around new teacher and principal evaluations, the Common Core State Standards, Race to the Top funding, and other initiatives have heightened the exigencies of giving and receiving feedback for educators within schools and across the system to achieve instructional excellence.[3] For example, between 2011 and 2013, almost every state in the US ushered in dramatic changes to its teacher evaluation systems—and, in ways both big and small, collaboration continues to infuse our educational milieu as part of the "New Normal" of contemporary life.[4] Everywhere one looks, new feedback measures and approaches—such as 360-degree feedback, S.M.A.R.T. goals, mini-observations, the Danielson framework, peer-to-peer feedback in teams and PLCs, instructional "rounds" and learning walks—all seek to improve student learning by framing, structuring, and delivering feedback to educators in strategic ways.[5] Within the realm of teacher education, too, administrators and evaluators have been found to use more kinds of feedback and outcome measures to assess program performance than leaders in any other profession.[6]

Despite this proliferation of feedback (formative and summative, formal and informal) throughout the education world, there remains a growing sense that we need to do something *different* in terms of feedback, not just something *more*. For one thing, the impact of the growing emphasis on professional feedback seems mixed at best.[7] In a recent empirical analysis, for instance, Hallinger, Heck, and Murphy pointed out that "there is remarkably little evidence that associates the new generation of teacher evaluation with capacity development of teachers or more consistent growth in the learning outcomes of teachers."[8] Importantly, this mixed bag of results extends beyond formal evaluation systems to include other forms of mentoring and collaboration—as educators often report that they are thrust into collaborative scenarios with little support or training about how to best work together in these new and essential ways.

Speaking to this point, research is beginning to suggest that educators in some contexts may be getting *too much* feedback, as it is not uncommon for teachers to receive different (and sometimes even conflicting) feedback from supervisors, mentors or coaches, colleagues, value-added measures, and other data streams (e.g., student and parent ratings, self-assessment tools).[9] Practitioners, too, increasingly report that these mountains of feedback do not necessarily translate into improved performance, as it can be difficult to filter, make sense of, prioritize, or even understand the large amounts of feedback they encounter, let alone act upon it.[10]

In other cases, a *lack* of quality feedback seems to be creating a different kind of problem for educators hoping to grow themselves and others.

For example, not too long ago, a staggering 74 percent of teachers who participated in a study of twelve large US districts reported that they received virtually *no* feedback or suggestions on their summative evaluations.[11] Likewise, research has documented the steadily disappointing dearth of feedback for teachers containing actionable specifics or meaningful opportunities for reflection and analysis.[12]

While these different feedback challenges inarguably have multiple roots and causes, we find it significant that teachers and administrators—like so many of us—describe a lingering uneasiness with feedback as an authentic process. Regularly, for instance, educators express that they find it difficult to make their feedback "stick" despite their best and most earnest efforts.[13] Some confide that they feel uncomfortable giving honest feedback to colleagues, as they worry it may damage relationships or cause tension. Others struggle to break the habit of giving feedback just as they themselves would like to receive it—even when their preferred feedback styles (e.g., very direct, crisp feedback, or feedback cushioned by positive affirmations) don't always work for everyone in their care. Still other educators explain that they repeat their feedback messages over and over again, striving for consistency and fairness, but repeatedly run up against what feels like resistance and frustration on the part of colleagues. Despite these educators' best and most thoughtful feedback efforts, they concede that things are not working as well as they'd like. Given the growing awareness that ineffective feedback can actually push employees to be *less* committed and/or more withholding of their best ideas, looking anew at feedback through a developmental lens can help all of us do and see feedback better as we strive to reach common educational goals.[14]

## A DEVELOPMENTAL PERSPECTIVE

It is our contention that a developmental perspective can help shed light on the very important feedback challenges, patterns, and statistics just described. Time and again, when we work with educational leaders of all kinds, we notice that their questions and concerns about feedback have developmental dimensions. For example, leaders frequently report the following feedback challenges:

- "It's hard for me to care for both the emotional and intellectual aspects of feedback in the moment."
- "Sometimes I don't feel comfortable sharing my honest thoughts and feelings with my supervisees."

- "Giving unsolicited or informal feedback is really hard, especially when I'm not in a supervisory role."
- "I find it challenging to refrain from criticizing or judging."
- "I'm working to remain mindful of my own internal states and capacities during feedback exchanges."
- "I want to get better at approaching conflict and difference as opportunities for growth, rather than moments to be avoided."
- "I want to learn more about how and why others interpret my feedback so differently."
- "One big goal I have for improving my feedback is balancing supports with constructive challenges."
- "I'm coming to see that my feedback style and preference may not suit everyone equally."
- "It's hard to simultaneously support *and* evaluate my colleagues' practice."
- "I'm never quite sure how best to follow up after giving feedback or receiving feedback."

As we will describe, these and other challenges related to giving and receiving feedback can actually be developmental in nature. By this we mean that these challenges can stem from a mismatch or misunderstanding of the internal, developmental capacities of the feedback giver and/or receiver. Accordingly, a deeper understanding of the developmental dimensions of feedback—and the qualitatively different ways of knowing in adulthood—can help us to effectively differentiate the kinds of supports and challenges we employ during feedback to best support the adults in our care.

Importantly, though, "appropriate" supports and challenges will look and feel different to people with different ways of knowing. To further illustrate this key point, it can be helpful to think of one's way of knowing as the audio frequency with which one speaks or hears. Put another way, you could imagine the range of feedback an individual receives from others as the different radio stations on an old-fashioned dial radio (remember those?). When not broadcast in ways "tuned into" the recipient's developmental orientations, feedback might sound more like static—or those in-between channels that don't quite come in clearly. On the other hand, when feedback is offered in ways that adults with different ways of knowing can actually hear and understand, it's more like finding that magical place on the dial where, suddenly, the music comes in loud and clear. And, if you're lucky, your favorite song is playing!

Like one's taste in music, ways of knowing can feel more like a manifestation of who one *is* than something one *has*. Yet, unlike our musical preferences, human development seems to follow a particular progression and order throughout the lifespan, with each way of knowing reflecting an increased capacity to stand back and reflect on oneself and one's work. While each way of knowing in adulthood has both strengths and limitations (and adults will move to and through these stages at different rates and trajectories), the transition to each new way of knowing reflects a significant expansion of a person's internal, developmental capacities. Because the mounting challenges we face in education today call for increases in these capacities over time, understanding the patterns of meaning making in adulthood can inform how we support and challenge each other—so that we *all* have deeper wells of self and interconnection to draw from. The real hopefulness of this approach and this book, then, rests on the fact that adults can and, most often, *want* to grow and learn—both when giving and receiving feedback and in general. Supporting growth, development, or transformational learning (we use these terms interchangeably) *is* possible and necessary in our schools and districts. And employing feedback for growth is one very promising path toward this essential and hopeful outcome.

## INTRODUCTORY EXAMPLE: LEDA'S FEEDBACK CHALLENGE

To ground some of the developmental dimensions of giving and receiving feedback in a real-life example, next we share the story of Leda, a district-level leader who bumped up against a very common feedback challenge in her important work supporting and coaching school principals. While the internal challenge Leda experienced resonates in profound ways with the stories and experiences of many of the principals, teacher leaders, and coaches with whom we've had the honor of working, her example also helps to highlight the key point that enacting a developmental approach to feedback involves looking inward—toward our *own* developmental capacities and preferences as feedback givers—just as much as looking outward, toward recipients'.

When Leda first assumed her position as a district-level coach, she confided that she felt uneasy offering direct feedback to her principals. While she had a great deal of expertise and insight to share, she worried that being too direct might upset her new colleagues or otherwise damage her ability to be genuinely helpful and supportive. Because of her hesitancies, however, Leda found herself holding back her best ideas and suggestions, and felt increasingly torn about her effectiveness.

After a conversation with Leda, it became clear that her worries about giving feedback were influenced as much by her own internal sense making—her underlying assumptions and constructions about feedback, authority, and relationships—as they were by her experiences with the principals themselves. More specifically, Leda had not yet developed the internal capacity to step back from her relationships with the principals, as her sense of self and success were so closely bound up with their affirmations and approval. Accordingly, "conflict" with these valued others felt too threatening and uncomfortable to her, and sharing her true thinking and feeling felt like too big of a risk. Yet, after several months of developmental coaching, Leda gradually came to realize that sharing her honest thinking with the principals wouldn't destroy her professional relationships. In fact, she realized, it could help her to push the work further! Learning and experiencing this—by "trying it on" in practice in safe ways over time—proved to be a great relief for Leda, and also a promising opening to her own growth and improved coaching and feedback giving.

## CAPACITY VERSUS EXPERTISE

As evidenced in Leda's example, leaders' internal capacities to offer feedback can be just as important as the content of what they share and the nature of their expertise. For example, Leda often had the skills, knowledge, and information needed to support principals to be more effective in their supervisory work with teachers, yet it was only *after* she developed her internal capacity to share what she was actually thinking (and to understand that the principals in her care were themselves ready for this kind of exchange) that she could most effectively help the principals improve their practice. In Leda's example, just as in life, expertise and capacity *both* matter immensely when one is giving and receiving feedback—and they need to work in tandem in order to strengthen an organization's or system's complex network of relationships and expertise.

As an alternate example, a school principal could be an expert on literacy initiatives, interpreting achievement data, or mathematics pedagogy, but if the principal did not have the *capacity* to communicate ideas and suggestions in ways others could understand and ultimately implement to improve practice, the students, staff, and school community would not benefit from this expertise. Likewise, if a teacher leader felt comfortable sharing best practices with only a few teachers, many colleagues would miss the opportunity to grow and learn from this leader's most effective work. Ultimately, then, while we need to understand key content and skills in order to guide another's improvement and practice (i.e., we need a good handle on the *what* of feedback), we must simultaneously build capacity around *how* we give feedback in order to harness and maximize educators' diverse gifts across the system.

Let's dive a bit deeper into this distinction between expertise and capacity, as it can shed light on two different but equally important kinds of learning needed to grow and improve our feedback. As we have discussed, expertise is a fundamental part of good and effective feedback. As leaders and feedback givers, we must keep abreast of the most recent and relevant content in order to be of best help. This is what we refer to as *informational learning*—and it is related to increasing our funds of knowledge and skills.[15] Put another way, informational learning is learning that relates to leveling up the knowledge, content, skills, and information we have—or *what* we know—and this is vital to being able to offer feedback that can help improve practice. While this type of learning is necessary in order to bring about changes in adults' skills, knowledge bases, attitudes, and competencies (e.g., employing higher-order questioning techniques, developing assessment rubrics that align with the Common Core State Standards, interpreting value-added scores or student data reports, or even learning the fundamentals of adult developmental theory), knowing more *may not be enough* if it is not coupled with an internal capacity for change.

Just as we saw with Leda's experience offering feedback to principals, sometimes what is most needed is an increase in our internal leadership capacities—or what we call *transformational learning*.[16] This different kind of learning involves changes in *how* we make sense of and interpret our experiences (including the ability to give or receive feedback), and is characterized by increases in our cognitive, affective, interpersonal, and/or intrapersonal capacities.

When transformational learning or growth occurs, there is a qualitative change in the structure of a person's way of knowing, not just what he or she knows. Psychologically speaking, this person has grown a larger and more complex self. Such growth enables adults to take a bigger and broader perspective on themselves, others, and the relationship between the two. Importantly, the more perspective we can take on ourselves (i.e., the deeper we can see into and understand our thinking, feeling, being, and acting), the more perspective we can take on others and our relationships with them. Related to this, the more perspective we can take on ourselves in relationship to and with others, the better able we are to manage the enormous challenges and opportunities of teaching, learning, leading, and exchanging feedback in today's world.

## ADAPTIVE VERSUS TECHNICAL CHALLENGES

Related to the important distinction between informational and transformational learning, Harvard psychiatrist and leadership development scholar Ronald Heifetz, who has devoted many years of his professional career to increasing capacity in organizations and societies, makes a valuable and powerful distinction between what he refers to as "technical" and "adaptive" challenges.[17] In fact, he and his colleague Martin Linsky maintain that leaders are increasingly encountering adaptive challenges in today's world.[18]

So what are technical and adaptive challenges? And what kind of learning—informational or transformational—can help us manage these and the many kinds of challenges mentioned previously (new teacher and principal evaluation systems, the rollout of the Common Core State Standards, new policy mandates, etc.)?

Technical challenges, Heifetz, Linsky, and Alexander Grashow explain, are challenges for which we can clearly identify both the problem and the solution.[19] In these situations, even if we do not have the skills, knowledge base, expertise, tools, or training to address the challenge ourselves, we can discern *what* the problem is, and we can find someone—such as an expert or specialist (or even an Internet poster!)—who knows how to address and fix it.

Undeniably, though, in today's complex and ever-changing educational world, we are facing an increasing number of adaptive challenges, which Heifetz characterizes as murkier and harder to define. For these problems and situations, no one—not even an expert—has a ready-made solution. To meet these profound and complex challenges, he and colleagues maintain that new approaches, capacities, and tools are needed. We must, for instance, have the internal capacity to manage the enormous complexity and ambiguity that are hallmarks of adaptive situations.[20] In addition, we must be able to solve problems *in the act of working on them*.[21]

It's important to note that informational learning, as you might suspect, can help us to manage the many important technical challenges we face in our work. It is also vital to understand that we need transformational learning (i.e., changes in *how* we know rather than *what* we know) to most effectively manage the mounting adaptive challenges in our current educational context—as well as those on the horizon. Significantly, research suggests that only 20–25 percent of us can spontaneously exercise the kinds of higher-order internal capacities needed for adaptive teaching, learning, collaborating, and leading today.[22] As this startling statistic makes clear, supporting adult development in our schools and organizations can make a big difference—but we cannot do this work alone. We need each other's help to grow and learn, and we need to support both informational and transformational learning through our feedback in order to develop the capacity to embrace and enact change.[23]

## A NOTE ABOUT CONTEXT

Of course, effective feedback (both in terms of content and a developmental approach) needs to take place in some *context*, so it is also important to consider the many organizational roles and structures that can influence a school's larger culture of feedback—including hierarchical relationships as well as how and by whom feedback is used. In addition, the culture of power in schools and districts is important to consider, since we know that feedback can feel different when it is tied to different sources (e.g., authority figures, policy makers, department chairs, leaders of PLCs, coaches, parents, students, trusted colleagues, or newcomers to an organization).

Likewise, we know that feedback can take place in many different ways—including formal observations and walkthroughs, informal encounters, private and public meetings, and various administrative routines. In all of these cases, the interpersonal and group dynamics can be multifaceted and multidirectional in terms of who is positioned as both the giver and receiver of feedback. A principal, for example, may give feedback to a large group, such as a department, or to a small group, such as a PLC. This sort of feedback is different from the intragroup feedback that occurs when members of a school improvement team or department are attempting to give feedback to each other. While all of these are important, we begin this book with the assertion that *the relationship between two people is the most important starting place for considering feedback for growth*. Toward this end, this book begins by illuminating the developmental underpinnings of self and other on an individual level, and then moves toward a more global approach for supporting larger groups and communities of adults.

In the end, however, and regardless of one's organizational or positional context, our construction of feedback for growth rests on the fundamental belief that growth is a worthy and noble aim of feedback—that it is indeed something worth giving and getting feedback "for." We hope you find the ideas, processes, and strategies outlined in this book helpful as we work to meet the pressing and unprecedented challenges at our door, and as we carve out—together—new possibilities for education and school improvement.

## A BRINGING TOGETHER OF VOICES:
## OUR FEEDBACK COLLABORATION

We want to emphasize right up front that we have seen a developmental approach to feedback work! I (Ellie) have had the honor of investing more than twenty years into teaching, researching, and consulting with thousands of educational leaders around the globe about the promise and power of leadership that supports adult development. A big part of this work, as you might imagine, involves talking and listening. It involves sharing and taking in—in the most earnest ways possible—new ideas, perspectives, and points of view, and it involves learning with and from educators of all kinds and from all over the world, together. I couldn't be more delighted to share the very best of what I've learned from my research and all of these treasured explorations with educators here with you. I am truly honored.

For more than seven years, Jessica has accompanied me in this journey as a research collaborator, teaching fellow, coinstructor, and writing partner. In all of these different contexts, Jessica has been learning about, employing, and contributing to the kinds of developmental feedback discussed in this book, and it has been our great pleasure to combine our perspectives and expertise to bring this promising feedback approach to life on the page.

Our hope, ultimately, is to raise up the power of developmentally oriented feedback as a tool for helping people grow, and for building instructional and leadership capacity throughout schools and school systems. Accordingly, this book builds upon our research, practical experiences supporting adult development, and key learnings from the feedback literature. And it adds another important layer: it offers educators of all kinds a new approach to improving and diversifying feedback (i.e., differentiating with developmental intentionality) so that others can better hear, take in, and grow from it. This is something that leaders yearn for—and something that we hope supports you, too, in your noble and important work.

We also want to share that, while we present many examples and anecdotes in this book, they draw from experiences and interactions that Jessica and I have had both together and independently. In many instances, we combine real-life details from our teaching and practice with different educators into single, representative scenarios that illustrate a particular aspect of feedback for growth, and we use pseudonyms or anonymously attributed quotations throughout to protect confidentiality, except when someone has asked us to use his or her name.

## ORGANIZATION OF THIS BOOK

Put most simply, this book is designed to guide you through the theory and practice of exchanging feedback for growth. Each step of the way, we draw from on-the-ground examples from educators and leaders of all kinds (principals, assistant principals, teacher leaders, etc.) and describe practical, research-based strategies that you can use to deepen and enhance your practice of growth-oriented feedback. In addition, we include a series of reflective questions in each chapter to help scaffold your thinking and enhance your practice.

We begin this journey by exploring the wider feedback "landscape" and literature in chapter 2. More specifically, given the mounting pressures pushing feedback front and center in educational reform efforts today, chapter 2 highlights many important lessons researchers and practitioners have already taught us about effective, actionable feedback. In addition, it begins to preview how a working knowledge of adult developmental theory can help *complement, deepen, and extend* this critical knowledge base and our practice of giving feedback for growth and improved performance.

In chapters 3, 4, and 5, we introduce the foundational principles of Robert Kegan's constructive-developmental theory, which sheds light on the qualitatively different ways adults make sense of their work and the exchange of feedback.[24] In particular, these chapters focus on (1) the four ways of knowing (or developmental meaning-making systems) found in adulthood, and their connections to our capacities for offering and taking in feedback; (2) the importance of a safe and productive holding environment (i.e., the context or relationship in which growth occurs) when adults are exchanging feedback; and (3) the kinds of supports and challenges (or developmental stretching) that adults with different developmental orientations will need in order to feel *well held* when engaging in any part of the feedback process. We pull these practical and theoretical threads forward and together throughout these chapters (and throughout the book more generally). More specifically, though, chapter 3 introduces key elements of this theoretical base; chapter 4 focuses on the ways our internal capacities will influence our propensities and preferences for taking in feedback; and chapter 5 focuses on how these same internal capacities inevitably connect with our abilities to offer feedback to others in our care.

In chapters 6, 7, 8, and 9, we look more closely at effective feedback approaches, strategies, and processes that can help you meet adults where they are developmentally—before, during, and after feedback. In chapter 6, for instance, we focus on the importance of nurturing the preconditions of trust, safety, and respect *before* engaging in feedback, and we offer a series of suggestions for developing, modeling, and sustaining a genuine culture of feedback that can build capacity in your school, team, or organization.[25] In chapter 7, we highlight the important distinction between constructive and inquiry-oriented feedback, and describe how understanding—and being intentional about—the continuum of purposes underlying feedback can help us frame our messages in the most meaningful, growth-enhancing ways. In chapter 8, we share seven key strategies for offering effective, actionable, in-the-moment feedback that others can truly hear, learn from, and implement. Connected to this, we emphasize in chapter 9 the great importance of following up on feedback in developmentally appropriate ways to support growth over time, and to help the adults in your care bridge feedback and action.

Next, in chapter 10, we stress the foundational importance of seeking out and receiving feedback as a leader (of any kind) in order to grow one's practice and internal capacities. Coming full circle, we present powerful strategies that can help you ask for and learn from feedback of different kinds (e.g., formal, informal) and from different sources (e.g., supervisors, colleagues, supervisees, students, families, and other stakeholders). Seeking out feedback with an open heart and mind, we've found, is one of the most powerful ways to grow as a leader and human being.

Finally, in the epilogue, we offer a few summative reflections about the power and promise of feedback for growth, and introduce a structured opportunity to synthesize and apply learnings from the book to your own practice. It is our hope that this and all that comes before (and after) supports you and your very important work.

## BEGINNING OUR JOURNEY TOGETHER

In the next chapter, we draw from our ongoing research and teaching with educators of all kinds, as well as from the literature about feedback in both the business and education sectors, to further unpack the possibilities and challenges of feedback for growth. In particular, we dive deeper into *why* a developmental approach to feedback is so important and needed at this very moment, and we highlight what researchers, theorists, and educators in the field say about feedback that works (and the challenges that can get in the way). For each focus point, we consider how a developmental lens *complements, deepens, and extends* key learnings with another layer of understanding. More specifically, we offer insight about why, with all we already know about feedback, many still wonder, *Why is feedback so hard—and how can I get better at it?*

Very recently, for example, at the close of a semester-long developmental institute for leaders in New York City, Katie, a principal of a very large middle school, raised her hand to offer this reflection:

> Over the course of the semester, one of the most important things I realized—and my colleagues [fellow principals] here at my table agree—is that supporting adult growth needs to be an even bigger part of our work as leaders. But while it's so important, it's also so hard. We've been talking about how, before this institute, we just sort of expected the adults in our schools to know what to do for kids and how to do it, or at the very least we assumed they'd be ready to give and receive feedback with open hearts. Now, we see that, really, our work—and our challenge—is to help our teachers build capacity so they can build capacity in others. There's nothing more important—or more adaptive—than that!

We share Katie's courageous reflection here, as a next step into our learning journey, because it shines a bright light on the challenge *and* the opportunity of a developmental approach to feedback. It also accords with the sentiments and excitement leaders of all kinds express to us in workshops, university seminars, conferences, and other professional learning sessions that feature developmental ideas. In all of these contexts, educators emphasize and agree that we must exchange feedback that is meaningful, timely, and developmentally oriented if we want to effect the greatest change in our schools.

Now, more than ever, we need each other to learn, and we need each other to grow. Supporting one another *as best as we possibly can* is the promise—and the hope—of feedback for growth.

## CHAPTER SUMMARY AND CONCLUSION

In this chapter, we introduced a new, developmental approach to feedback that we call *feedback for growth*. Given the increasing importance of feedback in education—and the mounting number of adaptive challenges on our doorstep and on the horizon—feedback for growth offers educators and leaders of all kinds a timely, promising approach for building capacity in individuals and organizations. This chapter also included an overview of the book's organization, and a few orienting examples to help illuminate the important connections between feedback and our internal capacities.

As we will explore in chapter 2, a developmental lens also sheds new light on the feedback challenges and strategies currently documented in the wider literature. Specifically, we describe how our developmental approach extends and enhances key learnings from the business and education sectors, and can help all of us give and receive feedback that others can even more effectively hear, take in, and act upon.

## REFLECTIVE QUESTIONS

Please take a moment to consider the following questions, which can be used for private reflection and/or group conversation. You may find it useful to reflect in writing independently first and then to engage in discussion with a colleague or team. These questions are intended to help you and your colleagues consider the ideas discussed in this introductory chapter and how they might inform your practice of giving feedback.

+ What are two of the more important technical and adaptive challenges you encounter in your work?
+ What kinds of informational and transformational learning opportunities do you have to help you with meeting the different kinds of challenges you listed in response to the first question? What additional kinds of opportunities might assist you in managing the complex challenges you encounter?
+ After reading this chapter, what are two or three insights, learnings, or connections that stand out for you about the process of giving and receiving feedback?

## CHAPTER 2

# What Do We Know About Effective Feedback?

*Listen to the voice of others and your voice will more likely get listened to.*

—CONSTANCE CHUKS FRIDAY

Originating in the Industrial Revolution, the term *feedback* was coined as a way to describe the return of energy, momentum, or signals to their point of origin in a mechanical system. It was only after World War II that the word was adopted by the business world to describe processes of performance assessment and management.[1] More specifically, *feedback* came to refer to the process of relaying—or of *feeding back*—information to individuals or groups about their performance in order to inform current and future behaviors in alignment with particular goals or desired results.[2]

Put most simply, feedback is information about others and ourselves, and about our thinking and behaviors (performance-related and otherwise). As Douglas Stone and Sheila Heen, two Harvard Business School lecturers and leading feedback thinkers, described it, "feedback includes any information you get about yourself. In the broadest sense it's how we learn about ourselves from our experiences and from other people—how we learn from life."[3] With this encompassing conceptualization of feedback, you could imagine giving or getting feedback that is deliberate (i.e., intended and presented to inform future actions) or indirect (i.e., reactionary or unconscious, like a valued other's facial expressions or an experiential encounter that teaches an important lesson). You could imagine feedback flowing to, from, and between human beings—both individuals and groups—or back and forth between humans and mechanical systems (e.g., adaptive learning tools or, say, a heart monitor during an exercise routine).

Despite this great variety in the nature and substance of feedback (all of which are important), our focus in this book is on feedback that takes place, intentionally and with care, between two or more people. Resting at the heart of professional learning and improvement efforts, interpersonal or relational feedback of this kind—in both the business and education sectors—is most often conceptualized as a tool to "help employees identify what they are doing well and build on those skills, correct problems, and develop new skills that improve the organizations in which they work."[4] In an article about feedback in *Educational Leadership*, for instance, Grant Wiggins defined feedback as "information about how we are doing in our efforts to reach a goal."[5]

But what *are* the goals and purposes of feedback in education? If the end goal of feedback in education is improved student outcomes and experiences, a developmental frame on feedback may help us even more effectively meet and exceed these important goals. As discussed in chapter 1, we conceptualize feedback for growth as a developmentally oriented exchange of ideas that honors adults' qualitatively different ways of knowing, and that seeks to build internal and organizational capacity, which helps to improve performance. Drawing from a constructive-developmental perspective, we argue that—when approached with developmental intentionality—feedback can enhance our funds of knowledge and skills (i.e., foster informational learning) *while simultaneously* supporting and challenging individuals to build the internal capacity needed to manage education's most complex challenges (i.e., support transformational learning).[6]

By attending to the stages and possibilities of growth in adulthood, a constructive-developmental approach to feedback also helps us see more deeply into ourselves and others, into the nuances of interpersonal dynamics, and into the supports different adults need to grow. In this way, you might think of feedback for growth as a process through which we can cultivate bigger and better selves for our personal, professional, and relational goals and commitments. This is essential because the greater our internal capacities, the more we can bring to our work, to each other, and to our students. Indeed, research has shown that leadership and professional learning that authentically support adult development have been linked to improved student achievement—and students have recognized educators' higher-order capacities as directly supportive of their own learning and success in the classroom.[7]

While we find the whole-person nature of feedback for growth promising and powerful, we want to emphasize that we also see developmentally oriented feedback as an essential part of larger evaluation systems and feed-back processes. In its most fundamental sense, feedback for growth is about helping educators to reach the highest performance standards, expecta-tions, and outcomes. It is about getting and *being* better in our work by in-fusing what we already know and do with new knowledge and sensitivities. In this way, a developmental approach to feedback can help us *pay attention* to potential enhancers and inhibitors of effective communication, supervi-sion, and collaboration, so that all of us can better enact and make good on the noble intentions driving our work.

## PRESSING FEEDBACK CHALLENGES

With the growing emphasis on giving and acting on feedback in educa-tion, researchers and practitioners have identified a number of common feedback challenges in schools and school systems. In this section, we de-scribe some of the biggest challenges to effective feedback named in the literature, and highlight what is known about effective feedback practices. We then go on to discuss how these important strategies and ideas could be further enhanced by a developmental approach.

Challenges to effective feedback include:

- the need for more effective feedback;
- the skill and knowledge of the person delivering feedback;
- the complexities of evaluation in a "culture of nice"; and
- the call for fuller understandings of feedback receivers.[8]

### The Need for More Effective Feedback: Broadening and Deepening Our Approaches

We've learned that when people are asked about feedback, what often comes to mind are their experiences with traditional, top-down communi-cations (e.g., from principals, administrators, or bosses). In fact, for many people, such formal, summative evaluations—those sometimes-anxiety-ridden meetings that address what they're doing well, and what they still need to work on in order to improve—are almost synonymous with feedback. Yet, as Richard DuFour and Robert Marzano argue, this kind of top-down, observation-based feedback "is a low-leverage strategy for im-proving schools, particularly in terms of the time it requires of principals."[9] Put another way, educators and researchers generally agree that the actual impact of principals' formal feedback is disproportionate to the tremen-dous amounts of time and effort principals caringly invest into pre- and post-observation conferences and official written reports.[10] As Kim Marshall succinctly states, "school leaders are spending huge amounts of time on a process that rarely improves classroom teaching."[11]

Principals and other supervisors bring great wisdom and expertise to feedback of all kinds, and we have the deepest respect for the hard and important work they do every day with heart and courage. Yet the well-documented limitations of new evaluation systems suggest that school leaders may not yet have the extra-institutional or professional learning supports they really need to effectively leverage new systems in mandated and hoped-for ways.[12] For example, leaders often share how difficult it can be to support colleagues' growth and professional development (i.e., help educators manage and sustain meaningful change in practice over time) *while also* attending to accountability demands (i.e., confirming or disconfirming an individual's compliance or "success" within a larger system)—especially when these underlying imperatives at times seem to work at cross purposes. Indeed, it is almost as if, in the current system, we are asking educational leaders to do it *all* in their feedback, and to do it well in the shortest period of time and without enough support. As Gera Summerford, the president of the Tennessee Education Association, characterized it, the philosophy behind some emerging evaluation paradigms feels a lot like "taking your car to the mechanic and making him use all of his tools to fix it, regardless of the problem, and expecting him to do it in an hour."[13]

That said, we absolutely recognize top-down and evaluative feedback as vital to educational improvement and change. In fact, one key aim of this book is to shine light on feedback for growth as a promising lens for enriching and expanding these foundational conversations in new, meaningful, and developmental ways. By recognizing and attending to ways of knowing, for instance, leaders can even more effectively meet supervisees where they are developmentally, and can infuse formal feedback processes (and other exchanges) with the developmental intentionality needed to support authentic growth *and* hold adults accountable for performance in compassionate, relational ways.

More specifically, this book responds to a call for broader, deeper, and more effective feedback—both formal and informal, top-down and lateral—in our schools and organizations. To most effectively meet its many purposes, feedback needs to undergo both a quantitative and a qualitative shift. By this we mean that we need to think differently about the technical, logistical aspects of feedback (e.g., the tools we are using, the amount of feedback we are giving) *and* about the kinds of feedback encounters, conversations, and cultures that could more fully encompass our experiences as growing professionals (both formatively and summatively). After all, it is not just about getting *more* or *less* feedback (as we learned in chapter 1), but about getting *better* feedback that more closely aligns with our evolving needs and capacities. Likewise, while current and emerging teacher evaluation systems may be incredibly effective at justifying rewards, promotions, and sanctions for educators, we must augment and supplement these foundational processes in order to more directly translate our feedback into increased human and organizational capacity.[14]

For example, scholars and practitioners now call for increases in content-area specificity during feedback, more involvement of experts or specialists in observing and evaluating teachers, and a general improvement in the applicability and usefulness of the feedback being shared.[15] One influential voice in teacher evaluation, Charlotte Danielson, likewise outlined a number of limitations characteristic of traditional observation/ feedback systems, including (a) the outmoded, checklist-style criteria of many evaluative rubrics, (b) the ubiquity of oversimplified and all-encompassing ranking categories ("needs improvement," "satisfactory," etc.), (c) the lack of differentiation in relation to teachers' career stage or level of experience, (d) the lack of consistency among evaluators, and (e) the one-way "gotcha" kind of feeling sometimes associated with administrative evaluations.[16] Danielson's model, *The Framework for Effective Teaching*, seeks to counter these common pitfalls by structuring and guiding the feedback provided to teachers, and has been adopted by more than twenty states.[17] Depending on where you are in the country or the world, you may already be using it!

In concert with these astute technical critiques, we argue that a developmental perspective can help us further enrich our feedback at every level in service to ongoing change and improvement. For instance, it can help us to see that—in addition to directives, incentives, and sanctions—educators at every step in the process will need carefully tailored supports and challenges that meet them where they are (in the psychological/developmental sense) in order to overcome stasis or ingrained patterns of behavior. In this way, feedback for growth highlights the crucial truth that, in education today, *external* progress depends fundamentally on educators' less visible reserves of *internal* capacities.

## The Skill and Knowledge of the Person Delivering Feedback

Related to the importance of growing educators' internal capacities, there is a call in the field for leaders who are better able "to assess accurately, provide meaningful feedback, and engage teachers in productive conversations about practice."[18] While schools and districts are investing a great deal of time, effort, and money into training leaders on the logistics of new evaluation systems, a strategic approach to growing educators' capacities for authentically supporting self and others through feedback is largely missing from these conversations. As we discussed in chapter 1, content and technical expertise are, for sure, vital components of the equation. And yet we also need to get better at understanding and honoring the different ways people take in, make sense of, and experience feedback, and how we ourselves orient to the process of exchanging ideas and information. Gaining this kind of knowledge and perspective, we have found, is a process that involves both informational and transformational learning (i.e., it involves learning about constructive-developmental theory and related ideas, and also ongoing investment in understanding and growing our internal capacities).

Put another way, a crucial component to the success or failure of feedback is the person in the role of feedback giver. Who that person *is*—in every sense of the word—holds important implications for the way his or her feedback will be interpreted and understood. "Is this a person who can be trusted?" feedback receivers might wonder. "Is this a person who understands me and my needs? Is this a person who can help me?" Inspiringly, many leaders we have learned from and worked with have told us that developing a greater awareness of their *own* preferences for and understandings of feedback (as a necessary complement to more technical skills and expertise) has helped them offer better and more meaningful feedback to others. Doing this kind of "inner work" and learning, they have shared, is both an imperative and an ongoing process.

For example, Mickey, an executive coach whose work is informed by a developmental perspective, explained that he always tries to "remain aware of [his] thoughts, feelings, and inner temperature" while giving feedback:

> Who I am on the inside and everything that entails—my emotional state, my knowledge of adult development, my perception of events, my way of knowing—will influence why and how I give feedback, which will in turn influence how well my feedback is received. For example, am I being reactive? Have I had time to process the situation clearly? Am I too emotionally invested? What's at stake for me? It's so important to think about these questions and hold them in your mind every minute as a coach, especially when your clients are bringing their own needs and perspectives to the work.

As Mickey's example illustrates, and as we will discuss in greater detail, this kind of developmental, reflective awareness *of both self and other* has implications systemwide.

## The Challenges of Offering Feedback in a "Culture of Nice"

Another well-documented challenge related to feedback is the general inclination to avoid or to turn away from hard conversations, even when they're urgently needed. Dubbed the "culture of nice" by Elisa MacDonald, this tendency toward satiating rather than disruptive feedback manifests in many ways in the education world and beyond.[19] MacDonald discusses how honest discourse, in general, and especially among teachers and within teacher teams, is essential to shifting school culture. Educators must be able to provide feedback and to feel safe and comfortable challenging one another's thinking, beliefs, assumptions, and practice as well as their own. This, she rightly maintains, requires the willingness to be vulnerable and a deep sense of trust. In addition, educators must nurture teams and the spaces where they can work in these authentic ways, which MacDonald refers to as *vulnerability-based trust*.[20] This means that educators must be willing to expose their challenges, mistakes, and questions—as well as their hopes, strengths, and successes—and be comfortable discussing *all* of these with their colleagues. In essence, she states that educators "must be willing to tell the truth," or educators and teachers in teams "will [only] go through the motions of collaborative inquiry but never see results."[21]

Unfortunately, these limiting effects can dramatically impede the effectiveness of feedback as well. For example, the New Teacher Project's 2009 landmark report, "The Widget Effect: Our National Failure to Acknowledge and Act on Differences in Teacher Effectiveness," found that the vast majority of teachers in America—upward of 99 percent in some districts—are rated as "satisfactory," usually by their own principals. Indeed, and as we mentioned above, enduring norms of affirmation have been shown to limit critical conversations between adults in schools and other organizations, and the apparent universality of positive teacher evaluations amid stagnating achievement scores has drawn the ire of both the media and politicians.[22] Importantly, this phenomenon of "niceness" is not limited to education. In a recent study conducted in the business world, for instance, 63 percent of surveyed executives explained that their biggest challenge to effective performance management was the fact that their managers lacked "the courage and ability to have difficult feedback discussions."[23]

Leaders on the ground in different fields similarly acknowledge the challenging dynamics of offering other adults difficult or critical feedback. As Dami, a principal from a middle school in Dubai, recently confided, "If I'm honest in offering feedback, I think it will ruin my relationships with teachers." Maura, the principal of a very large middle school in the Bronx, similarly lamented, "I cannot offer critical feedback—if I do my teachers won't like me, and my colleagues won't work well with me." This is not only true for principals (and we know that it is not true for all principals): we have also learned that coaches, teacher leaders, and district-level leaders often experience similar internal challenges when they need to give feedback to those they supervise and even those who supervise them.

While there are many possible reasons for the enduring culture of nice in schools, one is that the developmental orientations (or ways of knowing) of both those who give feedback and those who receive it can perpetuate these kinds of norms. As we will discuss in greater detail in chapter 3, norms of niceness may reflect more than an overreliance on politeness or rules of etiquette, because the ability to comfortably manage conflict or criticism is in fact a developmental capacity. More specifically, research suggests that, for the large majority of adults, conflict can be experienced as a significant threat to the very fabric of one's identity and relationships.[24] Promisingly, a developmental perspective also sheds light on the potential for all adults to grow the capacities for effectively managing conflict— given the appropriate supports and challenges—and for better managing constructive conversations and feedback with valued others.

### The Call for Fuller Understandings of Feedback Receivers

Just as it is vital for feedback providers to consider and grow their capacities for engaging in meaningful feedback, so too must they pay attention to the qualitatively different ways that receivers of feedback will experience and make sense of feedback. While experts insightfully recognize the importance of individualizing feedback in order to be of best help to diverse constituents, the literature is only now beginning to pay attention to the different ways that adults will take in and orient to feedback from others.

Stone and Heen, for example, recently argued that receiving feedback in constructive ways is actually a capacity—and a way of thinking—that can be learned and improved upon over time. Recognizing that we all have our own tool sets for interpreting language, actions, and feedback, Stone and Heen's work foregrounds and complements the research of Carol Dweck, a Stanford psychologist who emphasizes the great value of a "growth mindset" when approaching challenges.[25] Drawing from her work with youth who undauntedly engaged with very difficult puzzles, Dweck highlighted the fundamental power of approaching unfamiliar or difficult tasks as *skills to be developed* rather than as threats to one's sense of self or competence.[26] As she explained of the children she worked with, "Not only weren't they discouraged by failure, they didn't even think they were failing. They thought they were learning."[27] From this perspective, then, how one thinks and feels about feedback makes a tremendous difference in terms of what one hears and experiences during feedback sessions.

Like Dweck, Stone, and Heen, many leaders in the field recognize the critical importance of understanding the "place" from where feedback recipients are coming, and meeting them there. David, a management consultant and university professor, for example, offered the following powerful reflection: "I believe that in order to lead anyone out of where she or he is, we must first get inside and alongside and beside that other person . . . so that we can be company for him or her as they move and change and learn and grow and develop." Importantly, and as we will discuss throughout this book, adult developmental theory offers one very helpful window into the sense making and experiences of feedback receivers.

## TEN KEY TAKEAWAYS FROM THE FEEDBACK LITERATURE

Despite the very real and pressing feedback-related challenges just described, our exploration of feedback for growth builds off of, extends, and complements a very important and emerging literature about what we already know works well when giving feedback in both the education and business worlds. Drawing from research from the Gates, Carnegie, and Wallace Foundations, as well as the work of leading scholars such as Danielson, Linda Darling-Hammond, DuFour, John Hattie, Marshall, and Marzano, we have culled the following ten key feedback strategies from the business and education literature:

1. Individualize feedback for the receiver.
2. Offer specific, focused feedback.
3. Keep feedback objective and nonjudgmental.
4. Maintain a positive, compassionate focus during feedback and other communications.
5. Give feedback sensitively, and within the confines of safe contexts and relationships.
6. Make feedback regular and ongoing.
7. Be consistent.

8. Offer feedback in a timely manner.
9. Follow up on feedback.
10. Provide feedback recipients with opportunities to respond, reflect, and contribute.

Looking anew at these strategies through a developmental lens helps us enrich and complicate—in good ways—those aspects of effective feedback most prominently featured in current discussions. As a way into this important idea, we next present each of the "top ten" feedback strategies we found in our literature review, and then preview how a developmental perspective can help us support, extend, and further see into these key precepts in new, expanded, and significant ways. As always, it is our hope that the cross-pollination of good ideas—others' and our own, as well as those of writers in different disciplines and fields—will leave all of us standing on and tending to more fertile ground.

### Strategy 1: Individualize Feedback for the Receiver

Thinkers across domains recognize the importance of tailoring feedback to recipients' individual strengths and weaknesses, as well as personalities and preferences.[28] Just as when we give feedback to students and hope that it is received as "just-in-time, just-for-me information delivered when and where it can do the most good," we need to appreciate that adults, too, benefit from individualized feedback that recognizes and honors their unique needs.[29]

For example, Shana, an assistant principal at an elementary school, explained in response to one of our research survey questions that she feels "most successful" at giving feedback when she knows a person well, and when she understands "how they will interpret certain words, their background, their experience receiving high-quality feedback, and their openness to hearing comments (either positive or negative) on their work." In a similar way, a developmental perspective helps to make clear that underlying the many diversities that people inevitably and beautifully bring to feedback conversations, there are differing developmental orientations (i.e., ways of knowing) that will also influence and fundamentally inform their experiences with feedback.

### Strategy 2: Offer Specific, Focused Feedback

The literature also recognizes the importance of feedback that is both focused and specific.[30] By establishing clear expectations, offering direct communications, and referencing concrete situations, behaviors, and data, feedback givers can avoid the pitfalls of sharing too much, or of burying their most important feedback under less pertinent or tangential details.

Of course, all of this begs the questions of what people will actually understand to be "specific" and "focused," as well as how they will experience feedback offered toward these ends. For example, some adults will find direct, to-the-point feedback incredibly helpful, supportive, and meaningful, while others will prefer to receive focused feedback within the context of a larger, relational conversation and/or relationship. Either way, a developmental perspective helps shed light on the qualitatively different ways adults can define and interpret *even the same kinds* of feedback experiences.

### Strategy 3: Keep Feedback Objective and Nonjudgmental

Feedback experts also point to the importance of avoiding assumptions and judgments when offering feedback, and to drawing from multiple measures or data points to ensure greater accuracy.[31] Especially within the confines of high-stakes teacher feedback and evaluation, there is a growing sense that the measures we are using and the feedback we are offering need to be reliable, valid, data based, and objective.

On the flip side, however, is the fact that even the most objective-seeming data can reflect our very subjective priorities and points of view, and can also elicit intense feelings, emotions, and reactions (in both givers and receivers of feedback). As Stone and Heen aptly stated, and as we similarly pointed out earlier in this chapter, "The evaluation we give people is a reflection of our own (or our organization's) preferences, assumptions, values, and goals. They might be broadly shared or idiosyncratic, but either way they are ours."[32] Put another way, data is never truly value-neutral; what we pay attention to reflects what we care about and believe in, so even "objective" feedback can be incredibly personal. Moreover, understanding and navigating these complexities with and alongside one or more persons demands high levels of self-awareness and sensitivity, qualities which themselves can be developmental in nature.

### Strategy 4: Maintain a Positive, Compassionate Focus During Feedback and Other Communications

In both the business and education literatures, a compelling strand highlights the power of offering positive feedback in compassionate, meaningful, and constructive ways.[33] Different from the overcautious (and perhaps withholding) "culture of nice" described earlier, this body of research draws from Positive Organizational Scholarship and argues that affirming communications and authentic expressions of support among colleagues and team members can actually improve commitment, collaboration, affective-motivational well-being, productivity, and outcomes. In other words, this approach is not about making people feel good through empty platitudes. Rather, it involves offering genuinely constructive feedback in affirming ways so that recipients can take it in and hear it more effectively. As David Sousa, an educational consultant with a neuroscience background, further explained, "How we *feel* about a learning situation often affects attention and memory more quickly than what we *think* about it."[34]

While we agree wholeheartedly that an emphasis on what is "positive, flourishing, and life-giving" holds great promise for schools and other organizations, it is also our experience that building and modeling norms of safety, genuine care, and true collaboration require careful intentionality and an awareness of the developmental diversity present in virtually any team, organization, or district.[35]

### Strategy 5: Give Feedback Sensitively, and Within the Confines of Safe Contexts and Relationships

A fifth strategy highlighted in the literature about offering effective feedback involves remaining mindful of and sensitive to the inevitable emotional, relational dynamics of feedback.[36] From this point of view, ensuring a safe context (both literally and figuratively) for delivering feedback is just as important as the content of the message itself. For example, feedback givers need to remain sensitive to the personal and power dynamics that can be at play in meetings, and they need to offer feedback privately and respectfully while caring for the in-the-moment experiences of feedback recipients. Underlying all of this, one might argue, is the importance of trust. Indeed, in our own prior research with school leaders of all kinds, trust, care, and respect emerged as essential preconditions for effective leadership and capacity building.[37]

Yet, as we have noted—and as we will continue to discuss throughout this book—the ability to take another's perspective requires sophisticated developmental capacities that some leaders may still be growing. Moreover, it is likewise important to note that both givers and receivers of feedback can orient differently to professional relationships, and may accordingly bring different expectations and needs for support, challenge, and safety to the table.

### Strategy 6: Ensure Regular and Ongoing Feedback

Scholars also emphasize the essential importance of regular, ongoing feedback.[38] Unlike feedback that happens only once per year, irregularly, or not at all, the most effective feedback, research suggests, involves continued and authentic communications, frequent check-ins, and multiple opportunities to learn and grow. A developmental perspective helps extend this idea by explicating the foundational importance of meeting adults where they are in the psychological sense and remaining present to them as they change and grow over time. This kind of staying in place and being present can be a powerful support to improved practice—and will also mean different things to different people.

## Strategy 7: Be Consistent

Related to the power of maintaining ongoing feedback is the importance of staying consistent and *on message*.[39] Indeed, consistency in one's feedback can help allay ambiguity, bring needed clarity and focus to action steps, and give feedback recipients the time needed to digest, reflect on, and take in new ideas. It can also dispel some of the surprise or "gotcha" associations of feedback that we mentioned earlier.[40] As Josh, a New York City Department of Education leader responsible for supporting leaders' professional development, recently explained, "An employee that receives consistent feedback through the year will not approach the year-end evaluation with dread. Indeed, they should know *exactly* what feedback their employer is going to provide."

At the same time, a developmental approach to offering feedback for growth underscores that consistency, for its own sake, may not serve all people equally well. If, for instance, the same message, delivered in the same way, is not influencing needed and desired changes after repeated attempts, we need to think about different ways to share our intentions to be of service. We need to meet seemingly resistant adults where they are—with our hearts, minds, and ideas—so that they can best hear and absorb what we are trying to say. In other words, in their reluctance, resistant adults may actually be imploring, *"Tell me so I can hear you!"* In another vein, it is also true that the feedback we offer to adults will need to change and evolve over time as we—and the individuals we are caring for—continue to grow, build internal capacity, and learn from feedback. This kind of change can be fuel and incentive for growth.

## Strategy 8: Offer Feedback in a Timely Manner

Feedback experts likewise emphasize the importance of offering timely feedback—when and where it is needed.[41] If, for example, you observe a particularly excellent (or problematic) lesson or exchange, offering your best thinking and feedback right away, while the experience is still fresh, can be a powerful support and motivator.

On the other hand, remaining mindful—and engaging with developmental sensitivity—to the *readiness* of feedback receivers to hear, take in, and understand what you're trying to share is also critical. It may, for instance, be possible to offer feedback too soon (e.g., if someone is still upset about a situation, or if someone does not yet have the distance or perspective necessary to understand where you are coming from, developmentally or otherwise). Coupling timeliness with patience and remaining sensitive to self and others are key developmental extensions of this important feedback strategy.

### Strategy 9: Follow Up on Feedback

In both the business and education realms, following up on feedback remains a vital component of effective evaluation and professional learning.[42] It is usually not enough, for instance, to simply drop a suggestion, mandate, or new idea into a person's lap and then expect it to be implemented fully, independently, and in accordance with our expectations. Rather, feedback receivers may need ongoing support—and opportunities to ask questions, request clarifications, or add new ideas—as they work with us to achieve desired objectives.

Nevertheless, as you may already suspect, adults with different ways of knowing will probably experience follow-up supports in qualitatively different ways and have different expectations and hopes for the help being offered over time. For instance, some educators may prefer a very hands-on kind of follow-up, while others may prefer more freedom as they explore different options and alternatives for shared goals. Either way, it is critical that we, as leaders and givers of feedback for growth, understand and honor the supports that feel most comfortable and helpful to those in our care as we follow up.

### Strategy 10: Provide Feedback Recipients with Opportunities to Respond, Reflect, and Contribute

Finally, feedback cannot simply be a one-way street. Scholars and practitioners alike emphasize that recipients of feedback need opportunities to respond, reflect, and refocus future actions and directions—collaboratively and with some self-direction.[43] For instance, Len, a former veteran teacher and principal who now serves on the district level supporting adult development, recently shared that, from his view, feedback is really "an opportunity to begin a conversation, not an end unto itself." He continued, "It is an opportunity to learn more about one's practice, to reflect honestly and openly on strengths and challenges, and to problem-solve in partnership with trusted, trusting professional colleagues."

Of course, it is important to invite adults into such collaboration and self-direction with developmental mindfulness and care. Indeed, and as we will continue to explore throughout this book, adults will orient differently to these promising aspects of feedback, because taking a perspective on one-self and others—and voicing one's own opinions and suggestions—requires developmental capacities that may call for extra and differentiated support and challenge. Just as with all of the strategies offered in our top ten list, then, a developmental perspective on collaboration and self-direction in feedback can help to broaden and deepen our understandings of what it means to give and receive effective feedback for growth.

We hope that highlighting these ten practices from the literature—and the ways that a developmental perspective can begin to augment our understandings—will be useful to you as a jumping-off point for thinking about and employing feedback for growth. An overview and summary of these important strategies—as well as their developmental extensions—can be found in table 2.1. Of course, we will continue to consider and reference these ten tips in the chapters that follow.

**TABLE 2.1**

**A developmental perspective on ten best practices for effective feedback**

| Strategy | Description in the literature | Developmental extensions |
|---|---|---|
| 1. Individualize feedback for the receiver. | Effective feedback is tailored to a recipient's individual strengths and weaknesses, as well as personalities and preferences. | Feedback must take into account recipients' diverse ways of knowing (developmental orientations and capacities) to better *meet them where they are* in the psychological sense. |
| 2. Offer specific, focused feedback. | Feedback should reflect clear expectations, and reference concrete situations, behaviors, and data. It is important to avoid overbroad or unspecific feedback. | Different people will experience any kind of feedback differently—even if that feedback is offered in exactly the same way (e.g., specific, direct, or focused). Understanding this has implications for not only what we say, but *how* we say it as well. |

*continues*

**TABLE 2.1** (*continued*)

| Strategy | Description in the literature | Developmental extensions |
|---|---|---|
| 3. Keep feedback objective and nonjudgmental. | It is important to avoid assumptions and judgments when offering feedback. Drawing from multiple measures or data points can also be helpful and effective. | Understanding that seemingly objective data can reflect subjective priorities requires sensitivity and self-awareness—both developmental capacities. |
| 4. Maintain a positive, compassionate focus during feedback and other communications. | Positive communication and authentic expressions of support among colleagues and team members can actually improve commitment, collaboration, affective-motivational well-being, productivity, and organizational outcomes. | Building—and modeling—the norms of safety, genuine care, and true collaboration that undergird a positive individual and organizational approach requires intentionality and an awareness of developmental diversity. |
| 5. Give feedback sensitively, and within the confines of safe contexts and relationships. | Feedback givers must remain sensitive to the emotional, relational dynamics of feedback. Likewise, feedback needs to be delivered by trusted colleagues in safe spaces. | Fully taking another's point of view requires developmentally sophisticated capacities. Moreover, feedback givers and receivers alike will orient differently to professional relationships and bring different expectations for support, challenge, and safety. |
| 6. Ensure regular and ongoing feedback. | Effective feedback involves continued check-ins and frequent communications. | A developmental perspective underscores the importance of meeting adults where they are (psychologically) and remaining present to them as they change and grow over time. |
| 7. Be consistent. | Consistency in one's feedback can help alleviate ambiguity, bring needed clarity and focus to action steps, and give feedback recipients the time to digest, reflect on, and take in new ideas. | If consistency alone is not effecting desired change, it is important to think about different, developmentally oriented ways to share focal messages so that others can best hear, understand, and grow. |
| 8. Offer feedback in a timely manner. | Feedback needs to be offered when and where people need it. Waiting too long can limit effectiveness and impact. | It is important to remain mindful of a person's readiness for feedback so that recipients can hear, take in, and understand what you are trying to share. It is also important to balance timeliness with patience when offering feedback. |

**TABLE 2.1** (*continued*)

| Strategy | Description in the literature | Developmental extensions |
|---|---|---|
| 9. Follow up on feedback. | Receivers of feedback may need ongoing support—and opportunities to ask questions, request clarifications, or add new ideas—as they work to achieve desired objectives. | Adults with different ways of knowing will experience follow-up supports differently, and have different expectations and hopes for the help others offer over time. |
| 10. Provide feedback recipients with opportunities to respond, reflect, and contribute. | Feedback cannot be a one-way street. Recipients need opportunities to respond, reflect, and refocus future actions and directions—collaboratively. | It is essential to understand that adults will orient differently to self-direction, as taking a perspective on oneself and others—and voicing one's own opinions and suggestions—requires corresponding internal capacities. |

## CHAPTER SUMMARY AND CONCLUSION

In this chapter, we began by considering the origins and evolution of *feedback* as a term and concept, and shared our own thinking about what feedback is as we discuss it here and throughout this book. Then, we described some of the key challenges associated with feedback today, and highlighted ten best practices culled from the cutting edge of the feedback literature (in both the education and corporate worlds). In both of these sections, we previewed how a developmental lens can help enhance and extend these important learnings.

In the next chapter, we describe the theoretical underpinnings of feedback for growth in greater detail, with a specific focus on the ways in which Robert Kegan's constructive-developmental theory—and Drago-Severson's extensions of it—shed light on the qualitatively different ways that adults will orient to learning, teaching, leading, feedback, and life.[44]

## REFLECTIVE QUESTIONS

Please take a moment to consider the following questions, which can be used for independent reflection and/or group conversation. You may find it useful to reflect in writing privately first and then to engage in discussion with a colleague or team. These questions are intended to help you and your colleagues consider the ideas discussed in this chapter and how they might inform your practice of giving feedback.

+ What are two or three insights, learnings, or connections that stand out for you after reading this chapter?
+ How, if at all, does what you learned from this chapter connect with your own experiences of giving and/or receiving feedback?
+ What are two or three of your biggest hopes for your learning in reading this book? What do you think would help you most in terms of becoming even better at giving feedback? Receiving feedback? At this point, what would you name as your most important improvement goal in relation to professional feedback?
+ What are some of your burning, sizzling, and/or simmering questions about the processes of giving and receiving feedback at this time?

# CHAPTER 3

---

# Theoretical Foundations of
# Feedback for Growth

---

*Could a greater miracle take place than for us to*
*look through each other's eyes for an instant?*

—HENRY DAVID THOREAU

In this chapter we look more closely at the theoretical foundations of feedback for growth. In particular, we focus on constructive-developmental theory as one very promising lens for understanding, appreciating, and caring for the developmental diversity that exists in almost any group, team, or organization—and for recognizing this important diversity in our feedback.[1] As we will explore, constructive-developmental theory outlines four distinct meaning-making systems that are more common in adulthood: instrumental, socializing, self-authoring, and self-transforming. The last of these, self-transforming, is less common, but growing numbers of people are making meaning in this way so we include it here.[2]

As previewed in chapters 1 and 2, these meaning-making systems—or ways of knowing, as we call them—reflect qualitatively different orientations to learning, teaching, leading, and living, and serve as the lenses through which we filter all of our life experiences. In relation to feedback more specifically, they also serve as the "frequencies" with which we hear, and influence the aspects of feedback we can tune into, and those we tune out (even unintentionally). In light of this, understanding these ways of knowing—including their strengths and limitations—can help us build upon, deepen, and expand what we already know about effective feedback. It can also help leaders intentionally adjust, adapt, and *differentiate* their feedback to support ongoing learning and improved performance for adults who make meaning across the developmental spectrum.

35

As one aspiring principal recently shared after completing an intensive summer graduate course about leadership for adult development, "Our work [in schools] is hard, and adults need support in how to grow and learn that is differentiated for where they are in their ways of knowing." We agree that the mounting demands of new evaluation systems, standards, accountability mandates, and other reforms place unprecedented pressures on and opportunities for educators, and that they require new ways of working, learning, and leading. We must do this essential work together. And we also know that there is great hopefulness in a constructive-developmental approach to leading for change, as it emphasizes the buoying truth that all adults can grow, learn, and evolve in their work and lives if they can benefit from appropriate supports and challenges. We have witnessed this.

As another teacher and soon-to-be school principal recently shared with us, constructive-developmental theory offers "the knowledge of how to love people more and have deeper compassion for . . . colleagues while still being real, open, and honest with them." We hope that you, too, find a closer look at constructive-developmental theory helpful in underscoring the beauty, fragility, and potential within each of us, and in unlocking the promise of feedback for growth as a powerful, developmental tool for educational change.

## CONSIDERING CONSTRUCTIVE-DEVELOPMENTAL THEORY IN THREE DIFFERENT WAYS

Before focusing more closely on key principles of constructive-developmental theory and the four ways of knowing more common in adulthood, we invite you to consider (or "rent," as we like to say) the following ideas in three different ways. First, you may find it helpful to explore the theory as a general explanation of *how* adults orient differently to feedback and the world, as well as the underlying reasons *why*. Beyond this informational level, learning about constructive-developmental theory can be a jumping-off point for more personal reflections about the people around you, or—in this case—about how others might be making sense of your feedback and leadership. Finally, this chapter serves also as an invitation to look even deeper within, and to think further about how your own developmental needs and inclinations as a growing, learning, and complex human being might influence and inform your propensities for giving and receiving feedback. We will dive even deeper into the practical implications of constructive-developmental theory for giving and receiving feedback in chapters 4 and 5.

## CONSTRUCTIVE-DEVELOPMENTAL THEORY: ORIGINS AND KEY IDEAS

A neo-Piagetian theory of human development, Robert Kegan's constructive-developmental theory draws from more than forty-five years of research about how people grow, learn, and develop across the lifespan.[3] Building off of the pioneering work of Swiss psychologist Jean Piaget, who studied children's cognitive, moral, and social development, Kegan's theory extends these ideas to adulthood as a critical and potentially dynamic time of growth and change.[4] While, like Piaget's work, Kegan's theory outlines distinct developmental stages and recognizes *transitional* stages (points of growth between stages where two adjacent ways of knowing are operating at the same time), Kegan's theory differs from Piaget's in that it highlights four pathways of development rather than solely the cognitive line. To be more specific, Kegan's theory illuminates the affective, interpersonal, and intrapersonal lines of growth in addition to the cognitive pathway. His theory also emphasizes the vital interaction between a person's developmental capacities and his or her psychosocial context (e.g., relationships with people and society).

### Foundational Principles

Three principles sit at the heart of Kegan's constructive-developmental theory. These relate to both the structure and process of a person's meaning-making system: constructivism, developmentalism, and the subject-object balance.

First, *constructivism* recognizes that people actively interpret—or construct—their experiences throughout their lives, and that these constructions largely dictate their realities. Whether we experience something as positive or negative, or helpful or dissuading, depends on how we make sense of it and the experiences we bring to it. You could imagine, for instance, the very different reactions of, say, a bride-to-be on the morning of her wedding and a gardener who had just planted seeds if they both woke up to a rainy day. Objectively, the rainy day doesn't mean anything in and of itself. *It is what it is,* for the bride and the gardener. Yet, just as with these two individuals, each of us brings our own hopes, worries, remembrances, and reactions to every one of our experiences, and these aspects of ourselves imbue our days and encounters with meaning and significance. Put another way, constructivism has to do with how we actively make sense of our realities—moment to moment, hour to hour, day to day, and even in our dreams as we sift through experiences. It is the *motion of life.*

The second principle, *developmentalism*, highlights the important truth that people's constructions and ways of knowing can evolve—or become even more complex—over time. This happens when an individual is provided with developmentally appropriate supports and challenges for growth. In other words, developmentalism underscores the importance of receiving supports *and* challenges throughout our lives that can push us to make meaning in more complex, expansive, and sophisticated ways. Without developmentally appropriate supports, it can be difficult to grow, to reach within and find the person we want to become. Without challenges, on the other hand, we lack any real impetus to change, to consider alternatives and perspectives that may knock us off balance yet simultaneously open us to broader possibilities. With *both* supports and challenges (in just the right combination), we may find our way toward greater fullness and development.

Just as a "growth mindset" helps us see possibility in our personal struggles and limitations, developmentalism reminds us that adults' orientations to feedback and change are temporary constructions related to their experiences and developmental capacities, rather than permanent fixtures of their identities.[5] As we mentioned in chapter 2, Carol Dweck makes an important distinction between a growth mindset and a fixed mindset, and argues that the former helps us recognize potential and possibility in others and ourselves.[6] Giving feedback that takes a person's developmental orientation into account is one powerful way to honor and recognize the intrinsic promise of colleagues, and to demonstrate faith in this kind of important growth.

Third, there is the *subject-object balance*. This balance—in the truest sense of the word—constitutes a person's meaning-making system. More specifically, our ways of knowing hinge on (a) how much we can consciously see and actively be responsible for (or manage) about ourselves (i.e., what we can hold out as *object* and clearly look at, see, understand, and take responsibility for), and (b) those parts of ourselves that we cannot see or be responsible for and control or take a perspective on (i.e., these are things or parts of ourselves that we cannot see, or relationships that we cannot reflect upon because we are identified with them; they run us). Put another way, as we grow and develop more complex internal capacities and ways of knowing, we *shift the balance* between those aspects of our identity—and thinking and feeling—that run us (i.e., that we remain subject to) and those parts of ourselves that we can now clearly see, understand, reflect on, and hold as object. When this happens, we can see more deeply into ourselves, understand more about others, and reflect on the relationship between the two. We can take responsibility for more, understand more, and see more about why we do and think what we do. In other words, we can consciously hold out and reflect on or examine *more* parts of ourselves, our relationships, and the world, and are thus subject to (and internally run by) *less*. In this way, growth involves *renegotiations* of the subject-object balance (i.e., what is "self" and what is "other") that yield greater perspectives on our ways of thinking, working, and interacting in the world.

Much like the difference between gazing down from the balcony of a tall skyscraper and being embedded in the hustle and bustle of a big city (where everything is so close up and immediate), this kind of perspective taking offers a new and sometimes astonishing look at the way things work and fit together—at the way we work with and alongside those around us. Just as the skyscraper's height affords us a very different look at the city than the view from a crowded subway train, a greater developmental perspective can help us see and understand more about the parts of ourselves and our experiences that we were previously immersed in and subject to or identified with. Put most simply, developing greater internal capacities is really all about being able to take more and more perspective on ourselves, others, and the relationship between the two.

For example, one may begin to consciously notice thinking, acting, and/or behaviors that were once automatic or reflexive (e.g., a person may begin to recognize and wonder why he or she apologizes rather than engages in conflict, or asks for permission to speak before asking a question, or dismisses new ideas without really considering them). Both practically and developmentally speaking, it can be hard to step back and see things about ourselves and our work that might be *otherwise*, so learning about the possibility for and the trajectory of growth in adulthood is one powerful way to see deeper into the patterns of our own meaning making and recognize them as malleable. As Carl Jung aptly phrased it, "Until you make the unconscious conscious, it will direct your life and you will call it fate." Through our feedback and communications, we can help each other bring new consciousness, awareness, perspective, and intentionality to our thinking and acting (i.e., we can help each other take more as object and have more perspective on ourselves and others). And, as we loosen the grip of our former subjectivities (i.e., as we develop internal capacities to help us have perspective on what formerly "ran" us as automatic and reflexive), we can see some of our once taken-for-granted assumptions and behaviors and consider them as we work on and toward new pathways of growth and change.

## Strengths and Limitations of a Developmental Lens

While we recognize the great promise and potential of applying developmental ideas to our feedback and communications, we know that understanding constructive-developmental theory is not a panacea for everything related to school improvement. Like all theories, constructive-developmental theory has both strengths and limitations, and illuminates one particular aspect of who we are as human beings and active makers of meaning. For example, while it helps us to understand more about how we see, hear, and interpret the world, constructive-developmental theory does not directly address the ways in which racial identity, gender, religion, or age might influence our development (though researchers are investigating this as well). It may be helpful, however, to know that development has been shown to follow similar pathways across cultures and around the world.[7] In addition, research shows that a person's way of knowing is not determined specifically by gender, race, age, or life phase (i.e., both men and women, and people of all ages, can make meaning with any of the ways of knowing we are going to discuss).[8]

All that said, developmental psychologist William Perry maintained that in order to understand anything well—including ourselves and others—we need at least three good, working theories, since no single lens can fully shed light on all of the complex dimensions of a person's experience.[9] While we know that each of us brings many different perspectives and experiences to learning and leading, we hope that you find constructive-developmental theory to be one useful theory for exploring and deepening the feedback processes.

## Ways of Knowing

According to constructive-developmental theory, adults generally make meaning with one of four different meaning-making systems, which we call ways of knowing. These four ways of knowing—instrumental, socializing, self-authoring, and self-transforming—reflect qualitatively different systems of logic that underlie and infuse all that we think, see, hear, and understand. In life and therefore in the context of education, our ways of knowing shape the fundamental ways we orient to our roles and responsibilities as teachers, leaders, learners, feedback givers, and feedback receivers. In fact, and as we noted earlier, our ways of knowing are so intimately entwined with our experiences and sense making that they may feel more like a part of who we are than something we have.[10]

While, generally speaking, our ways of knowing remain consistent for periods of time and across contexts, it is important to understand that we *can* continue to grow developmentally throughout our lives—to acquire more complex and sophisticated capacities for relating, reflecting, and perspective taking—provided we have opportunities to benefit from appropriate supports and challenges. By "appropriate" we mean the kinds of supports and challenges that *feel like* supports and challenges to us on our growing journeys.

It is also important to note that, while constructive-developmental theory (just like other stage theories of development) is hierarchical in nature, "higher" is not necessarily better from our perspective. *All* ways of knowing have both strengths and limitations. Moreover, adults with any way of knowing can be as generous, hardworking, and caring as anyone else. (They will, however, tend to express their generosity, kindness, and care in different ways depending on their ways of knowing.) That said, "higher" or more complex ways of knowing *are* useful when we need greater capacities to meet the implicit and explicit demands of working, leading, learning, and living. In fact, in his seminal book, *In Over Our Heads*, Kegan argues that there is often a "mismatch" between our internal capacities (ways of knowing) and what is expected or demanded of us in our multiple roles as leaders, workers, parents, and citizens.[11] For this reason, we find it most helpful when thinking about development to consider the *goodness of fit* between an adult's developmental capacities and the implicit and explicit demands she or he faces.[12] In other words, it is the match between what is asked or expected of a person and her or his internal capacities to do it that matters most. If an adult can meet the demands and expectations placed on her or him, then there is a good fit. If, however, demands and expectations exceed an individual's internal capacities, then there is a need for further growth and development to be of best support to that person.

With this in mind, please note that many roles in education today, particularly leadership roles, require at least some degree of self-authoring capacities (such as the ability to consider others' views while holding firm to one's own).[13] More than twenty years ago, Kegan conducted an analysis of research related to adults' developmental capacities and approximated that less than 20 percent of adults in the United States were making meaning in this way.[14] While the number of people with more complex ways of knowing has grown along with the challenges we face, it is still the case that many of us want and need to better manage these challenges, and to better understand how internal growth (our own and others') can be a powerful force for educational change.[15] Constructive-developmental theory offers such a lens and opportunity, as it provides us with new insights about *how* to best support professional learning and internal capacity building. Also, as we will continue to describe throughout this book, adult development plays a very important role in how we orient to both giving and receiving feedback.

There is one last point we'd like to make about ways of knowing regarding the importance of context and its influence. On the one hand, there are some contexts and relationships in which we, as adults, feel safe demonstrating our biggest or most complex versions of our selves. These are contexts that invite us, whether intentionally or by good fortune, to bring our fullest selves out to shine and to test our emerging skills and capacities (e.g., a willingness to voice our ideas, to disagree with someone in authority, or to stand more firmly for a position). On the other hand, some contexts or relationships can threaten or undermine our growth. In these contexts, we might not try on or try out our fullest selves or developing capacities because we do not feel safe psychologically, and the perceived penalty is too high (e.g., we perceive that our expressions of self would be unwelcomed or unacknowledged—or we could even lose our jobs!). As you might imagine, context is especially important in relation to feedback, and what we feel comfortable sharing or risking with others.

In the next sections we describe important features of each of the four ways of knowing found in adulthood. Our intention is to offer a working understanding of these qualitatively different meaning-making schemas as a foundation for employing feedback for growth. By way of preview, you may find it helpful to explore table 3.1, which provides a detailed overview of the four ways of knowing. For more information about ways of knowing, please see Drago-Severson 2009, 2012; Drago-Severson, Blum-DeStefano, and Asghar 2013; and Kegan 1982, 1994.[16]

### The instrumental way of knowing

Adults with an instrumental way of knowing have a "what do you have that can help me/what do I have that can help you?" orientation to others (e.g., colleagues, supervisors, valued others) and the world. They generally understand their experiences in concrete terms (e.g., What can you give me? What can I get from you? How will it help me? What do I need to do to get things right?). Importantly, adults with this way of knowing can take perspective on their impulses and perceptions (i.e., they can recognize and hold them out as *object*), but they are still run by (or *subject* to) their needs, interests, desires, and wishes, as table 3.1 shows. In other words, adults who make meaning in this way have developed the internal capacity to understand and control their impulses, yet still operate from a place of wanting and needing to meet their own desires and objectives. They do not reflect on these because they do not have the capacity to do so.

**TABLE 3.1**

## Ways of knowing most common in adulthood according to constructive-developmental theory

| Way of knowing (meaning-making system) | Subject-object balance | Defining orientation of self | Preoccupying concerns | Guiding questions for self |
|---|---|---|---|---|
| Instrumental ("Rule-oriented self") | Subject to (run by and identified with): one's own needs, interests, wishes, and desires (usually concrete needs).<br><br>Can hold as object (take perspective on, look at, and be responsible for): one's impulses and perceptions (views). | Orients to and is run by one's own self-interests, purposes, and concrete needs. | • Self orients to rules.<br>• Self seeks to do things the "right" way and to behave in the "right" way. If the person does not follow the rules, he or she will work to avoid being caught or punished.<br>• Self is most concerned with concrete consequences of own and others' actions.<br>• Self makes decisions based on what the self will acquire and on following the rules.<br>• Other people are experienced as either helpers or obstacles to meeting one's own concrete needs.<br>• Self does not yet have the capacity for abstract thinking in the psychological sense or for making generalizations from one context to another. | • "How can I get the things I want and need?"<br>• "What's in it for me?"<br>• "Will I get caught or punished if I do something wrong or do not follow a rule?"<br>• "How can I avoid getting caught if I do something wrong?" |
| Socializing ("Other-focused self") | Subject to (run by and identified with): the interpersonal (relational), mutuality (felt by each; shared).<br><br>Can hold as object (take perspective on, look at, and be responsible for): needs, interests, desires, and wishes. | Orients to valued others' (external authorities' or loved ones') or society's expectations, values, and opinions about the self and one's work and thinking. | • Self depends on external authority or society for values and judgments about self. Self adopts others' standards and values.<br>• Acceptance, approval from important others, and affiliation are of primary importance.<br>• Self is defined by important others' judgments.<br>• Self orients to inner states.<br>• Self feels responsible for others' feelings and holds others responsible for own feelings. | • "Will you (valued other/authority) still like/love/value me?"<br>• "Will you (valued other/authority) still approve of me?"<br>• "Will you (valued other/authority) still think I am a good person?" |

*continues*

TABLE 3.1 (continued)

| Way of knowing (meaning-making system) | Subject-object balance | Defining orientation of self | Preoccupying concerns | Guiding questions for self |
|---|---|---|---|---|
| Self-authoring ("Reflective self") | *Subject to (run by and identified with):* authorship, one's internal government, identity, psychic administration, ideology (system of beliefs).<br><br>*Can hold as object (take perspective on, look at, and be responsible for):* the interpersonal, mutuality. | Orients to self's values (internal authority) and the smooth running of one's own internal system. | • Self generates and replies to one's self-generated internal values and standards (i.e., bench of judgment).<br>• Criticism is evaluated according to internal standards.<br>• Ultimate concern is with one's own competence and performance.<br>• Self can balance contradictory feelings simultaneously.<br>• Conflict is viewed as a natural part of life, work, and leadership and can enhance one's own and others' perspectives to achieve larger organizational and systemic goals. | • "Am I maintaining and staying true to my own personal integrity, standards, and internal values?"<br>• "Am I achieving my goals, and being guided by my ideals and values?"<br>• "Am I competent?"<br>• "Am I living, working, and loving to the best of my ability and potential?" |
| Self-transforming ("Interconnecting self") | *Subject to (run by and identified with):* interindividuality, interpenetrability of self-systems.<br><br>*Can hold as object (take perspective on, look at, and be responsible for):* authorship, identity, self-government, psychic administration, ideology (system of beliefs). | Orients to multiple self-systems; open to learning from other people; wants to grow and improve different aspects of self; engages constantly in process of discernment about self. | • Self is committed to self-exploration.<br>• Engaging with conflict is an opportunity to let others inform and shape one's own thinking.<br>• Conflict is viewed as natural to life and can enhance individuals' and one's own thinking.<br>• Self can own one's part in conflict and wants to explore it with others.<br>• Self is able to understand and manage tremendous complexity and ambiguity.<br>• Self is substantively less invested in own identity and more open to others' perspectives.<br>• Self constantly judges and questions how self-system works and seeks to improve it. | • "How can other people's thinking help me to enhance my own?"<br>• "How can other people's thinking help me to develop and grow?"<br>• "How can I seek out information and opinions from others to help me modify my own ways of understanding?" |

*Adapted from:* Eleanor Drago-Severson, *Leading Adult Learning: Supporting Adult Development in Our Schools* (Thousand Oaks, CA: Corwin/Sage Publications and the National Staff Development Council, 2009).

Instead, they orient toward seeking to fulfill their needs, wishes, and desires. Also, instrumental knowers do not yet have the capacity to think abstractly in the psychological sense or to make generalizations from one context to another.

Because of this, instrumental knowers tend to have dualistic thinking and orient most closely to "rules" as the key to achieving their own goals and/or objectives. They believe, for instance, that there are right and wrong answers to problems, and right and wrong ways to do things, think, and behave. They feel most supported by tangible, action-oriented suggestions, and want to know what they did correctly and what, exactly, they did wrong. For example, they often wonder, "Did I get it right?" or "What specific things do I need to do differently?" Step-by-step guidelines and models really help adults who make meaning in this way feel supported. Conversely, and although they can be as kindhearted as anyone else, instrumental knowers typically find it challenging to take others' perspectives fully, as they have not yet developed the internal capacity to do so. Similarly, since instrumental knowers' goals, needs, and worldviews are often automatic and reflexive (rather than reflective), other people are largely experienced as either helpers or obstacles to these ends.

### The socializing way of knowing

Socializing knowers have developed more complex reflective capacities, including the ability to think abstractly, reflect on others' feelings and actions, and make generalizations across contexts. As table 3.1 indicates, they have grown to have the internal capacity to reflect on, be responsible for, and manage (i.e., hold as object) their needs, interests, and wishes. Nevertheless, socializing knowers are run by or subject to their relationships, society's expectations of them, and their interpersonal connections. More specifically, socializing knowers feel responsible for valued others' feelings, and in turn hold other people responsible for their own feelings and emotional states. Because of this, they can experience conflict as a threat to their very selves, and tend to subordinate their own opinions, needs, and interpretations to those of important others (e.g., supervisors, feedback givers, authorities, loved ones).

This means that socializing knowers will internalize supervisors' ideas, suggestions, and solutions as "best" or "true" in order to avoid conflict and/ or to maintain their approval. And, importantly, others' judgments about them and their instructional practice *become their own*. Put another way, socializing knowers respond to and participate in important interpersonal interactions (such as feedback sessions) by thinking, "What you think of me as a leader, teacher, or person, I think of me. If you think I am doing a good job, then I am." Understanding this has important implications for both the supports and challenges you offer socializing knowers as you accompany them in their professional development.

### The self-authoring way of knowing

Adults with a self-authoring way of knowing have developed the internal capacity to take perspective on their interpersonal relationships and society's expectations. In other words, they are no longer run by or subject to them. Additionally, self-authoring knowers can identify their own values, beliefs, and purposes, and have the internal capacity to assess other people's expectations and judgments of them and their work in light of their own. For self-authoring knowers, demonstrating competency, achieving goals, and working to one's fullest potential are of primary concern (as table 3.1 illuminates). When receiving feedback on instructional practice or leadership, for example, these knowers assess others' feedback in light of what *they* think is best. They have their own internal bench of judgment, so (for better or for worse), self-authoring knowers will decide *what* to do with the feedback they receive.

Yet adults who make meaning in this way remain run by their own ideologies, theories, and values. Therefore, they cannot critique the way *they* feel things should be done (e.g., their ideologies and internal theories about what makes for good teaching and effective leadership). In general, it is especially difficult for these knowers to hear or take in perspectives that are diametrically opposed to their own. This is often true even when new ideas could support their personal or professional growth. Accordingly, to be of good developmental support to self-authoring knowers, it can be helpful to propose questions that are aimed at more deeply and carefully considering different types of solutions, as well as alternative paths and strategies.

### The self-transforming way of knowing

Increasingly, more adults are developing a way of knowing beyond self-authoring, which we call the self-transforming way of knowing. While adults who make meaning with at least some degree of self-transformational capacity total only 8–11 percent of the US population, this number may be on the rise given the complexities of modern living—and still represents nearly 40 million people according to research in the United States.[17] We think it's important to describe this way of knowing given the qualitatively different way adults experience feedback beyond the self-authoring way of knowing.

For example, adults with a self-transforming way of knowing have developed the capacity to see into and through their self-systems, and are no longer identified with the smooth running of their own ideologies. In light of this, self-transforming knowers are less invested in their Identities (with a capital *I*), and can be more open to others' points of view, standards, and beliefs. More specifically, self-transforming knowers are able to examine issues—and feedback—from multiple points of view. In addition, they can even see the way seemingly opposing perspectives can overlap. While, like any developmental transition, the shift from self-authoring to self-transforming can be disorienting and even painful, it opens new possibilities for interconnection and the management of complexity and ambiguity.

Again, a detailed overview of each of these four ways of knowing—including general orientations, preoccupying concerns, guiding questions, and the subject-object relationship—can be found in table 3.1.

## Ways of Knowing: Looking Below the Surface

While we have begun to explore the qualitatively different ways of knowing more commonly found in adulthood, we want to underscore here how important it is to remain mindful of adults' *internal* experiences when attempting to understand them in developmental terms. In other words, it's not just *what* we do or say as leaders when giving feedback that matters developmentally; it's also *how* we and those receiving the feedback make sense of our experiences (and what is at stake for us on the inside) that illuminates our meaning making.

For example, learners of developmental theory often recognize that, from the outside at least, one way of knowing may look a lot like another. Both instrumental and self-authoring knowers, for instance, may hold firm to a particular vision or ideology, although, as we've discussed, they do so for very different reasons. Likewise, both socializing and self-transforming knowers can orient strongly to others' perspectives, feelings, and experiences. However, while socializing knowers are made up of and dependent upon valued others' assessments and reactions, self-transforming knowers have grown to understand that opening themselves to others' ideas and experiences in deeply intimate ways actually helps them feel *more* complete and fulfilled. In each case, the important thing to remember is that leaders' internal experiences will be significantly and qualitatively different, even when some of the surface behaviors may appear to be quite similar on the outside.

While there is no quick and easy "questionnaire" you can use to definitively identify your own or others' way of knowing—formal developmental assessments are conducted via an intensive ninety-minute Subject-Object Interview—we have found that for incredibly busy leaders like yourselves, one powerful way to begin to meet people where they are, and to peek under the surface of external behavior, is to share key ideas from constructive-developmental theory and engage in conversation about collective hopes, worries, needs, and experiences.[18] What, for instance, feels most supportive to others and to us in our work? What feels most challenging? What personal needs and preferences can we identify in relation to collaboration, leadership, and the exchange of feedback? Thinking and talking together about these important questions can help shed light on some of the developmental dimensions of our leading, teaching, learning, and feedback.

By way of example, in exhibit 3.1 we offer a series of vignettes, compiled from the reflections of real-life educators, that illuminate four different teacher leaders' experiences participating on a schoolwide data team. The teachers in the vignettes respond to these questions:

- How do you feel about your work on the data team?
- What do you like most about it?
- What, if anything, do you find challenging?

As you will see, all of these teachers—who make meaning with qualitatively different ways of knowing—appreciate different aspects of their collaborative work, and identify different parts as challenging. Yet, as we have explained, what is most significant from a developmental perspective is not necessarily the specific supports or challenges named by the teachers (although these are important, of course), but rather the rationales they provide for *why* they experience these aspects of their work in the ways they do. As you read the vignettes that follow and look for clues to help you identify each teacher's most dominant way of knowing, we invite you to consider *what* the teachers seem to appreciate and find challenging (e.g., what they like and dislike, the different strengths and limitations they bring to the work) and also their *underlying thinking, feeling, and meaning making* (i.e., their different orientations to collaboration and teamwork). We hope you find this application activity helpful as a first peek underneath observable behaviors and into developmental ways of knowing.

*Diving deeper: Analyzing the vignettes*

As a careful read of the vignettes in exhibit 3.1 makes clear, adults can bring a great diversity of perspectives to their professional work and relationships, even when they are engaging in very similar activities. Providing

EXHIBIT 3.1

**APPLICATION EXERCISE**

### Advancing Your Practice:
### Four Teachers Making Meaning on a Team

In this application exercise, four teachers reflect on their experiences on a school-wide data team. As you read, please consider the following questions:

- With which way of knowing do you think each teacher is primarily making meaning? You may find it helpful to underline or circle evidence that points to one way of knowing or another. For example, what seems to be a preoccupying concern for each teacher? (You may find table 3.1 a helpful point of reference.)
- What do you notice about how each of these teachers experiences other colleagues on the team? How might this be connected to adult development?
- Do you think that these teacher leaders could all be members of the same team? Why or why not?

**DEVIN'S REFLECTIONS**
One of my favorite parts about the data team is that it gives me a chance to spread my wings. It's invigorating to be in a group of like-minded adults who really care about doing the best they can for kids, and to have some space to share my thinking and ideas about improving our school. I'm a relatively new teacher—this is my fourth year—but I have a strong vision for education, and I do my best to live by and enact my convictions each and every day. I've come to really believe that data can play an important role in addressing the achievement gap—which is a big part of why I became a teacher in the first place—so it feels good to be trusted by the principal with such high-leverage, high-priority work. I also appreciate the opportunity to take on a bigger leadership role with my peers. A lot of the teachers in the group sort of look to me for answers and ideas—and it's rewarding to help guide the direction we take as a team.

In terms of challenges, I guess what frustrates me most is when teachers don't take initiative or contribute ideas during meetings. I really enjoy working with data, but a few of my colleagues need a lot of hand holding to get their work done, and I find myself questioning their commitment. I know that, for the most part, we're all doing our best, but still. It's good work, and important work, but it feels like a lot depends on me, you know?

**JORDAN'S REFLECTIONS**
When my principal asked me to be on the data team, I was flattered but nervous. Not everybody here agrees with the administration's plan for using student data and test scores, and, honestly, I prefer to stay out of these kinds of arguments. I'm comfortable using data to guide my own practice—I have a strong statistics background—but it feels like my principal is counting on me now to be an advocate for

*continues*

*her* view on data, and some of my teacher friends are really worried about how the proposed changes will affect *them*, so being on the data team is kind of like being caught between a rock and a hard place, so to speak. Not to mention the fact that a few of the other teacher leaders on the team have their *own* strong opinions about data—and they aren't shy about sharing them. At this point, it's pretty clear to me that I can't make everyone happy, so mostly I'm not sure what to do, even though I really want to help and make a difference. I just don't like disappointing people.

**REESE'S REFLECTIONS**
One of the things I like most about working on the data team is the clarity of the work. Looking at student performance data helps us zero in on who's most effective in the classroom and who needs more help, and it gives us the same kind of insight into our curricula. I mean, it's all right there in black and white. Can't argue with that, right? For me, personally, I know that analyzing my students' data helps me be a highly effective teacher. It's like making a roadmap—or a blueprint—that tells me *exactly* what I need to do to perform better for my students and for my formal evaluation.

In general, then, I'd say that I'm pretty satisfied with my work on the team—we even get a special stipend. The only challenge is when some of my teammates get bogged down in discussion or debate. When this happens, I do my best to keep us focused on our objectives and the numbers right in front of us. *That's* what we need to be talking about.

**TYREE'S REFLECTIONS**
Joining the data team was one of the best and hardest parts of my work this year. As a team, we sit at what I consider to be the epicenter of the changes happening in our school right now, and it's also an opportunity to come together around some of the larger issues and challenges we face as educators more generally. It's a complex time to be a teacher, I think, and what I love most about our meetings is simply having some time and space to really talk with other teachers about the nature of our work together. It's a rare privilege to learn from the different perspectives my colleagues bring to the table—although it can be discouraging when certain teachers on the team want to push an agenda or "get things done" without much reflection. Over the years, I've learned that there are no hard-and-fast rules in teaching and school improvement. It really is a process and a big responsibility, since the work we're doing on the team has far-reaching implications for all of us, our colleagues, and our students and families.

opportunities for adults to talk about and reflect on these important differences and similarities can help shed light on some of the developmental dimensions of our experiences, so that we can better understand and meet each other where we are.

In terms of the vignettes, we hope that each helped illuminate how a way of knowing might be characteristically experienced and expressed in living, breathing form. Devin, for instance, evokes a more self-authoring way of knowing (e.g., Devin works to "live by and enact" strong convictions and a personal vision, and enjoys being a leader on the team). Like other self-authoring knowers, Devin is strongly committed to internally generated values and beliefs (e.g., using data to address the achievement gap), but may not yet have grown the internal capacity to take a larger perspective on these. More specifically, Devin seems to be almost exclusively invested in influencing the direction of the data team's work, and interprets other teachers' disagreement, passive acceptance, or alternate styles of contributing as lack of commitment. How might a deeper understanding of colleagues' internal experiences and sense making help Devin even more effectively lead and participate on the team?

Representing a more socializing way of knowing, Jordan's reflections help to complicate some of Devin's assumptions about the nature of commitment and participation. It seems clear that Jordan has a lot to offer (including a statistics background and a sincere desire "to help and make a difference"), but carrying the weight of others' contrary and competing expectations (e.g., the principal's, other colleagues') makes it hard for Jordan to chart a path forward in a way that brings these skills and qualities to bear. As with other socializing knowers, Jordan's identity seems to be so deeply and almost completely influenced by valued others' assessments that acting authentically when these external voices conflict feels "like being caught between a rock and a hard place."

Interestingly, while the experience of working on a data team for Jordan feels rife with contradiction and internal conflict, Reese seems to approach the work with a more straightforward, "right and wrong" mentality. Indicative of a more instrumental way of knowing, Reese's reflections highlight both the strengths and limitations of looking at the world in dualistic terms. While, on the one hand, Reese's clarity—much like Devin's—could help focus and ground a team, Reese's emphasis on finding *one* right solution (e.g., "who's most effective in the classroom and who needs more help") and meeting personal needs (e.g., learning "*exactly* what I need to do to perform better for my students and for my formal evaluation") may delimit or crowd out some of the deeper complexities of the work at hand.

By contrast, it is these very complexities—and unpacking and exploring them in the company of others—that seem most important to Tyree, whose meaning making represents a more self-transforming perspective in the vignettes. For Tyree, the data team is a deeply valued context in which to "come together" to learn from colleagues' different perspectives, and to co-construct a path forward. Unlike Jordan, however, whose identity seems so connected to the expectations of valued others, Tyree's preference for listening to different voices seems rooted in the idea that school improvement is "a process" in which no one person has all the answers.

While the vignettes do not definitively suggest whether or not Devin, Jordan, Reese, and Tyree are part of the same data team, it seems clear to us that they certainly *could* be; many real-world teams operate with just such a range of developmental orientations. In fact, it seems clear that for all four of the teacher leaders in the vignettes, engaging in conversation about adult development—and posing questions about how they and others make meaning—could be one powerful step toward making this often-overlooked form of diversity more visible, and toward working together even more effectively.

### HOLDING ENVIRONMENTS FOR EFFECTIVE FEEDBACK: DEVELOPMENTAL SUPPORTS AND CHALLENGES FOR GROWTH

As the preceding discussion and vignettes suggest, adults who make meaning in different ways will feel supported and challenged by *different* things, and this has important implications for the ways we work and lead together. As we prepare to look even more closely at the developmental dimensions of feedback in the chapters that follow, it may be helpful to know that for feedback, just as for growth more generally, the journey and process of development (i.e., moving from one way of knowing to the next) always takes place in some context, which Robert Kegan refers to as a *holding environment*.[19] By definition, a holding environment is a nurturing context in and out of which we grow, and can be a relationship, a series of relationships, carefully designed collaborative practices, or a complex organization like a school.[20]

As principals, assistant principals, superintendents, teachers, coaches, and educational leaders of all kinds, we need to give feedback in holding environments that honor and take into account our colleagues' ways of knowing. Doing so allows us to maximize our communications, better tune into each other's best thinking and ideas, and be of best support for enhanced instructional practice and for leadership growth. In fact, offering feedback that is carefully tailored to adults in this way can actually make it more relevant and actionable—key outcomes as we work to build capacity and improve performance. It is important, then, to understand that effective holding environments serve three key functions:

- First, and most importantly, effective holding environments meet adults where they are developmentally, without an urgent press to make them change. In other words, they recognize and value a person's current way of knowing and offer supports and appropriate challenges tailored to an individual's needs. It can be helpful to think of this as the "holding" part of a holding environment. In other words, this means meeting a person where he or she is, at this moment in time.
- Secondly, holding environments need to gently encourage adults to step beyond their current internal capacities. Kegan, like us, describes this implicit challenge as one of *letting go*.[21] This is the second key component of a good holding environment, and involves a kind of caring push toward change and internal growth.
- Finally (and simultaneously), the third function of an effective holding environment is remaining in place (or as Kegan puts it, *sticking around*) as the person within begins to exercise new internal capacities.[22] At the heart of this third function is continuity—though with an intuitive sense of presence and flexibility to accommodate the new, bigger selves of the adults we are supporting. Put another way, we must continue to "be there" for those in our care over time, but as those we care for learn, grow, and change, we need to be there for them in different ways.

As you consider these three key functions of an effective holding environment, you may notice that we often do these things intuitively when we care for children (e.g., when we help them learn to walk or ride a bike, we both "hold" and "let go," all while letting them know we are "right there"). Indeed, in guiding and nurturing youth toward independent mastery of skills and new emerging internal capacities, we scaffold them. As they grow, we gradually shift levels of support and challenge and stand in relationship with and for them differently. This similarity is no accident. The term *holding environment* was first used by psychologist D. W. Winnicott in reference to the evolving kinds of care children need from their caretaker as they grow out of infancy.[23] Kegan extended this idea by arguing that people can benefit from holding environments throughout the lifespan, and that adults, like children, need different supports and challenges as they grow and learn.[24]

Similarly, for adults just as children, it is the interplay of both supports and challenges that matters immensely in creating holding environments. As we discussed earlier, we need a healthy balance of both to maximize our learning and development. As one aspiring principal recently told us after learning about these ideas in a university leadership preparation graduate course, "Every adult deserves to be both supported *and* challenged. Without either one of these components we are not honoring the fullness of each other." It is the genuine recognition of this fullness—this human possibility—that underlies the great promise of feedback for growth in our schools and school systems, and that we will continue to explore in greater detail in the chapters that follow. As another aspiring school leader said after completing the same course, "We owe it to ourselves and to each other to hold one another. I never realized the power of a holding environment, but now I see that I can create a space for adults where they are able to learn, share, and explore openly without inhibition. Everyone deserves to have that, and I feel empowered to bring that to my school." Ultimately, learning about and sharing developmental principles is one of the most powerful ways we can begin to shape our feedback—and our leadership and professional relationships more broadly—as holding environments for growth.

## CHAPTER SUMMARY AND CONCLUSION

In this chapter, we explored the key principles of constructive-developmental theory—including constructivism, developmentalism, the subject-object balance, the four ways of knowing more common in adulthood, and holding environments—as foundational elements of feedback for growth. In chapter 4, we will dive even deeper into the practical applications of this important knowledge, and consider the fundamental ways that adults' developmental capacities will influence how they "tune into" and receive feedback, as well as the different supports and challenges they will need to best hear, learn from, and implement new ideas and suggestions for professional improvement.

Next, we invite you to consider a series of reflective questions that can help you think more about the ideas in this chapter, how they connect to your important experiences and practices, and how you might be able to use them moving forward. First, however, we will share a sentiment that many educational leaders have found inspiring and deeply resonant: namely, we encourage you to remember that supporting adult development for others and ourselves is not always easy (in fact, it can be incredibly hard!). It is, however, always vitally important, and can even be downright magical. *That*, in the end, is the gift we can offer to each other and ourselves.

## REFLECTIVE QUESTIONS

Please take a moment to consider the following questions, which can be used for independent reflection and group conversation. You may find it useful to reflect in writing privately first and then to engage in discussion with a colleague or team. These questions are intended to help you and your colleagues consider the ideas discussed in this chapter and how they might inform your practice of giving feedback.

+ After reading this chapter, what are two of your biggest takeaways?
+ In what ways has learning about the four ways of knowing in adulthood and the foundational principles of constructive-developmental theory helped you think differently about feedback? About yourself? About your colleagues and associates?
+ At this point, how would you describe your own way of knowing? Do you see any connections between your way of knowing and your feelings about giving and/or receiving feedback?

# CHAPTER 4

## How Do Different Ways of Knowing Influence How We *Receive* Feedback?

*No one cares how much you know, until they know how much you care.*

—THEODORE ROOSEVELT

After learning about ways of knowing, you might be wondering what they mean for your leadership in general, and for the ways you give and receive feedback in particular. We've found that these kinds of questions are quite common after one learns about constructive-developmental theory, no matter one's current way of making meaning. In this chapter, we offer an even closer look at the practical applications of developmental theory for making feedback more actionable and effective, with a particular focus on the ways adults' internal capacities will influence their experiences *receiving* feedback.

By way of example, you might fondly remember the supportive and just-right suggestions of a trusted principal, advisor, or mentor. You might conversely recall (with equal vividness) less pleasant conversations with a curmudgeonly boss, seemingly shortsighted supervisor, or even someone you love and admire. Yet a quick water cooler conversation in a professional setting could reveal that a supervisor you consider curmudgeonly and curt (a construction) could seem to your colleague like a no-nonsense motivator with an effective tough-love approach (a qualitatively different construction). Similarly, a boss who seems wishy-washy and ineffective to your colleague could feel to you like a supportive and sensitive guide.

Ultimately, these impressions are largely a matter of interpretation, and of our active and ongoing meaning making of our experiences.

As we started to explore in chapters 2 and 3, adults who make meaning in different ways can experience even the same leader, feedback strategy, or team context differently, and will require qualitatively different kinds of supports and challenges to feel well held developmentally. While this diversity of experience and meaning making may, at first, seem to warrant a "can't please them all" approach to feedback (or a scenario in which the feedback giver simply sticks with a style that feels most comfortable to him or her), a developmental perspective can actually help us expand and diversify the kinds of feedback we offer so that others can more effectively hear, take in, and act upon our communications. In the sections that follow, we further unpack the connections between our developmental orientations and the specific feedback strategies and holding environments that will help us grow and learn.

## REVISITING WAYS OF KNOWING: HONORING THE DEVELOPMENTAL DIVERSITY OF FEEDBACK RECEIVERS

As we described in chapter 3, feedback for growth needs to be given and received within holding environments that fit us well developmentally and gently stretch our developmental edges and boundaries. With this in mind, we thought it would be helpful to expand our discussion of ways of knowing to illustrate how adults' different developmental orientations will influence their experiences as *receivers* of feedback. For each of the four ways of knowing more common in adulthood, we consider how adults' orienting concerns for receiving feedback accord with particular supports and challenges, and we highlight areas for growth—what we refer to as "growing edges"—for adults who make meaning across the developmental spectrum.

As we did earlier, we invite you to consider, or "rent," this information in three different ways: (1) to learn on an informational level about the theoretical and practical implications of how our ways of knowing influence our capacities for receiving feedback; (2) to deepen your understanding of how best to offer developmentally oriented feedback to colleagues, supervisees, supervisors, and other adults in your care; and (3) to gain deeper insight into your *own* experiences with receiving feedback. It is our hope that the following discussions, applications, and reflective invitations presented in this chapter open new possibilities for further strengthening your practice of feedback for growth in all three ways, and that they begin to illuminate the promise of feedback for growth as a critical element of effective holding environments.

## Instrumental Knowers as Feedback Receivers: "Tell Me What I Need to Do"

As we began to consider in chapter 3, adults who make meaning with an instrumental way of knowing tend to see the world in concrete, dualistic terms: they believe that there are right and wrong answers to problems, and right and wrong ways to think and behave. Because instrumental knowers are run by fulfilling their needs, wants, and desires, they respond well to feedback that helps them understand *exactly* what they need to do to achieve these ends, and what kinds of obstacles might get in their way. In light of this, adults who make meaning in this way feel most supported by (a) tangible examples to guide practice and change (e.g., models, rubrics, step-by-step instructions); (b) the perception of a supervisor's consistency and fairness (i.e., the feeling that leaders do not offer conflicting directives or ask different things of different people); and (c) external rewards for good performance (e.g., public recognition, high evaluation scores, increased pay, or other forms of promotion). As one teacher leader recently shared, "I want to feel like I'm walking away from feedback with my principal with pragmatic strategies and a clear understanding of what's expected of me. I like to know what's expected of me. In fact, I really need that."

Of course, there are times when all of us need concrete information and clear expectations in our work and professional learning. For adults with *any* way of knowing, for instance, it is incredibly important to become familiar with organizational policies and routines, especially when beginning a new job or taking on a new role. (Plus, it's always helpful to have a clear sense of what's most important to one's boss or supervisor, and rewards tend to feel good to most people, too.) For instrumental knowers, though, the need for explicit, concrete feedback runs deeper than just "learning the ropes." For these adults, concrete feedback accords with the fundamental ways they are making sense of their work and the world, and thus are not means to an end, but rather ends in and of themselves.

### Growing edge: Instrumental knowers

While it can be incredibly powerful to offer concrete feedback to colleagues who are more instrumental in their meaning making—as this can serve as a "tuning in frequency" to help them best take in, learn from, and implement your suggestions—teaching and leading today often require adults to look beyond "right" and "wrong" solutions, and to think abstractly and make connections across contexts and situations (all of which would likely feel like a stretch developmentally for instrumental knowers). That is why, thinking back to our previous discussion of holding environments, we need to offer a careful balance of both supports *and* challenges when offering feedback for growth and change. In other words, while it is important to first meet someone where she or he is developmentally so she or he can hear and take in what you're trying to say, feedback for growth also involves tapping gently at the edges of a person's thinking or meaning making in order to support growth. By this we mean carefully and caringly encouraging a person to "reach up" and "try on" some of the skills and capacities that currently lie just beyond her or his reach (much like Vygotsky's famous conceptualization of the *zone of proximal development*[1]). This kind of intentional stretching can help all of the adults in your care grow more sophisticated internal capacities for managing their work and responsibilities. For instrumental knowers in particular, it can help them more effectively approach the mounting adaptive challenges in education that, by definition, come without clear or ready-made answers.

### Socializing Knowers as Feedback Receivers: "Make Me Feel Valued"

While socializing knowers have developed greater internal capacities for abstract thinking and relating, and are no longer run by their needs, interests, and desires, they *do* feel responsible for valued others' feelings—and in turn hold those others responsible for their own. Since socializing knowers orient so strongly to the interpersonal dimensions of feedback (e.g., kindness, care, relationships), it is important to acknowledge and attend to these when giving feedback to educators who make meaning in this way. As discussed previously, the feedback, opinions, and assessments of important others actually *become* socializing knowers' own self-assessments. Understanding this helps us to see that they will feel most supported by feedback that: (a) couples constructive feedback with authentic affirmations and demonstrations of confidence (e.g., acknowledgments of hard work, contributions, and/or positive characteristics); and (b) *de*couples critical assessments from larger personal or professional judgments (e.g., "You're a really good teacher/person, and I think it's important to work on X"). In other words, you can support socializing adults' growth by helping them to understand that while they may still be learning (as we all are), their hard work is appreciated, and they are valued members of your organization. As one teacher who makes meaning in this way expressed it, "When I feel cared for and respected, my confidence just soars. When somebody believes in me and cares what's happening, I feel like I can do anything!"

*Growing edge: Socializing knowers*

Because socializing knowers tend to subvert their own ideas and assessments to those of valued others and authorities in order to avoid conflict with them and/or maintain important relationships, it can be hard for them to really take in, respond to, or implement critical feedback if it is not offered with developmental intentionality and care. As Nelson, a middle school science teacher, recently told us: "Critiques from my principal leave me doubting my own abilities. I'm constantly apologizing for things I'm not even sure I did wrong, and it takes me a pretty long time to recover and get my confidence back after meeting with him. And it's too bad, because instead of putting myself out there and trying new ideas, I'm holding back and playing it safe by focusing on what I already do well. I guess I just don't want to look incompetent."

Importantly, when working with socializing adults, you can establish feedback encounters as safe contexts—holding environments—that convey important information *while simultaneously supporting the development of adults' emerging internal capacities.* For example, offering constructive feedback with developmental intentionality can help socializing knowers take in critical assessments in ways that feel supportive and actionable, rather than threatening or deflating. You can also approach feedback conversations with adults who make meaning in this way as invitations to explore and express their *own* ideas and opinions, even when they conflict with your own. In other words, by caringly and genuinely encouraging socializing adults to share their thinking, assessments, and beliefs about practice as part of feedback conversations, you can help them to gently stretch their capacities for communicating, collaborating, and contributing in new ways. One educational leader recently captured this powerful idea as follows: "Feedback can sometimes be a tool for helping people to realize their untapped potential."

## Self-Authoring Knowers as Feedback Receivers: "Let Me Demonstrate Competency"

Unlike socializing knowers, self-authoring knowers have grown the capacity to more comfortably take a stand for their self-generated values, assessments, and ideas. They also assess other people's expectations for and judgments of them in light of their own. So, when considering another person's feedback—whether a colleague's or a supervisor's—self-authoring knowers will decide *for themselves* what they want to improve and what they're doing well (even while understanding that some things may be mandated or non-negotiable).

For example, Andrés, an elementary school principal, recently shared the following about his experiences receiving feedback as a self-authoring knower:

> I have really strong personal preferences about receiving feedback, which I don't think I always consider in the people I manage. I really crave space in a conversation. I'm creative, and I'm results driven, so I love to think about problems and generate creative solutions. That's what I live for, really. So I really value my intellectual engagement and autonomy. It's important for me that the person giving me feedback recognizes that—even just the fact that I care about it. So if they have to be directive, I really appreciate someone saying, "I know you'd like the time to think deeply about this, but what I'm telling you now is X has to change in this way, because . . ." That recognition means a lot to me.

Like Andrés, self-authoring knowers tend to value opportunities during feedback sessions to voice their opinions, offer suggestions and critiques, and formulate their own strategies and goals. Perhaps not surprisingly, they may even have some feedback for you! Nadine, for instance, highlighted her need for reciprocity during feedback as a teacher leader: "When receiving feedback I always have a lot to say and I want to be given the time to explain why I did what I did. In addition, I usually have questions for the person giving me the feedback, and I think it's important to have time for this. Feedback should not be an A-to-B format. It should be a back-and-forth dialogue between the two parties."

*Growing edge: Self-authoring knowers*
Because self-authoring knowers are deeply invested in demonstrating competency and excellence *as they define it*, they can have a hard time opening themselves to critical feedback, especially when they perceive that feedback to be in conflict with their own plans or ideas. As one school principal recently said, reflecting on her stance as a self-authoring leader: "I have a really strong sense of vision, and a firm stance on what excellent teaching looks like. I work hard to listen to my teachers and their feedback, but I know what I want to accomplish and what needs to be done in my school. I just do. It's not quite tunnel vision, but it *is* intense focus and determination." Understanding that self-authoring knowers cannot yet objectively see their own value propositions and ideologies (or critique them) has important implications for how you accompany them in their professional

development with your feedback. Gently encouraging these adults to con-sider and then explore new ideas, alternative framings (e.g., "Have you considered...?"), and directions—in your private conversations, on teams with other colleagues, or even through new leadership roles that require the negotiation of differing perspectives and agendas—can help them more effectively seek and see common ground, and more openly embrace new possibilities for improving practice over time.

## Self-Transforming Knowers as Feedback Receivers: "We Can Figure This Out Together"

For self-transforming knowers, receiving feedback is often understood and experienced as a cherished opportunity to co-construct interpretations, un-derstandings, and value propositions with colleagues and supervisors. Put another way, self-transforming knowers recognize the value of juxtaposing and learning from different perspectives, paradoxes, and ideas, as these ap-parent differences can illuminate new knowledge and open paths of pos-sibility. One veteran educator who makes meaning in this way recently reflected on the value of feedback as follows: "We require an 'other' both to point out the areas of growth we did not know about, and also to point out the areas that we did know about, but were too afraid to address." Offering feedback to self-transforming knowers is really about inviting them into conversations, about learning with and from them in genuine, intimate, and promising ways. Creating spaces for the two of you to learn together—with and from each other—is vital as well. As another self-transforming educational leader said, "Feedback is an invitation to grow—to experiment, take risks, excel, and to stumble—and all of these are good things."

*Growing edge: Self-transforming knowers*

Even though self-transforming knowers have developed the capacity to see and seek commonality in seemingly opposing viewpoints and perspectives, it can be incredibly hard and painful for adults who make meaning in this way to engage in feedback encounters that do not position them as active and collaborative participants. For example, Evette, a veteran teacher at a charter high school, was very disoriented and disappointed when her prin-cipal gave her an "emerging" rating on her interim teaching evaluation for instructional technology use, but would not debrief or discuss the mark with her at length. "Can you please help me understand this feedback?" she asked, genuinely curious about the rating. "Evette," the principal replied, "you're sterling at just about everything—top notch. Everyone has some-thing they need to work on. Just let it go." Because Evette was genuinely interested in learning more about teaching with technology, she asked again for a chance to dialogue with her principal in order to learn more about her principal's ideas. When he told her that he "didn't have time to dive in right now," and that she should "just talk to some colleagues" about their strategies for incorporating technology in the classroom, Evette left the meeting feeling disappointed. As she shared, "I understand that I still have many things to learn, and that there will always be new things I could do to grow myself and my teaching. Still, it would have been so much more effective—so much more meaningful and respectful—if my principal tried to understand the thinking and intention behind my practice, and shared at least something about his own understanding of the issue." For Evette, the problem wasn't just that she didn't have a chance to defend her current use of instructional technology (although part of her was willing and prepared to do so), or that the principal wasn't forthcoming with helpful tips to guide next steps; what was really hard for her, she explained, was that she felt "in the dark about the thinking *behind* the rating"—that she didn't even have a clear sense of the principal's perspective on instructional technology and its purposes in the first place. As she continued, "I feel badly that I didn't have a chance to learn from my principal's reasoning, or a chance to expand my own. I'd really like to come together around this."

While the principal's "drop and go" feedback style, as Evette referred to it, may have felt just as uncomfortable to adults with other ways of knowing for these and other reasons, this example helps illustrate the importance of being of good company with and for self-transforming knowers during important moments of collaboration and feedback. Given the implicit contradictions, paradoxes, and tensions of education today—and also the urgent pace of learning and leading in schools—adults who make meaning with a more self-transforming way of knowing may need extra support and acknowledgment when leaders need to make unilateral decisions or act without consultation. Helping self-transforming adults more clearly recognize and understand the rationale behind these actions, and remaining open to involving them in other ways moving forward, can support these knowers as they strive to take even greater perspectives on themselves, others, and the intricacies of working together.

## Ways of Knowing and Receiving Feedback

As we have now explored in some depth, adults who make meaning in different ways will have different needs and preferences as feedback receivers, and this has important implications for the kinds of feedback we give to others with caring attention. To summarize, in table 4.1 we highlight key

**TABLE 4.1**

**Feedback supports and challenges for adults with different ways of knowing**

| Way of knowing | Feedback supports ("tuning in" frequencies) | Feedback challenges (stretches for growth) |
|---|---|---|
| *Instrumental* | • Offer concrete suggestions, models, and examples.<br>• Recognize what went right and wrong.<br>• Provide clear and explicit expectations.<br>• Remain consistent with your message, suggestions, and directions. | • Encourage looking beyond only one "right" and "wrong" solution or path for teaching and leading.<br>• Scaffold abstract thinking and comparison of ideas across different situations. |
| *Socializing* | • Voice appreciation for effort and contributions.<br>• Validate progress and personal qualities.<br>• Begin with a sincere acknowledgment of personal value of the person's instructional practice and/or leadership. | • Invite expression of recipient's own beliefs about practice in safe contexts.<br>• Model and role-play conflict that does not threaten relationships.<br>• Distinguish constructive feedback as separate from your assessment of colleague as a person. |
| *Self-authoring* | • Acknowledge competence and expertise.<br>• Provide opportunities to discuss recipient's own ideas, develop recipient's own goals, and critique and design initiatives.<br>• Invite person into leadership roles. | • Encourage exploration of new and different ideas, values, and approaches—both professionally and personally.<br>• Invite person to be a facilitator in general and especially in relationship to a proposal about which there is disagreement. |
| *Self-transforming* | • Invite into collaborative reflection on practice and exploration of alternatives, contradictions, and paradoxes (internal and systemic). | • Gently support the management of the implicit frustrations and tensions of transformation and change.<br>• Offer support as recipient makes sense of internal and systemic contradictions and inconsistencies. |

developmental supports and challenges you can use to shape your feedback conversations as genuine holding environments for adults who make meaning with instrumental, socializing, self-authoring, or self-transforming ways of knowing. Importantly, these strategies can help us imbue our feedback with a developmental component regardless of content or context (i.e., be it a formal or informal feedback relationship, team, professional learning community, or other collaborative practice). In the chapters that follow, we will dive even deeper into the process of giving, receiving, and differentiating feedback within, and as an expression of, genuine holding environments that support professional growth and capacity building.

To further synthesize the connections between adults' developmental capacities and their orientations to receiving feedback, we offer in table 4.2 a concise overview of ways of knowing and feedback that can be easily shared with colleagues. In working with educational leaders of all kinds over many years, we have found that sharing the language and ideas of constructive-developmental theory—even in small ways at first—can make a powerful difference in the collaborative culture of any school, team, or organization. We hope you find this a useful takeaway as well.

Of course, when you are reflecting privately about and/or sharing these ideas with others, it is important to acknowledge the complex business of both having and "diagnosing" ways of knowing in our feedback and leadership. No matter where we fall on the developmental spectrum, or where those around us are and aspire to be, we often live much of our lives in transition, or in the spaces between two dominant ways of knowing. Indeed, as we stretch and strengthen our developmental reach and expand our internal capacities, we inch forward toward more sophisticated and more complex ways of seeing and being in the world and with others. Because of this, and because surface behaviors alone (i.e., what we notice people *doing*) are not always indicative of a person's way of knowing, it is imperative that we consider these ideas with and for each other with open hearts and open minds. The chance to walk with another person in good company and confidence as you explore questions, problems, and hopes for practice can be an incredibly powerful gift and opportunity, one that recognizes the fundamental dignity and fragility of the people around us (and ourselves) without letting go of the urgency of the demands we face together.

*Applying your learnings*

As we have been exploring, adults' ways of knowing directly influence how they orient to, feel about, interpret, and take in leadership, authority, and suggestions for improved practice. All of these are key as we strive to make our feedback more meaningful and actionable. Because leaders of all kinds often need to listen carefully and caringly to others as a first step in understanding how colleagues might be making meaning (and especially before building a shared developmental language), in exhibit 4.1 we present a series of vignettes that illustrate four different teachers' reflections on their experiences receiving feedback from supervisors. We present these without

**TABLE 4.2**

## Understanding how adults with different ways of knowing orient to receiving feedback

| | WAY OF KNOWING | | | |
|---|---|---|---|---|
| | Instrumental<br>"me" | Socializing<br>"you" | Self-authoring<br>"I" | Self-transforming<br>"we" |
| When receiving feedback, I . . . | Need to understand the rules—that's what helps me in my work. | Internalize others' feelings and assessments of me and my instructional practice as my own. | Listen and yet feel that I still hold firm to my own values and beliefs. | Seek to grow myself further through interconnection with the person offering feedback. I want to grow myself. |
| When receiving feedback, I am most concerned about . . . | Meeting my own needs and getting it "right." It's important to me. | Ensuring that others think highly of me and like me regardless of my work. | Demonstrating my competencies and sharing my perspectives. | Seeing deeper into myself and my practice with trusted others. I want to talk with my supervisor. I want to grow from our conversation. |
| When receiving feedback, I wonder . . . | What's in it for me? What did I do right? What did I do wrong? What do I have to do to get a reward and/or avoid punishment? | What do you think of me? Do you still like me even when I'm not teaching as you think I should? Do you think I'm doing a good job? Do you think I'm a good person? | How will your feedback better help me reach my goals? Do your suggestions and ideas align with my own understanding of next steps to grow my practice and myself? | How might you see into me and my practice in new and important ways? How can I learn from your perspective? How can I become a better teacher and leader? |

*continues*

**TABLE 4.2** (*continued*)

| | WAY OF KNOWING | | | |
|---|---|---|---|---|
| | Instrumental<br><br>"me" | Socializing<br><br>"you" | Self-authoring<br><br>"I" | Self-transforming<br><br>"we" |
| **When receiving feedback, I feel most supported when you . . .** | Offer me concrete suggestions, models, and examples so that I can get things right in my practice of teaching. Clear and explicit expectations really help me. I need to know so that I can get better. | Offer me sincere appreciation for my work and contributions. It feels supportive and I feel good about it and you. Personal and professional validation means a lot to me. | Explicitly recognize me and my competence and expertise. It feels like you respect me. Opportunities to discuss my own ideas and develop my own goals when we meet feel supportive to me. I appreciate that a great deal. | Invite me to collaboratively reflect on my practice and yours, and when we explore new ideas, alternatives, and paradoxes together. It feels supportive to me, and I hope it does to you as well. |
| **When receiving feedback, it feels challenging when . . .** | I am asked to reflect on competing alternatives or decide between multiple options when there is no clear answer. I would like you to tell me what I need to do, please. | I am asked to share my thinking without knowing how you or other leaders feel first—especially if I am given negative or critical feedback about my performance. | I am presented with ideas or perspectives that directly oppose my own, or that call my competency into question. | Others do not include me in the processes of feedback or planning for next steps. It's hard for me when there are so many rules and when we do not address paradoxes—both systemic and on our team. While I understand that conflicts and differences of opinions that are resistant to resolution are part of our work, it's still hard for me. |
| **In terms of receiving feedback, I think I need to get better at . . .** | Understanding others' feelings and perspectives; acknowledging when challenges may not have one right answer. I wish everyone would just follow the rules. | Taking in constructive criticism without experiencing it as dislike of me personally. | Navigating, exploring, and "hearing" seemingly opposing viewpoints or ideas that are so different from my own thinking. | Accepting that I cannot solve every problem and conflict; I really want harmony. Recognizing when I need to hold back in hierarchical systems and structures. |

identifying each teacher's way of knowing and in no particular order. We hope you find this a meaningful opportunity to apply your learnings from this chapter to practical case examples. These vignettes can also be a helpful heuristic for sharing and discussing key aspects of feedback for growth with colleagues.

To help guide your reading, we invite you to consider the following investigative prompts:

- With which way of knowing do you think each teacher is making meaning? You may find it helpful to underline or circle evidence in each vignette that points to one way of knowing or another. (You may also see a glimpse of two ways of knowing operating. If that is the case, please try to determine which way of knowing is dominant.)
- What seems supportive to each teacher? Challenging? How might this relate to his or her way of knowing? (You may find tables 4.1 and 4.2 helpful points of reference/comparison.)
- Do you think that it could be the same leader offering feedback to each of these teachers? Why or why not?

*Diving deeper: Analyzing the vignettes*

When analyzing the vignettes for developmental clues, we've found it helpful to zoom in on indicators that point specifically to meaning making (e.g., orienting concerns, things that seem to be either "subject" [something a person is "run by"] or "object" [things a person can take a perspective on and control]). More specifically, what is each person able to take responsibility for? What, for each person, seems to be outside of or within his or her control? What do you think is *most* important to each? Next, we briefly revisit all four of the vignettes and highlight specific evidence that suggests, from our view, each teacher's particular way of knowing. We hope this is useful to you.

Beginning with the first vignette, Andy's reflections point strongly to a socializing way of knowing. What seems most important for Andy is having the principal's approval, and the sense of her genuine care. Specific feedback supports named in the vignette include expressing appreciation, engaging in private conversations, and, as Andy puts it, highlighting "the good things I'm already doing." Challenges, or growing edges, arise for Andy when the principal solicits reflections and ideas *without* first sharing her own. Ultimately, Andy's identity and self-assessments as a teacher seem intimately bound with the principal's. As Andy explains, when the principal communicates confidence and encouragement, "it makes me want to

EXHIBIT 4.1

**APPLICATION EXERCISE**

## Advancing Your Practice: Four Teachers Making Meaning of Their Supervisor's Feedback

ANDY'S REFLECTIONS

My principal gives *great* feedback. Her comments make me feel like I'm doing a good job, and they give me confidence. Even when she offers suggestions for improvement or little critiques on my practice and leadership role, I know that she's offering them because she really cares about me—not just as a teacher, but as a human being. That makes a huge difference to me—that she cares about me as a person. It makes me want to do more for her, and really, she gives me the courage to try new things to be an even better teacher. I want to be a better teacher, and I know my principal can help me be better. She has a lot of great ideas and suggestions, and I'm very grateful that she's willing to share her expertise and experience with me. Sometimes, when she has an idea for me, she pulls me aside privately to talk about whatever it is that she's thinking about. It might be about something she observed in my classroom during an observation or an idea for how I might help out in a faculty meeting or school event but—whatever it's about—she always shares it in a way that feels constructive, and also points out the good things I'm already doing. I like that she doesn't embarrass me; that means a lot to me.

Sometimes, when she tells me that I didn't do something quite right in my teaching, I feel so badly. I don't like to disappoint her. But, when she says something like this, she also lets me know that she can tell I'm really trying, and that makes me feel better. She makes me feel like I am an important part of the school— like I am contributing—even if I'm still learning about a lot of things. And she is very patient with me. I feel like I matter to her. If she didn't do that, I think I'd feel like, "What am I doing here? Maybe I should just leave this school and find somewhere else to go." I've been in situations like that before, and the mean feedback I've received from other bosses never helped me do better at all. They pretty much just made me more nervous and I felt like I actually did worse, even though I was *really* trying to do better. My principal now, though, she works really hard at helping us all to feel appreciated, and to have a sense of our school as a real community—a place where we're all making a difference. She likes us. It's hard being a teacher, I think, and she lets us know that that's okay. I feel like she really understands, even when she doesn't say that out loud. I just feel it—do you know what I mean?

In terms of something that I find unhelpful, I'm not really sure. A lot of times at school, she'll say, "Andy, what do you think you should do?" Or, "Andy, what do you think about this or that?" Or she'll ask me what I thought of a colleague's idea or something that I'm struggling with in my teaching. It's really not helpful to me when she does this after I've asked her a question about something that I don't understand and ask for her help with. I'm not sure how I'm supposed to learn new instructional practices if she doesn't tell me what she thinks I should be working on. I ask her questions when I'm not sure about what's best. Plus, when my colleagues give me feedback on my instruction, they usually just say what I do well.

**TAYLOR'S REFLECTIONS**

My principal is most supportive in her feedback when she speaks with me openly, honestly, and without artifice. I feel that she really understands that what motivates me the most is the fluidity and mutuality of our conversations about teaching and our school, and the chance to explore new possibilities for improvement together. After observations, I always bring ideas about what I can or should be doing differently in my classroom, but it's incredibly helpful to consider my practice from her perspective. I obviously can't do that alone. In this way, I truly welcome my principal's feedback—whether it's positive or critical, formal or informal. We've actually come a long way together, and I really value our relationship and the unique lens she brings to my teaching and to our school. Her experience is both similar to and different than mine—and I consider her a valued and insightful thought partner.

Related to this, something I really admire is her commitment to empowering everyone in our school—teachers *and* students—to shape the vision of the school. We work together collaboratively; we *are* community. We develop our own goals, and try on different roles in grade level and vertical teams, professional learning experiences, and even school governance. I really like that I'm able to experiment with colleagues while encouraging and enacting a learning process I believe in.

In terms of something I would offer to my principal as a suggestion that could help everyone—and I have told her this directly, so I'm not talking behind her back—I find it frustrating when she presents certain initiatives as "non-negotiables." As I said, I've actually told her this, so I don't feel like I'm speaking out of turn. I understand that we live and work in a very high-pressure context as educators today, and that—as the principal—she is especially accountable to outside stakeholders. But still, I feel that a closed approach to school improvement limits our school and our students' potential. I think that if we kind of joined together in exploring more thoughtfully—and critically—what we are doing and what alternatives might also foster change, we could further develop our school's potential and programs even more! I understand, though, that moving away from what we're told to do by the DOE isn't always easy, comfortable, or possible—especially today. Still, I think we could get there.

**GERRY'S REFLECTIONS**

My principal is very helpful to me in her feedback—she's very clear. She always tells me exactly what I need to do, which takes a lot of guesswork out of things, you know? That helps me a lot. In our school there are rules and policies so none of us can say that we don't understand what to do. I like that. It helps me understand what I need to do and how I need to do it. She also helps me after observations because—when she gives me feedback—she tells me what I did right and what I did wrong. She always recognizes my hard work and offers clear directions about what I need to do next. When I get something wrong—like not asking students

*continues*

enough higher-order questions—she gives me charts from books, based on research, to help me learn what to say, and that really helps. I know what to do to get it right. That's very helpful. Plus, when she gives me feedback, she explains the steps and then she directs me to more resources and tools I can use. Sometimes she even tells me to go to someone on my team who, say, is better at classroom management than I am. Plus, every policy is written out for us in our faculty handbook. That's really good.

And it's not just that. If I have a question or need help with something, she usually has a clear answer, too. She's very objective in terms of her feedback, and I feel like she holds all of the teachers to a fair and equal standard. I've worked in some places where different people seem to play by different rules, and that honestly drives me crazy. It makes me feel like people play "favorites" in ways that undermine what we're all trying to do. It was a big relief for me when I started here that my principal wasn't like that. She's quite fair, and very straightforward.

The one thing that I'm confused about in terms of her feedback is that she sometimes asks me to consider different options for my teaching. Like, do I think this or that would be more effective? It's a little frustrating for me when she asks questions like that after observations, because it sort of leaves me in limbo about what to do next. I already know what I'm thinking, so why can't she just tell me what she needs me to do to get it right? I'm completely committed to my students and my work—I want my job to be in education for many years. I just wish that she would focus on what I need to do for my annual evaluation. That's what would really help me.

## NOEL'S REFLECTIONS

My principal gives very effective feedback because she encourages me, and everyone at school, to think for ourselves. We learn a lot from each other—and I truly feel that is essential. I've had other principals who didn't do this; they just wanted me to follow their rules and do whatever they want. I understand that needs to happen sometimes when you're rolling out a new policy or gathering data on a new initiative. But not in all situations—especially with all the mandates from our district right now. I also really appreciate that my principal makes room for us to discuss my teaching thoughtfully after observations. She asks me what I personally think about the lessons she observes, and invites me to share my thinking before offering hers. And during evaluations and goal setting meetings, I can pick my own goals—things I really care about and want to get better at. And I tell her. I mean, I feel I can be honest with her. That means a lot to me. I know what I do well, and what I still need to work on. I also know what she's really good at, and what she might be able to improve. Despite our frequent back-and-forth, I'd say our relationship is one of mutual respect—and I think she would too. She trusts me as a competent professional and respects my decisions about her feedback—even when I don't always do what she suggests. And I really do appreciate her feedback, even if she might not always know that. I think that, mostly, she knows that. On another note, my principal doesn't need or want me to check in with her about every instructional choice I make in my classroom or with my team. *That* is very helpful, too.

> The part that is hardest for me is that she doesn't always take my advice or feedback when I offer it to her with best intentions. Like the time when a bunch of teachers in a recent grade-level team meeting were upset about the changes she was making to our weekly meeting policy. Some of the teachers—including me—preferred the old system and just didn't understand her reasoning. I told her about that and how I thought she could help. At my school, in my team, and in my life, I question things. Just because she's the principal, and just because she's in an official leadership position, I'm not going to stop that. I'm not going to take something as truth just because she says so. I guess that's something that I find unhelpful.

do more for her, and it gives me the courage to try new things to be an even better teacher."

In many ways, Taylor's reflections evince a similarly relational orientation. However, Taylor's meaning making suggests a more self-transforming perspective on feedback and collaboration. It is, for instance, "the fluidity and mutuality" of Taylor's conversations with the principal that feel most supportive (i.e., not just her approval). In addition, Taylor clearly communicates an openness to learning and growing from others' perspectives (e.g., "[I]t's incredibly helpful to consider my practice from her [the principal's] perspective. I obviously can't do that alone"). Like many self-transforming knowers, Taylor also finds it challenging to accept "non-negotiables" at face value, and yearns for greater opportunity to "join together" and explore the deeper complexities of such mandates.

In the third vignette, Gerry's reflections are more indicative of an instrumental way of knowing. For instance, Gerry's preferences for "rules and policies," "right" and "wrong" answers, evidence-based suggestions, and a single standard for "fairness" reflect a concrete, dualistic orientation to the work at hand. Unlike Taylor, then, Gerry *prefers* when the principal "just tell[s] me what she needs me to do to get it right." Like other instrumental knowers, Gerry finds exploring different options and alternatives (each of which may be "right" in one form or another) disorienting, and a little bit like being "in limbo."

Finally, Noel's reflections suggest a strong appreciation of autonomy, and a self-authoring perspective on teaching, authority, and feedback. More specifically, Noel demonstrates an internal capacity for self-reflection and awareness (e.g., "I know what I do well, and what I still need to work on"). In addition, Noel expressly appreciates opportunities to direct goal-setting conversations and share internal assessments with others—even those in authority (e.g., "Just because she's the principal, and just because she's in an official leadership position, I'm not going to stop that"). Yet Noel still finds it challenging when others don't share the same assessments, ideas, or points of view, and may need support to take a larger perspective on these internal values and judgments over time. For example, Noel has a hard time understanding when the principal—despite their "mutual respect"—"doesn't always take my advice or feedback when I offer it to her with best intentions."

### IS RESISTANCE ALWAYS RESISTANCE? A DEVELOPMENTAL REFRAMING ON A COMMON CHALLENGE

As all of these examples show, it is vital to understand the kinds of developmental supports and stretching that adults will need to best hear, take in, and act upon your feedback. It is equally important to recognize that when feedback is *not* offered in the confines of a safe holding environment or in ways that meet people where they are developmentally, it can fall quite flat. This is another reason why a working knowledge of the developmental aspects of feedback for growth is so needed and promising. Indeed, because of the frequent (if unintentional) developmental misalignments that can occur in almost any group, team, or relationship, it can sometimes seem to feedback givers that colleagues are being resistant, when in fact they may have misheard, misunderstood, or not heard at all what was being shared in the first place. In these cases, the gap between how feedback is offered and how others receive it can feel almost like a language barrier or, to return to an earlier analogy, a staticky radio signal. As one New York City principal recently characterized it, when this happens it is much like a "misfire in the messaging"—albeit one we can actively work to correct.

Put another way, in our roles as feedback givers, we may sometimes wonder why people are not acting on the *really good* feedback we provided. Understanding the potential developmental dimensions of resistance can help, as another leader put it, make perceived pushback "less 'ouchy' and personal."[2] Accordingly, when we encourage people to do things or entertain new perspectives as part of our feedback, we must carefully consider the developmental *fit* between their strengths and capacities and what we are asking them to do. We must also be intentional about the supports and challenges we offer to colleagues as they work to demonstrate new skills and abilities, as simply telling individuals what is needed or required is not always enough. Is the person ready, for instance, to develop and reflect on goals for practice (knowing that "reflect" can mean different things to different people)? Will he need carefully tailored supports to implement a new initiative or take on a leadership role, or is this something that would already feel comfortable and rewarding? Does she agree with your assessments and suggestions? Understanding the developmental landscape—for both ourselves and others—can help us better build the human capacity that will enable us to meet and exceed the mounting demands of teaching and leading today.

## Educators' Reflections on Reframing Resistance

While there are inarguably many reasons for and forms of resistance, educators nevertheless often wonder and worry about adults who do not seem to be keeping pace with their feedback. In our work with educational leaders of all kinds, for instance, many voice concerns about "dealing with difficult people," "understanding why people act the way they do," or managing adults who are "skeptical and critical." As we have discussed, however, understanding the developmental roots of some kinds of resistance can be empowering and liberating—for both feedback givers and receivers. It can, for instance, help us to offer feedback with more empathy, compassion, and insight into others' sense making. As many educators have similarly expressed after learning more about constructive-developmental theory and related practices, developmental mindfulness can help us lead and offer feedback more effectively when things (and people) are not changing as fast as we might otherwise like.

For example, after learning about ways of knowing in a professional workshop, Brendan, a leader at an urban middle school, described an important "a-ha" moment. "Now I understand why some of my teachers can't understand my feedback," he shared excitedly. As part of his school's efforts to improve test scores and find its way out of struggling status, Brendan had been encouraging his teachers to use more high-level questions as indicated in Bloom's taxonomy. Some, however, still weren't doing it. Realizing through his learning in the workshop, though, that some of his teachers were likely making meaning with an instrumental way of knowing, he decided to offer these colleagues more concrete examples and models of practice to scaffold the transition and help them improve their instructional practice.

Another leader from this same school offered a parallel insight about providing feedback to teachers with a socializing way of knowing. While this leader identified as self-authoring in her own way of knowing and tended to offer colleagues what she described as "direct and crisp written feedback," learning about ways of knowing helped her to understand that many socializing teachers likely couldn't hear her fully when she offered feedback only in this way. It wasn't necessarily that these adults were resisting her feedback, as she initially thought, but that perhaps they felt overwhelmed or threatened by it. More specifically, referencing the "glow" and "grow" comments she outlined in the written feedback forms (i.e., positive and critical remarks for improved practice), this leader wisely concluded that shifting the order of her comments to focus first on the positive, as well as finding more sincere "glows" to share up front, could help her socializing colleagues better learn from and take in the feedback she was offering.

## CHAPTER SUMMARY AND CONCLUSION

As these examples and this chapter make clear, understanding constructive-developmental theory has important implications for the kinds of feedback colleagues can best hear, understand, take in, and act upon. As we have also begun to explore, adult developmental theory can help us better recognize and deepen the ways in which we ourselves orient to feedback, both as givers and receivers. In chapter 5, we will further consider how these ideas offer insight into why we and others *offer* feedback in the ways that we do, in terms of the gifts we bring as well as the challenges we face—and how we can continue to grow ourselves and our feedback.

## REFLECTIVE QUESTIONS

Please take a moment to consider the following questions, which can be used for independent reflection and group conversation. You may find it useful to reflect in writing privately first, and then to engage in discussion with a colleague or team. These questions are intended to help you and your colleagues consider the ideas discussed in this chapter and how they might deepen your understanding about ways of knowing and receiving feedback.

- ✦ After reading this chapter, what are two ways you will use what you have learned to enhance your practice of giving feedback so that others can best hear it or take it in?
- ✦ At this point, what would you name as your most important improvement goal—something you feel you need to get better at—to make your professional feedback more accessible to and actionable for others?

✦ What insights do you have about your own way of knowing or growing edge, especially as they relate to receiving feedback? What would
feel like a good feedback holding environment for you?

✦ With your growth opportunities for giving and receiving feedback in
mind, what small steps might help you work toward these goals? How
might you collaborate with colleagues to achieve them?

# CHAPTER 5

# How Do Different Ways of Knowing Influence How We *Give* Feedback?

*Adult growth and development is as much about growing and developing yourself as it is about growing and developing others, about both giving gifts and receiving gifts. There is much to be said for leaders who can look inside themselves and examine their own assumptions and ways of knowing in order to better develop others, and who are willing to learn from those around them as well.*

—ASPIRING PRINCIPAL

Feedback relationships are always—and at least—a two-way street. As feedback givers, we need to constantly consider and remain mindful of how our *own* ways of knowing intersect and interact with the developmental capacities of the adults we are supporting. In this chapter we offer a closer look at this important coming together of developmental preferences and orientations. More specifically, here we invite you to consider how feedback givers' ways of knowing are just as important and integral to the process of feedback for growth as the developmental capacities of those on the receiving end.

Remember, for instance, the leaders we described in the opening of chapter 4 (who some adults considered "curmudgeonly" or "wishy-washy" in their feedback, while others did not). We explained how understanding ways of knowing helps illuminate how and why different adults might experience these leaders and their feedback styles differently, but we have not yet considered why these hypothetical leaders tended to give feedback in the ways that they did. How, for example, might their ways of knowing have influenced the nature and style of their feedback? How might a deeper awareness of their own ways of knowing and their preferences for giving feedback have helped them more effectively reach the adults they were caring for? This chapter focuses on us as feedback *givers* and how our own ways of knowing, and thus our own internal developmental capacities, are at the heart of how we give feedback. They matter greatly.

As we will explore throughout this chapter, leaders' ways of knowing inevitably inform how they think about, conceptualize, and offer feedback—just as they influence the ways receivers hear, take in, and make sense of the feedback they are provided. Understanding these differences, and their strengths and potential limitations, can help us enrich our *own* propensities for giving feedback so that colleagues can best take in and learn from it. This kind of self-knowledge is also key when considering the match between feedback giver and receiver, which research suggests is very important.

For example, a leader who makes meaning primarily with an instrumental way of knowing would have difficulty taking the perspective of a colleague transitioning from a socializing to a self-authoring way of knowing, so it would be hard for that leader to "reach up" (developmentally speaking) beyond his or her current internal capacities to truly meet that colleague as a learning guide. More specifically, there could be a problematic gap between an instrumental leader's emphasis on the "right" way of teaching and the hopes and needs of a colleague working to develop her or his own perspective on classroom practice (i.e., growing toward a self-authoring way of knowing). Conversely, if a principal solidly rooted in a self-authoring way of knowing lacked knowledge of development and its implications for feedback, it could be equally challenging for him or her to effectively support colleagues with a less complex meaning-making schema.

You could imagine, for instance, how painful it might be for adults with a socializing way of knowing to receive *only* critical feedback from a self-authoring principal if it were not offered with developmental intentionality—even if it were shared with best intentions to improve their instructional practice or leadership. In other words, since we now know that adults with a socializing way of knowing feel supported by authentic affirmations of their practice and personhood, and we also know that self-authoring knowers have the capacity to take the perspectives of colleagues who feel this way, understanding ways of knowing could help this principal more intentionally offer feedback so that these educators could take in and learn from it (e.g., by acknowledging what went well and offering admiration and appreciation for their hard work and successes *before* diving into suggestions for growth and improvement). Similarly, research suggests that developmental mindfulness can help adults reach up (developmentally speaking) to support colleagues who make meaning in slightly more complex ways (i.e., up to half a stage beyond their current way of knowing).[1]

Still, when it comes to feedback more generally, it has been shown that, more often than not, "birds of a feather flock together."[2] Put another way, it seems to be the case that adults often feel most comfortable giving feedback to people who take in and orient to constructive criticism, new ideas, and authority in ways similar to their own, and may also like to receive feedback from people who give it the way they like to get it (i.e., from people who share a similar feedback style and/or way of knowing). Indeed, in our work with school leaders of all kinds, we have found that people often operate on "default" feedback settings that align with their own developmental preferences and orientations.

For example, Jonah, the CEO of a K–12 charter school in the northeast United States, recently told us that he used to give feedback as a new principal in the very same way he liked to receive it. His preferred mode of receiving feedback—as a self-identified self-authoring knower—was in the vein of "Give it to me straight." He didn't want a lot of appreciation because he "already knew" what he did well. "What I needed," he explained, "was direct, critical, honest feedback—no sugar." However, based on his early experiences giving this kind of direct feedback to his teachers and leadership cabinet members, he grew to understand that what worked for him did not always work well for everyone. In order to best support growth in instruction and leadership in his school, he needed to realize (as he soon did) that "people need different things." As Jonah put it, "They needed to be held in ways I didn't." This was a "lesson learned" for him, and he explained that he changed his practice to accommodate adults' ways of knowing when offering feedback for growth. For example, when working with many of his teachers, he realized that he needed to slow down and reaffirm the underlying professional relationships—to "honor the integrity of their feelings," as he put it—before diving into constructive suggestions. He also recognized that, despite initially feeling more comfortable supporting self-authoring adults who oriented to feedback as he did, learning about ways of knowing helped him grow more adept at effectively supporting *all* colleagues and their growth through feedback.

As this example illuminates, there is a real hopefulness in learning about one's own way of knowing, and in sharing developmental ideas with colleagues so that they, too, can look within and outside themselves when giving feedback, with best intentions. Just as it did for Jonah, understanding ways of knowing can help us better understand ourselves *and* how to create holding environments for others so that they can hear and take in feedback to improve practice. Indeed, when we recognize each other and ourselves in developmental terms, it becomes clear that the match between feedback givers and receivers isn't entirely dependent upon luck or happenstance. We *can* deepen and strengthen our capacities for giving and receiving feedback. We *can* better meet each other where we are developmentally. And we *can* challenge ourselves and those around us to grow more and more, in ways big and small, every day.

## REVISITING WAYS OF KNOWING: EVOLVING CAPACITIES FOR GIVING FEEDBACK

Of course, the first step in enacting change both internally and organizationally is self-knowledge. As Osterman and Kottkamp remind us, "real change begins with us."[3] To address this important insight, in the next sections we expand our discussion of ways of knowing to illustrate how adults' different developmental capacities can influence how they tend to give feedback—the kinds of things they may be inclined to emphasize, their potential strengths as feedback givers, and their growing edges (i.e., areas for improvement and internal capacity building).

### Instrumental Knowers as Feedback Givers

As you now know, instrumental knowers, in general, are run by their deep preoccupying orientation to meet their own needs, wants, and desires by successfully navigating "the rules." When offering feedback, educators who operate primarily with an instrumental way of knowing orient to "right" and "wrong" solutions and strategies in their assessments of teaching practice and other key school initiatives. Whether they are run by a desire for external rewards or concrete recognition (e.g., a raise or promotion, higher ratings on a professional evaluation or school report card) or by a firm but unquestioned sense that a particular approach is the correct path for the school community, leaders who make meaning in this way feel most effective when colleagues are acting as they are "supposed" to: when they adhere to deadlines, follow directions, and meet outlined expectations to "get the job done." While these may be aspects of work that are important regardless of our way of knowing, for instrumental knowers this—a concrete, dualistic, "right and wrong" point of reference—*is* their orientation to learning, teaching, leading, and living.

Importantly, educators with an instrumental way of knowing can be very effective at providing concrete information and helping colleagues navigate complex and important tasks like completing forms and applications, setting up and learning new technologies, and inventorying outlined expectations. For example, Mark, a district-level financial officer, recently reflected on his approach to offering feedback to colleagues on his team:

> All of my team members know there are two big things for me. First—and I know this might sound like a little *and* a big thing—is that I need my team to reply to my e-mails right away. We've had lots of conversations about this. When they don't respond right away (which, for me, means within the hour), it causes me to be late on *my* deadlines, so responsiveness is really important to me. Second, I make it really clear to everyone that there are policies we need to abide by—that there are rules we must follow. Some of these rules come from the state—I mean, they're literally the law—and some of them have been developed by the district for our team. But all of them are important and keep things moving smoothly and equitably. I'm kind of a stickler for the rules because there's really no wiggle room when you're the one signing the documents at the end of the day, you know? So it's really frustrating to me when people sidestep or forget about the policies, especially since I've spent so much time making sure they're clear.

While, like Mark, adults with any way of knowing can do a good job with compliance and fiscal management matters, Mark came to see through his reflections—after learning about ways of knowing—that he was making meaning in his work and in his life more generally as an instrumental knower. This knowledge, Mark explained, was power for him. "It's actually a big comfort for me to know this," he explained, "because I understand my frustrations better." While his concrete approach had served him very well in many ways for a long time, Mark came to see that what made him most effective in certain aspects of his job also proved to be a growing edge when leading his team and supporting *their* professional growth. While, understandably, Mark still valued responsiveness and compliance, he set an improvement goal for himself to be more patient with his team. "It seems counterintuitive," he shared, "but I think being patient might actually help the team work more efficiently to meet our goals."

*Growing edge: Instrumental knowers*

As Mark's experience helps illustrate, a leader making meaning with an instrumental way of knowing finds little room for interpretation or "gray areas," as things tend to be black or white, right or wrong. Since adults with this way of knowing tend to see things dualistically, they may orient toward rewards and punishments when offering feedback, and may more easily interpret divergence or noncompliance as failure or resistance.

As an additional example, please imagine a leader with this way of knowing offering feedback in the spirit of, "If you're not with me, you're against me." Reflecting on some of her biggest professional challenges, for instance, another practicing district-level leader, Sandy, offered the following: "It really upsets me when adults don't come to the trainings I organize. This makes my job a lot harder than it needs to be, and creates a lot of extra work on my end. I don't think the teachers even realize how hard this is on me. And even when they do come, many don't retain the information they're provided. That's probably the hardest part of my work right now."

While it can be difficult to assess anyone's way of knowing from just a few snippets of dialogue, it seems clear from Sandy's framing here that, from her perspective, compliance and retention are key indicators of a quality employee. Moreover, like Mark's, Sandy's reflections point toward a developmental edge for growth in instrumental knowers. In this case, Sandy had a hard time taking the perspective of her colleagues; she was not able to "stand in their shoes," nor did she consider asking them *why* they were having trouble making the training sessions. From her view, "if everyone would just show up, they'd know what to do."

Indeed, adults who make meaning with an instrumental way of knowing may not yet understand how others experience their feedback, passion, or urgency. As yet another leader explained, describing her propensity to "call out" colleagues as soon as she saw a problem (even in front of students or other teachers), "People need to be made aware of what they are doing wrong immediately, as there simply isn't a minute to waste when educating children." In the complex context of education today, with so much up in the air and so much at stake, the fact that adults who make meaning in this way have not yet developed the capacity to see situations abstractly or take another's perspective fully can make giving feedback—and leading for change—difficult in the long term without continued growth.

Of course, we recognize that there might be times when educators with any way of knowing might want or need to adopt a more directive approach to feedback that echoes the characteristics of instrumental knowers. And, as we acknowledged earlier, regardless of our ways of knowing, there are times when we all must follow rules and policies or otherwise comply. Thus, it is important to understand that we are not describing the relative merits or detriments of any particular feedback or leadership style when discussing ways of knowing. Rather, our hope is to highlight, in big broad strokes, the difference between consciously *choosing* to adopt a particular style, and *being compelled* to enact that approach in our feedback because it still runs us psychologically (i.e., we remain subject to it, and cannot see or take perspective on it). Take, for example, the leaders we considered earlier in this chapter and in chapter 4, whom some adults experienced as "curmudgeonly" or "wishy-washy." While it may be tempting to make certain assumptions about these leaders' ways of knowing based on their feedback styles, we wonder how much anyone could really tell, with the limited information available, about these leaders' developmental sense making and experiences of feedback. Was the curmudgeonly boss operating with a right/wrong orientation to leadership (i.e., an instrumental orientation)? Or a principled stance based on self-authorship? Was the wishy-washy supervisor struggling internally to avoid conflict at all costs (a socializing orientation), or inviting colleagues to express their ideas and come to their own conclusions (a more self-transforming orientation)? Regardless of the answers, it seems clear that understanding more about what we and others are thinking and feeling internally can shed new light on *all* of our feedback encounters, and can help us grow ourselves and each other more fully.

## Socializing Knowers as Feedback Givers

When giving feedback, just as when receiving feedback, adults with a socializing way of knowing will orient strongly to pleasing important others (e.g., loved ones, valued colleagues, authorities, as well as societal expectations) and maintaining their approval, whether they be teachers, parents, supervisors, students, or other key stakeholders. Because they are essentially defined by their relationships, educators who make meaning in this way feel most comfortable, well held, and successful when school and classroom operations, and especially the interpersonal relationships within a building or organization, are running smoothly for them and for others. Accordingly, socializing knowers can be especially adept at offering positive, supportive feedback (or "glows," as many educators put it) but will likely shy away from more critical assessments—especially when they feel that offering these may threaten their relationships. As one high school principal shared with us, "I feel very comfortable *supporting* adults, and find it very easy to offer applause, but it's a lot harder to point out something that's not going well." While adults who make meaning in this way may not always share all of what they are truly thinking and feeling (especially when they fear that critical feedback may damage their relationships), they can be especially good at celebrating colleagues' genuine successes and contributions, and are also able to see into and understand how colleagues are feeling during feedback conversations.

*Growing edge: Socializing knowers*

As you know, educators with a socializing way of knowing will feel responsible for how colleagues feel during feedback sessions, and they will also hold colleagues responsible for how *they* are feeling as leaders and feedback givers. Because they orient to giving feedback in this way, it can be particularly difficult for them to offer critical or constructive feedback (or feedback that they feel will disappoint or upset someone), even when they want to or know that they should. For example, reflecting on some of her biggest feedback challenges, one instructional coach confided, "I struggle with having difficult conversations. I have strategies that I use, but don't always hold myself accountable for making them happen because they create so much anxiety in me." Another aspiring principal realized that, for her, "the hardest part of offering feedback to another person is finding a way to relay the critical information in a constructive way without hurting anyone's feelings."

Recently, Dora, a state-level leader who supports professional development (PD) throughout a northeastern state, reflected on a conundrum she was facing in her work. Dora was in the midst of planning a statewide professional learning day, and was tasked with selecting and organizing a series of sessions proposed by educators from across the state. As part of this work, Dora was working closely with eighteen district leaders, each of whom was pushing for particular topics and sessions to be included in the PD day. Anxious about pleasing these leaders, yet simultaneously hoping to offer the best and most coherent workshops possible for all attendees, Dora confided that she was "able to incorporate seventeen of the eighteen leaders' requests for the day," but one colleague—who had "*very* strong opinions"—proposed a session she needed to reject. As Dora explained, "The proposal just wasn't up to par, and it didn't align with our larger theme or purpose. I know I'm going to have to let my colleague know I can't accept her session for the PD day, and I know she's going to be *very* disappointed. Logically, I know I can't please all of the people who report to me. But I feel like I need to, and I really, really want to." After a moment of silence, she added, "Actually, I'm *dreading* telling her. I know she's going to be really up-set with me, and I'm not sure how she's going to take such critical feedback. I'm really dreading that call."

While, as this example highlights, socializing leaders and learners can bring many strengths and great sensitivity to their work, giving feedback can be very painful for them. Facing a constant stream of conflicting voices, demands, and expectations, leaders with a socializing way of knowing may feel torn apart by their work and their feedback. Reflecting on how hard it can be to lead and make meaning in this way, for instance, another school leader, Ginny, shared the following:

> I remember how hard it was for me emotionally when I first became a principal. I can see now that I was a socializing knower at that time. I would go home almost every night and just cry because each day— or at least that's how it felt to me then—I was constantly disappoint-ing some of my teachers. They would be really mad at me, and they would tell me that. My husband would always ask me, "Why do you care so much about appeasing all of your teachers? That's not your job. Your job is to do what *you* feel is best for the kids, your school, and the community. You're the principal!" It took a long time for me to feel that way—what I mean is that it took a long time for me to understand that I cannot please all of the teachers and staff and that it's actually okay if they're mad at me. I'm in a much better place now. I no longer feel torn apart and sad and hurt when my teach-ers are upset with me, angry about decisions I've made, or upset in other ways. I do my best to listen and care for them—and I think most of them know that. And I realize now that I sometimes need to make decisions that will disappoint some of my staff. And it's so helpful to understand *why* it was so hard for me as a new leader and to now have a language to describe this. I can see now that I'm in a different place, and how I've grown.

While everyone prefers to be liked (and few or none of us enjoy deliberately hurting others' feelings or making decisions that disappoint those we care about), for socializing knowers the need to be liked and approved of goes far beyond simple preference. In other words, without the acceptance and approval of others, these adults will feel incomplete and inadequate, just as Ginny did, so giving their fullest and most authentic feedback can be a real growing and important developmental edge.

## Self-Authoring Knowers as Feedback Givers

As we noted earlier, research suggests that in today's high-stakes educational climate, leaders need to develop at least some form of self-authoring capacity to be most effective in their work, and the same is likely true for giving feedback. When it comes to sharing their ideas, suggestions, critiques, and assessments with colleagues, for instance, self-authoring knowers have the developmental capacity to see into and understand others' perspectives while simultaneously holding firm to their own. In fact, educators who make meaning in this way often have little or no trouble sharing constructive feedback, standing up for principles or ideas, or challenging authority, even when they know their perspectives may not win any popularity contests. It's not that they don't care about interpersonal relationships. They can and do. However, they are not *defined* by these relationships or society's expectations of them. They can take a perspective on them, and they can prioritize and reflect on them. Moreover, self-authoring knowers have reflectively selected and developed their positions (unlike instrumental leaders, who adopt external stances as "right" or "wrong") and have consciously chosen and nurtured them in relation to who *they* are as leaders, teachers, and human beings.

When it comes to giving feedback, then, adults who make meaning with a self-authoring way of knowing feel most successful and effective when they are leading according to their own values, commitments, and ideals, and when they are demonstrating their own competency, working to solve problems, or finding appropriate solutions on behalf of a larger school or district mission.

Another experienced school principal, Ben, voiced a sentiment characteristic of a self-authoring stance on feedback: "Great feedback has to start with a strong vision." From Ben's prospective, "onboarding" people to his particular way of thinking, seeing, and doing is one foundational aim of feedback, as it can help "close the gap between the reality and my vision." Describing, more specifically, how he used his feedback as a tool for helping colleagues to understand and come around to his point of view, Ben explained: "By positively or constructively addressing the things that you really care about as a leader, you send a strong message that others should be caring about these things as well. What I mean is, I give people feedback about X and Y, because they should be focusing their work on X and Y, too."

Interestingly, while self-authoring knowers like Ben can be very invested in recruiting others to their own way of thinking and doing, and may pride themselves on providing effective solutions, we've discovered that many leaders with this way of knowing also express interest in helping colleagues to be more independent, self-directed, or self-sufficient themselves. As one instructional coach recently explained, describing her hope for supporting other adults through her feedback, "I want to work on capacity building and being more explicit about that work, so that the adults with whom I work do not become dependent on me, but rather they take the coaching and run with it." Similarly, another district-level leader, whose job entails supporting teachers' instructional practice, offered the following: "I aim to build capacity in adults by getting them to solve problems on their own with some support and not necessarily fixing a problem for them or giving them the answers."

### Growing edge: Self-authoring knowers

As these examples make clear, self-authoring knowers may experience something of a paradox in their feedback giving. On the one hand, they find it satisfying to solve complex problems of practice and draw people into their vision. On the other hand, however, they recognize how challenging it can be to hold all of this complexity for colleagues, and are usually invested, too, in helping adults grow their own capacities for self-authorship. In fact, some leaders with this way of knowing may have trouble looking back on their earlier experiences of making meaning, and can forget how difficult (or even painful) it can be to grow and learn from feedback in prior stages.

For example, after learning about ways of knowing in a workshop, a leader who self-identified as self-authoring recently wondered (with genuine incredulity), "Why would someone *want* to be socializing?" Of course, the big idea here is that ways of knowing are not simply a matter of choice or preference, but rather manifestations of an individual's most central tendencies for making meaning. That said, remembering—and honoring—that some adults may be in different places developmentally (and also that meaning making is not static) can be a growing edge for self-authoring knowers, especially those without an awareness of developmental theory and its implications for feedback and leadership.

Related to this, educators with a self-authoring way of knowing will often find it challenging (a growing edge for them) to remain open to diametrically opposing points of view—during feedback or otherwise. Like instrumental knowers, self-authoring adults can appear closed in ways that seem to limit possibilities for more expansive, collaborative constructions of practice and culture. Yet the internal reasoning behind this shared outward certainty is very different. More specifically, instrumental knowers hold firm on what needs to be done based on external directives, rules, and authorities, while self-authoring knowers put a stake in the ground because of their own internal thinking and feeling (i.e., bench of judgment). Nevertheless, like instrumental knowers, self-authoring knowers can sometimes gravitate more naturally to the "challenge" side of feedback as they work to "onboard others" to their ways of thinking or theories of action.

One leader who participated in our survey research that informs this book, and who leads a team in her developmental work, recently shared, "The one thing I think is really easy to do in giving feedback is to criticize— to say what's wrong with something." Acknowledging, though, how important it is to also "help fix things," this leader, like many self-authoring knowers, recognized that she needed to improve at offering challenging feedback that honors the receivers' experiences. As another self-authoring leader recently told us, this is a strong hope and need for professional growth. "I want to learn how to give constructive feedback without giving offense," she explained. "I want to learn how to show my mastery while being humble and approachable." While sometimes it can be challenging for self-authoring leaders to recognize the need to express appreciation for what socializing knowers are doing well before offering them critical feedback, meeting all adults where they are in this way can lead to more productive feedback exchanges and outcomes over time.

### Self-Transforming Knowers as Feedback Givers

As we discussed in chapter 4, self-transforming knowers orient to feedback as an opportunity to co-construct interpretations, understandings, and future directions. For educators who make meaning in this way, giving feedback (like receiving it) is about *mutual* growth, and involves "engaging in discussion to build meaning and think together" (as one self-transforming leader described her work supporting teachers' instructional practice in schools). Similarly, Daniel, who makes meaning in this way and teaches aspiring leaders in schools, universities, and businesses, said that for him the goal of feedback is "to help us—you and me and whoever are participants in the feedback exercise—to become better, to improve *our* capabilities, capacities, and competencies for handling the complexities of work and life and living together in more effective and successful and even joyful ways."

As these examples help show, giving feedback for self-transforming knowers is really about inviting other adults into conversations, learning with and from them in the spirit of reciprocal growth and transformation.

*Growing edge: Self-transforming knowers*

Although, ostensibly, self-transforming knowers have grown through and beyond the challenges of giving feedback associated with the instrumental, socializing, and self-authoring ways of knowing, giving feedback can still be complex for educators who make meaning in this way. Like being a person in general, giving feedback is *hard*—no matter one's way of knowing. This is a very important point for all of us to hold in our hearts and minds.

For example, it can be difficult and even painful for leaders at this developmental stage to align their own desire for interconnection and mutual generativity with the expectations and needs of the adults in their care, especially without an explicit knowledge of constructive-developmental theory or ways of knowing. As Daniel later acknowledged, "It's hard for me to tell other people what to do, how to do it, when to do it, etc. I tend to think such directive behavior demeans the other person and his/her dignity."

James, a self-transforming educational leader in a large urban city, similarly explained that there are times when leaders are very much expected to make decisive and commanding decisions, even if they prefer a more collaborative approach. In fact, withholding ideas and solutions in these cases (even when done in the spirit of building bridges and community) can be interpreted by some colleagues as a kind of failure, weakness, or lack of support on the part of the leader. Capturing the kind of unintentional misalignment that can complicate a self-transforming knower's approach to feedback, James shared a particularly challenging but enlightening exchange he had with a colleague:

> After wrapping up an important meeting, one of my colleagues turned to me and said, "Man, that meeting was so frustrating." I knew it had been hard for him, and I said, "Yup. I notice that you get so upset when there isn't a clear answer." He stood there, just sort of looking at me, and asked, "Why didn't you say anything?" So I told him the truth: "I wanted to see how you would handle the situation." And that's when he told me. He said, "Look, I didn't care one way or another. I appreciate you wanting to hear everyone's opinion, but you're the *leader*. Right or wrong, sometimes a decision has to be made. I just wish you would speak up in those meetings and say a decision."

As James later realized, his own preferences for and orientations toward feedback as a dialogical exchange were, ironically, "getting in the way" of his effectiveness as a leader for this particular colleague. Yet receiving (and really hearing) such explicit feedback about his approach allowed James to further consider and reevaluate his feedback stance, and "understand a little bit more" about how to best support this colleague and his team.

## THINKING MORE ABOUT OUR OWN WAYS OF KNOWING AS FEEDBACK GIVERS

We hope that this discussion of the different ways adults across the developmental spectrum orient to giving feedback has been helpful as you consider and reflect on your own leadership and experiences with feedback. By way of both summary and takeaway, we offer in table 5.1 an overview of key ideas from this chapter. We hope you find it helpful when sharing these ideas with others. It is also, we hope, yet another way to loosely place *yourself* on the developmental continuum, and to think about how you would like to grow in your own ways of giving feedback.

## CHAPTER SUMMARY AND CONCLUSION

Understanding and growing ourselves and others can be the hardest kind of leadership and work. It is also, from our perspective, the most important and profoundly gratifying. In this chapter, we looked closely at how leaders with different ways of knowing think and feel about giving feedback to colleagues and their direct reports. While we know that there are many ways to place oneself on the developmental continuum (and that this kind of "diagnosis" is complex in and of itself), we hope this discussion has provided you with even more insight into your own and others' ways of knowing, and the connection between our internal capacities and the successful exchange of feedback. After all, from a developmental perspective, giving and receiving feedback are really just two sides of the very same leadership coin.

Moreover, as we will continue to explore in the chapters that follow, this kind of rich, developmental understanding provides the foundation for the effective practice of feedback for growth, and is the firmament on which any growth-enhancing culture or organization must rest. As Kegan and Lahey similarly argue, in order for a school or organization to truly "become a home for the continuing transformation of talent," leaders must actively take on and communicate a developmental stance in their work.[4] In our feedback, just as in our leadership, we must convey with certainty and passion a few unwavering beliefs: namely, that (1) "We can all keep growing"; (2) "We will need to, in order to accomplish our goals [as an

**TABLE 5.1**

**Understanding how adults with different ways of knowing orient to giving feedback**

| | WAY OF KNOWING | | | |
|---|---|---|---|---|
| | Instrumental<br>"me" | Socializing<br>"you" | Self-authoring<br>"I" | Self-transforming<br>"we" |
| **In relation to giving feedback, I . . .** | Adhere firmly to tangible rules and policies. | Prioritize others' feelings and opinions. | Stay true to my own values and beliefs. | Seek interconnection and co-constructions of meaning. |
| **When giving feedback, I am most concerned about . . .** | Meeting my own personal goals or organizational goals and objectives. | Maintaining positive relationships and feeling liked. | Guiding individuals and groups in accordance with my values and larger vision. | Inviting others into a shared and mutually reflective space. |
| **When giving feedback, I often wonder . . .** | Are you doing things the right way? How can I get you to do what I need or want? | How will you feel if I tell you what I really think? What will you think of me if I do this? | How can I get you to subscribe to my vision or belief system? | How can I best support you as a growing, learning human being? |
| **When giving feedback, I feel most comfortable . . .** | Assessing what colleagues have done "right" and "wrong." I am good at offering concrete directions. | Offering praise and "glows." | Sharing my own assessments and suggestions that align with my beliefs. | Engaging in mutual reflections and open-ended discussions. |
| **When giving feedback, I find it challenging . . .** | To see the "gray" in seemingly black and white situations; to understand how others think and feel about my feedback. | When I need to have hard conversations or share ideas that I know will upset or disappoint colleagues. | To support adults who do not share my beliefs about education and/or thinking about best practices; to question my own theories about what needs to be changed. | When I cannot meet others in their thinking and feeling in ways I would like; when adults hold back or are overly defensive in demeanor. |
| **In terms of giving feedback, I think I need to get better at . . .** | Standing in my colleagues' "shoes" and better understanding their perspectives. | Sharing my true thinking and feeling with others, as I know this is also an expression of care. | Recognizing that others may bring different and important ideas to the table that I could also learn from. | Recognizing when it would be helpful to step in and offer direct solutions and when I need to step back and allow others to find their own way. |

organization, department, or team]"; and (3) "We will want to, in order to experience the greatest vitality and satisfaction in our work."[5]

Ultimately, if we are truly to leave "no teacher behind" (as one leader said during a recent workshop), we need to commit to modeling and expressing these powerful ideals in our leadership, practice, and feedback. The next chapters will help you learn, more specifically, how to do just that.

---

## REFLECTIVE QUESTIONS

Please take a moment to consider the following questions, which can be used for independent reflection and group conversation. You may find it useful to reflect in writing privately first, and then to engage in discussion with a colleague or team. These questions are intended to help you and your colleagues consider the ideas discussed in this chapter and how they might inform your practice of giving feedback.

+ After reading this chapter, what are two of your biggest takeaways?
+ After reading this chapter, what insights do you have about your own way of knowing or growing edge, especially as they relate to giving feedback?
+ After reading this chapter, what are one or two things you would like to grow about the ways you offer feedback to others? What feels most exciting about this? What still feels hard?
+ With these hopes for growth in mind, what are two or three small steps you could take to build these into your practice? How might you collaborate with colleagues to achieve them?

CHAPTER 6

# Building a Culture of Feedback and Trust

*The degree to which I can create relationships which facilitate the growth of others as separate persons is a measure of the growth I have achieved in myself.*

—CARL ROGERS

In this chapter, we address the fundamental question, "What has to happen *first*—after one learns about constructive-developmental theory and its implications for individual meaning making—in order for one to offer the most meaningful feedback for growth and improvement?" In particular, we highlight the critical importance of building a *culture of feedback* in your school or organization as the foundation for productive, growth-enhancing conversations about educational and instructional change. In our work with educators of all kinds, we have learned that meaningful, effective feedback is largely dependent on the holding environments in which it is offered. As reflections and extensions of one's sensitivity to developmental diversity, these contexts and relationships for feedback are key aspects of how ideas and communications will be interpreted, experienced, and valued. Therefore, in this chapter, we shine a bright light on the preconditions that need to undergird growth-oriented conversations, and describe developmental strategies for establishing trust and sustaining a generative feedback tone in your leadership.[1]

## PRECONDITIONS FOR GROWTH

In a longitudinal exploration of how a group of educational leaders went on to use a developmental approach to building capacity years after learning about constructive-developmental theory and related practices as part of a graduate school course, we found that nearly *all* of the leaders in the study described the vital importance of building mutually respectful, trusting relationships as a first step in their learning-oriented work.[2] While we did not explicitly ask these leaders about their feedback practices, they emphasized the fundamental importance of establishing *trust, safety,* and *respect* before undertaking *any* initiative designed to challenge or stretch—in a developmental sense—colleagues' thinking, feeling, and/or work in order to support enhanced practice and growth of self.

We agree that trust, safety, and respect are essential preconditions to the very personal and often sensitive business of supporting growth in others and ourselves. You might even think of them as the DNA of supporting growth and giving feedback that can really be acted upon. In our research we have found that these critical elements can be especially vital when it comes to feedback, as they can help alleviate anxiety, instill a sense of confidence and security for all participants, and contribute to a shared understanding and purpose—regardless of our ways of knowing. After all, no matter how we make meaning of our experiences and relationships, we all want and need to feel safe and respected in our life and work. While building trust, establishing safety, and demonstrating respect can sometimes be easier said than done (and may mean different things to different people), it is also true that when we find ourselves "well held" in these mutual and authentic ways, we know intuitively how much it means and how much it matters.[3] While it can be hard to put the power of the preconditions into words, one principal's recent announcement to his staff comes close. "I have your back and feel your touch on mine," he assured a group of his teachers about the upcoming school year. His poetic words point to the genuine reciprocity we have in mind when talking about preconditions for supporting adult growth and development, and serve as an important reminder that we have to be in this work *together* if we hope to enact meaningful change, especially when it comes to giving and receiving feedback.

### Starting Fresh, Starting Anew: Anticipating the Challenges of Building Trust, Safety, and Respect as Preconditions for Effective Feedback

While much of this chapter is dedicated to strategies you can use to help build this kind of trust and confidence with and for colleagues, we want to acknowledge up front how often educators confide initial feelings of fear, hesitation, or even confusion about starting to give or get "real" feedback. They worry that their courage or vulnerability might be held against them in some way, especially if feedback of this kind falls outside of a school's established culture or norms. As one school principal recently reflected, "feedback isn't always offered (or welcomed) in the spirit of mutual growth." In fact, authentic invitations to share and grow can seem far from many people's realities and hard for them to imagine. As this principal explained (and this is a common sentiment we've learned from): "Most feedback to which we're initially introduced [as people in general] is negative: parents/teachers/coaches/directors telling us what we did wrong, police telling us we broke the law, employers telling us we will be fired if [we do this or that] . . . These are not great introductions to feedback."

We have found in our research and collaborations with leaders of all kinds that understanding and acknowledging this very reasonable and initial uncertainty can be an important first step in building mutual trust, safety, and respect. Indeed, without acknowledging the histories we share with our colleagues, our past experiences in the world with feedback more generally, and the mistakes that may have occurred along the way (even with the best of intentions), we will not be able to figure out just what it would take to see each other in different ways—or to venture forward in more promising directions.

Echoing Antonio in William Shakespeare's *The Tempest*, who famously declared, "What's past is prologue," we agree that, when it comes to feedback for growth, educators will often need to work to understand (and in some cases overcome) the feedback practices of yore. Especially when colleagues' prior experiences have not been positive (and even more so when, as a leader, you are hoping to change, shift, or improve practices that implicate or involve *you*), it is important to recognize that building a genuine culture of feedback will take time and intentional investment.

## STRATEGIES FOR BUILDING A CULTURE OF FEEDBACK

In this section, we will describe a number of strategies that you can use to help you even more effectively set the foundation for feedback for growth in your school, team, or organization—and in relationships more generally. Employing and embodying the following six strategies over time can help you and your colleagues create a more fruitful *present* that, as it becomes the past, can in turn serve as a powerful new "prologue" for all that's to come:

- Finding value in mistakes
- Modeling vulnerability and an openness to feedback
- Attending to and caring for the interpersonal

- Clarifying expectations
- Sharing developmental ideas
- Building an infrastructure for collaboration

Importantly, while these strategies are effective on a universal, human level (in the sense that they can support adults who make meaning with *any* way of knowing), remaining mindful of the different ways diverse adults will orient to and experience these strategies is also essential as you grow a culture of feedback in your school or organization. Accordingly, we interweave key developmental considerations into our discussions of each strategy.

### Finding Value in Mistakes

As a point of entry into the first strategy, *finding value in mistakes*, imagine an elementary school classroom filled with student work. In this particular classroom (which we've based on a real one), the students hang their projects from clotheslines draped from the ceilings. Upon entering, one is struck by how the room feels nearly bursting with paintings, handwritten essays, quizzes, and other kinds of materials. While it is easy to feel inspired by the pride and community spirit evident in this very special classroom, the feeling deepens once it becomes clear that the students display not only the work they are proud of but also a beautiful lack of self-consciousness about the "mistakes" they may have made on that work. They comment, out loud and in writing, on what they did well each month and on what they need to improve, and demonstrate a deep confidence in the value of mistakes as part of growing and learning. It is quite inspiring.

In other words, the projects the students hang from the clotheslines aren't all "perfect" specimens (in the traditional sense of having perfect scores or grades), but they are *theirs*, and they mean something to them. When visitors arrive, for instance, students are proud to share their work as evidence of a learning journey in progress. "Here's my spelling test!" one student points out before continuing, "I got a 70 because I didn't know how to spell 'crocodile' last week, but now I do, so that's okay." Embodying the kind of growth mindset that we've been interweaving into our discussions in this book, these students (clearly emboldened and encouraged by their teacher) understand intuitively that mistakes are an integral part of growth, and that sharing their "mess-ups" can actually help them develop more than keeping those mistakes concealed.[4] What would happen, we wonder, if more adults—teachers and educational leaders of all kinds—approached their work with this same kind of transparency and vulnerability?

While, promisingly, some educators are courageously beginning to share the more challenging aspects of their practice with supervisors and each other, the authentic *growing conversations* they have about instructional practice and leadership happen most frequently, we have found, within small circles of trusted colleagues and advisors rather than schoolwide. We recognize that emerging teacher evaluation systems and mounting accountability demands place unprecedented pressures on educators to almost always put their best foot forward. In fact, as many educators have shared with us, defaulting to a "glossy display" during formal observations, classroom intervisitations, student test preparation initiatives, or other professional encounters (all while disguising or hiding areas for growth) makes perfect sense in our current system, given the stakes involved. After all, if you know the feedback heading your way will be written down and preserved indefinitely in a folder with your name on it, influence your job security or pay, or even become part of the public record, you'd want that feedback to be as glowing and as positive as possible.

Perhaps even more fundamentally, we have found in our research and teaching with educators of all kinds that adults tend to equate "being professional" with demonstrating desired competencies, showing off one's best work, or proving one's worth or value to an organization. While these are inarguably important and desired outcomes, it's almost as if we begin our professional lives by presenting a very singular slice of who we are (e.g., during interviews and other "first impression" kinds of moments), and then spend the rest of our time trying to preserve and augment these favorable images of ourselves. Importantly, this can be true whether we make meaning as instrumental, socializing, self-authoring, or self-transforming knowers (i.e., whether we do this in order to obtain a reward, feel accepted by colleagues, meet our own standards for excellence, or recognize a larger organizational imperative).

In the business world, for instance, Kegan and his associates point out that most people spend a good deal of their time and energy at work *concealing* possible weaknesses while striving to promote their greatest assets.[5] Students, too, recognize and lament this kind of "hiding" in their teachers as a detriment to their own learning and school experiences.[6] So we have to ask: with the stakes so high in education (in terms of both the external measures at our doorstep and the priceless students in our care), *might there not be a better, more effective way for educators to expend these vital stores of time, energy, and self?* After all, as Kegan and his colleagues put it, "to a greater extent than we want to admit, most people at work, no matter how dedicated they may be, are diverting some portion of their valuable energies to a second job [i.e., maintaining appearances] no one has hired them to perform."[7]

With this enlightening and vital idea in mind, we maintain that carving out even more time and space in schools, districts, and school systems for authentic adult learning, development, and collaboration can help us achieve more—together. While capstone, summative, and formal evaluations of course play very important roles in teacher feedback and evaluation (and adults will always want to do their "best" on these measures), creating opportunities for more formative, ongoing, and informal feedback throughout the school year—vertically, between leaders and teachers, and horizontally, between colleagues and team members—can help us open up a culture of feedback in which asking for help is a sign of strength, and in which mistakes, like those in the classroom described earlier, are evidence of a learning journey.

Interestingly, in the corporate sector, a new kind of company—called *deliberately developmental organizations* (DDOs)—are gaining traction with their mounting successes. DDOs, which we'll discuss more later in this chapter, are companies that recognize "immersive cultures for continuous individual growth as the necessary means of achieving superior business results."[8] We argue that, like this emerging and promising kind of organization, schools could more explicitly encourage educators to "surface and value their growing edge, and experience themselves as still valuable *even as they are screwing up*—potentially even more valuable, if they can overcome the limitations they are exposing."[9] While a few schools and leaders are beginning to explore what this kind of openness to learning could really do and mean in education (and we've got our fingers crossed that such a growth orientation will "go viral," so to speak), it is important to remain mindful of the different ways adults will orient to new kinds of vulnerability and transparency in their work.

For example, to help such a learning-oriented feedback stance really take hold in your school or on your team, you could: (a) help instrumental knowers recognize it as the "right" thing to do (e.g., that it is supported by research and will be valued by the organization), (b) assure socializing knowers that you will still like and respect them if they share issues of practice openly and honestly, (c) invite self-authoring knowers to identify their own areas for growth, and to point out more systemic areas for organizational improvement, and (d) engage self-transforming knowers as partners in these shifting processes and transitions. Educational leaders who are already working in these promising ways acknowledge that, "yes, it takes more time and a big investment (both logistically and emotionally)," and yet firmly agree that "it is well worth it!" As one principal of a large elementary school, reflecting on her work expanding the role and scope of feedback in her school, said: "These kinds of learning conversations where I'm helping teachers along the way make a huge difference. I can see that teachers are *really* getting something out of it. I can see it. They can see it. They are growing and improving their practice. It is making a tremendous difference."

## Modeling Vulnerability and an Openness to Feedback

So how does one begin to promote and nurture this kind of vulnerability and transparency? How does one harness the power of learning from mistakes so our schools can function even more effectively as holding environments for stretching and flourishing, for both children and adults? In our work and research with educators of all kinds, we have found that one of the most powerful strategies for creating change involves *modeling* the attitudes and behaviors one hopes to support in others.[10] In terms of giving and receiving feedback, modeling can be especially effective in setting—and maintaining—an authentic growth orientation. For example, acknowledging that you do not have all the answers (as either feedback giver or feedback receiver), seeking out and learning from feedback on your own work, and growing your own capacities for taking in others' perspectives can all help foster a more genuine culture of feedback over time.

Leading in this way takes both courage and practice, and aligning your "audio" with your "visuals"—and being transparent about it—can set a powerful example for others. In other words, making sure that your actions (i.e., the visuals) align with what you say (i.e., the audio) is essential. Toward this same end, there is a quote about character—usually attributed in some form to Ralph Waldo Emerson—that we often share with educators when talking about the fundamental importance of modeling: "What you do speaks so loudly that I cannot hear what you say." For us and in relation to feedback, this quote points to the importance of seeking out and *valuing* feedback, not just giving it to others (which we know is not always an easy thing!). As one aspiring school leader recently acknowledged about the challenges of taking in critical feedback, "It's not easy to get feedback, especially when you're just starting out and trying to do a really good job." Still, this same leader shared that "practicing" and "staying open" to what others had to say made a big difference for him, to the point that he eventually found himself "learning to love getting feedback after all—and wanting more." Importantly, modeling openness to feedback and learning can help create new possibilities for feedback for growth by deepening colleagues' feelings of trust, safety, and respect; and, it can also help *you* grow yourself and your leadership. We will discuss this circular benefit of seeking out feedback in more detail in chapter 10.

## Attending to and Caring for the Interpersonal

Now that you've read in previous chapters about how much our ways of knowing matter, we hope it is clear that most everyone likes to be liked and that everyone needs to be cared for, even if adults with different ways of knowing will orient to and experience interpersonal connections in different ways (e.g., as a means to an end, as the firmament of one's selfhood, as an affirmation of competence, or as a context for mutuality). As Morrissey of the band The Smiths once sang, "I am human and I need to be loved / Just like everybody else does." We pull from our shared '80s music memory here in order to highlight the key point that *attending to and caring for the interpersonal* dimensions of feedback is one important way to help build trust, safety, and respect for all in your care (not just colleagues with a socializing way of knowing).

We'd like to make a clear distinction up front between "attending to the interpersonal" as an integral part of your feedback and leadership (on the one hand) and "blurring the boundaries" with supervisees in extracurricular contexts (on the other). Aspiring and practicing leaders often confide an understandable uneasiness about being friends with subordinates, and this concern is even more prevalent among teacher leaders—including those who become coaches within their schools—since they do not have the same kind of positional authority as administrators but are tasked with leading colleagues through different initiatives. "How can I be someone's friend in one context, and their supervisor in another?" they wonder. "How close is too close?" While we agree that interweaving supervision and friendship can be complicated and confusing (especially if one or more colleagues in the relationship are not developmentally ready for that kind of permeability), we will leave it to someone else to write the (sure to be bestselling) book, *How to Have a Beer with Colleagues and Still Be a Top-Notch Boss*. Instead, our emphasis here is on the importance of thoughtfully and intentionally harnessing the power of interpersonal connections *in the workplace* (and in your feedback). Our suggestion is not, in other words, to be "friends" with colleagues per se, but to care for and about *who they are*—as teachers, leaders, individuals, and community members—in all of your communications and collaborations. Just as good teachers can genuinely connect with students without pursuing a "let's be BFFs" approach to teaching and learning, building a positive rapport with colleagues is a precursor to feedback for growth. By this we mean that genuinely caring for and about the ways colleagues' meaning making and life circumstances (whether positive or negative) inevitably influence their performance and contributions can make a tremendous difference. We have found this is a principle many educators embrace readily for children and youth, yet sometimes unintentionally neglect when working with adults.

No matter the message we want to convey in our feedback, demonstrating that we care deeply about and empathize with the person receiving it can be a powerful first step. Mary, a very experienced and successful principal of a highly effective school, shared that she quite consciously bases her feedback to teachers not just on their outward performances, but on the entirety of their circumstances as human beings and in light of their professional relationships with her as principal. As she put it, "I consider what else is going on in that person's life, the degree of trust we have in each other, the ways that they have shown themselves able to be resilient, and their processing needs." As you might imagine, holding and navigating this innate, interpersonal complexity helps Mary differentiate feedback on developmental *and* personal lines so that adults can more readily "tune in" to the heart of what she's trying to share.

Moreover, understanding developmental diversity can help us be even more intentional about *how* we communicate our care along developmental lines (which, as you know, is one important dimension of our experience). For example, adults with any way of knowing will appreciate kind gestures or acts, but instrumental knowers may particularly appreciate concrete shows of support (e.g., giving them a thank-you note or cup of coffee, procuring additional resources, scheduling time during a busy day to talk), while socializing knowers may prefer more intangible gestures (e.g., noticing and asking about how they are feeling, offering genuine compliments).

"But," you might be wondering, "don't educators have a really important job to do?" "How can we hold them accountable in our feedback if we spend so much time caring for their personal and internal experiences?" "Shouldn't *students'* needs and development trump an emphasis on educators'?" As we consider these important questions, we think there is great value in looking once again at the ways that deliberately developmental organizations—the emerging kind of company mentioned earlier—address such conundrums. Take, for example, the powerfully simple and profound idea embedded in DDOs that companies needn't choose between "development" and "outcomes" in any hierarchical prioritization. For organizations that operate in these ways, it is not a matter of one *over* the other, or even one *or* the other. As Kegan and his colleagues explain: "In a DDO, the goals of profitability and fostering development are not a 'both/and'; and they are not an 'either/or.' Rather a DDO looks at the way *very bold institutional aspirations*, on the one hand (such as high profitability, or breaking the mold in one's sector), and *further-developed human capabilities*, on the other, *are part of a single whole*. They depend on the other."[11]

Substituting "student success" for "profitability" in this equation, you can imagine how this kind of deliberately developmental approach could translate into educational contexts. Just as *"bold institutional aspirations . . . and further-developed human capabilities . . . are part of a single whole"* in DDOs, so too may desired student outcomes and educators' troves of internal capacities be intimately intertwined in schools. Related to this, we can never truly disentangle the personal from the professional dimensions of our experiences as teachers and educational leaders; each matters immensely and informs the other. As Kegan and his colleagues similarly acknowledged: "Everyone who has ever worked anywhere knows that work is intensely personal. We all bring our whole selves to work every day. In ordinary organizations, we regard this as an inconvenient truth we would rather ignore, and we essentially try to 'manage around' the inevitable manifestations of the personal. In a DDO, routine practices openly encourage, and seek to make regular room for, the personal and the interior, on behalf of explicitly *welcoming* the whole person into work every day."[12]

### Checking in and out

So, given that personal/professional engagement can have a direct and positive effect on desired outcomes, what kinds of routine practices might better support this in schools and other educational organizations? One practice that we've found to be very helpful in building trust, motivation, and interconnection in teams, groups, coaching, mentoring, and professional relationships in general is *checking in and out*.[13] More specifically, setting aside time at the start and end of meetings for colleagues to share a few words about what feels most pressing for them in the moment (whether it be personal or professional or, if time allows, both) can help all in the room better appreciate and understand the similarities and differences individuals bring to their work as living, growing human beings. Again and again, we have found that being there with and for each other in this way really matters and makes a difference!

One of the most interesting and effective aspects of this practice is that it is open and flexible enough to work for emerging *and* established groups, as well as for individuals who make meaning across the developmental continuum. In exhibit 6.1, for instance, we offer a few sample prompts that

EXHIBIT 6.1

## Caring For and About the Personal and Professional: Sample Prompts for Checking In on Two Levels

Emerging team check-in ideas—getting to know each other to support working well together:

- Did anyone do anything special over the weekend?
- Does anyone have a birthday coming up soon?
- Does anyone have a special event coming up soon?
- Is there anything anyone would like to share with us?

Established team check-in ideas—maintaining strong connections and caring for and about each other:

- Does anyone have an announcement or experience that you think would be important to share with the group?
- How was your day/week/month since we last met?
- Any updates since we last met?
- How are you feeling about _____ (e.g., some new initiative, our last meeting, or something specific that occurred during our last meeting)?

can be used to facilitate check-ins with new and established groups to introduce and build upon interpersonal connections.

Similarly, we have found that checking in and out is a practice that can "hold" adults with different ways of knowing in different ways. Instrumental knowers, for example, can exchange important logistical updates; socializing knowers can learn more about how others are thinking and feeling while safely expressing some of their own hopes and concerns; self-authoring knowers can offer anecdotes, insights, and expertise they think would be helpful to the group; and self-transforming knowers can build connections while learning more about individual and group dynamics. While, at first, some adults (particularly instrumental or self-authoring knowers) may find checking in and out an unnecessary or artificial luxury in our fast-paced educational world (as one leader recently said, "There's just so much to do!"), we have invariably found that adults who make meaning in these ways soon become some of the most active and articulate check-in participants over time. In the end, no matter one's way of knowing, the chance to genuinely come together with colleagues can be a powerful, supportive, and surprisingly rare treat.

Of course, we also want to acknowledge that adding (or enhancing) an interpersonal dimension to your leadership and feedback isn't about making the work easier—it's about making it better. As we discussed in chapter 1, educators frequently work in a "culture of nice," so knowing more about the complexities of colleagues' lives can actually make it *harder* for many leaders to share their honest thinking and feeling, especially if there aren't explicit expectations and norms in place about this.[14] It can feel much more difficult, for instance, to think about whether someone is a good fit for your school or a particular position if you know he or she is struggling with painful or challenging situations outside of work. As one educational leader put it, "I work in an environment where relationships are highly valued, so it is difficult to be sufficiently, clearly honest."

While we understand how hard it can be to appear approachable and understanding on the one hand, and firm about excellence on the other, we do not see interpersonal sensitivity and high expectations as mutually exclusive. In fact, approaching difficult conversations and/or decisions with empathy and understanding can actually make hard things a little "softer," we have found, when you consider them in the context of what is truly best for the person and for all involved. In light of this, thinking carefully about your *own* comfort with holding and caring for the multidimensionality of colleagues' experiences is an important component of attending to the interpersonal. And, as we will describe in greater detail next, communicating and clarifying expectations about feedback and collaborative work is a close second. In chapter 9 (which focuses on following up on feedback), we will further explore how acknowledging interpersonal feelings and understandings can continue to be powerful and helpful.

## Clarifying Expectations

As we've been exploring, understanding and reflecting on your own orientations to leadership and feedback—as they relate to your internal capacities—is only one part of the job. It is just as essential to learn about and take into account others' perspectives, and to come to some kind of common and transparent understanding about how feedback will work and what it will be for (i.e., the purposes and intentions behind it). Toward this end, we strongly recommend *clarifying expectations*—from both sides—at the start of feedback relationships, and revisiting these core agreements repeatedly and over time, whether the relationships are one-on-one or part of ongoing feedback systems for teams or organizations. After all, there are so many aspects of feedback that warrant upfront and ongoing consideration. Will the feedback you share be formative or summative? Formal or informal?

Solicited or unsolicited? Immediate or delayed? What feels most important to the involved individuals about the processes as well as the goals?

To help illustrate the importance of clarifying expectations, we offer the story of Georgia and Jeremiah, a couple who spent weeks carefully planning a party in honor of their 25th anniversary. To mark the occasion, and as a special part of the celebration, Georgia and Jeremiah agreed to have a private dance to a special song—just as they had at their wedding. Despite all of their careful planning and preparations, however, the couple never talked about or practiced the *kind* of dance they were going to do ahead of time. As Georgia later explained, "I never really thought about the dance itself, because it seemed so obvious to me that it would be a slow dance. I mean, it's a *slow* song." You could imagine her surprise, then, when Jeremiah stepped onto the dance floor, hamming it up with a high-energy disco!

In some ways, the lightheartedness of this example distances it from the higher-stakes urgencies of teaching and leading, but we think it's a helpful analogy for what can happen when two parties enter into a seemingly simple endeavor with very different expectations or assumptions. Just as this couple approached the dance in completely different ways, despite knowing each other very well and agreeing on the song, different people— even people who have worked together previously and may think they are "on the same page"—will often orient to supervision, mentoring, and other feedback relationships differently depending upon their ways of knowing, personalities, and prior experiences.

Take, for example, the experience of Denise and Sylvia, two teachers who were engaged in a mentoring relationship. As an early career teacher, Denise was excited to have Sylvia—a veteran colleague and "super star teacher," as the principal often described her—to support her professional learning and growth. As a more socializing knower, however, what Denise really wanted from the mentorship was a safe context in which to talk and learn, and a trusted ally who could support her growth in an expert *and* caring way. This was important to Denise because she felt particularly vulnerable when things didn't go well during her lessons, and sometimes had a hard time talking about her practice without getting emotional. Sylvia, on the other hand, was more self-authoring in her meaning making, and felt that what would be of best help to Denise were straightforward tips about what she could do better, as this was the kind of feedback she herself would have preferred. Although Sylvia offered her ideas and critiques to Denise with the sincere intention of being of best help, Denise was privately becoming more and more overwhelmed and discouraged by Sylvia's lack of positive feedback, and failed to make much progress on her goals (which, in turn, was frustrating for Sylvia). It wasn't until Sylvia and Denise learned about ways of knowing in a workshop that they were able to really come together to discuss their hopes and intentions for their working relationship. "Why didn't you ever tell me how you were feeling?" Sylvia asked Denise, genuinely sorry that she hadn't been meeting her needs or expectations. "I didn't want to disappoint you," Denise replied honestly. It was a relief to both of them that they were finally able to explore and understand what would feel like a safe and productive mentorship for both of them.

As this example helps illustrate, creating opportunities to consider and talk about what feedback relationships mean to you as well as the other person(s) involved is a step in the right direction, wherever you are in the process, and a straightforward strategy for alleviating potential frustrations, miscommunications, and unwelcome surprises when working with others. More specifically, clarifying expectations can increase transparency, foster awareness of participants' personal and developmental needs, demonstrate respect, and build trust with those you work with, whether as a supervisor or colleague. In light of this, in exhibit 6.2 we offer a list of questions you can share with colleagues to help guide reflective discussions about feedback preferences and expectations. Exploring these questions (privately and collaboratively) *before* offering or receiving feedback can help ensure that all parties come to the table with the clearest possible understandings of the process, and of each other. Also, as you may already suspect, not all adults will feel comfortable answering these questions directly or out loud (e.g., socializing knowers may need time to consider their own responses before hearing valued others'), so providing opportunities for private reflection and/or small-group sharing can also be quite helpful.

While these questions can be useful on a very practical level (in that they will give you direct insight into the kinds of things adults in your care will expect and find supportive), colleagues' answers can also provide clues about their underlying meaning-making system. Of course, "diagnosing" anyone's exact way of knowing is beyond the scope of a few quick questions. (As mentioned earlier, there is a detailed, tested, and sophisticated protocol, the Subject-Object Interview, which a trained facilitator would need to employ to determine this.)[15] Still, it can be incredibly helpful to think about how, if at all, colleagues' responses to these key questions align with the kinds of supports and challenges for growth outlined in table 4.1. For example, do your colleagues prefer concrete and explicit directions (like instrumental knowers), or do they respond better to more relational, sensitive feedback (like socializing knowers)? Do they crave autonomy and independence (like self-authoring knowers), or seek feedback partnerships

EXHIBIT 6.2

### Questions For Exploring Colleagues' Feedback Preferences

- What do you see as the purpose of feedback?
- What's most important to you about the process of feedback? The outcome of it?
- What kinds of things tend to feel most helpful and supportive to you when receiving feedback? Can you think of a time when getting feedback worked very well for you?
- What, if anything, tends to feels hard or challenging to you about getting feedback? Giving feedback? Why do you think this is?
- What could I do to make our feedback sessions more meaningful for you?

grounded in the mutual exchange of ideas (like self-transforming knowers)? Genuinely welcoming and honoring your colleagues' responses to these kinds of questions—all while looking for patterns of thinking, meaning making, and acting—can be a powerful tool for meeting and exceeding expectations during feedback sessions and beyond.

*Identifying the "hat" you are wearing*

When we talk with aspiring and practicing leaders about giving and receiving feedback, another issue that frequently comes up is confidentiality. Especially for teacher leaders or other mid-level administrators, there is a real sense of being torn between supporting colleagues on the one hand, and reporting to their bosses on the other. What can they keep confidential? And what are they obliged to disclose? Of course, these matters are complex. From our perspective, though, issues of confidentiality will only be compounded if there is a lack of transparency or if parameters are not clearly set in advance. Explicitly acknowledging the challenging power dynamics of leadership roles and hierarchies up front can help build trust and establish clear ground rules, regardless of a person's way of knowing.

In fact, we have found the practice of identifying the "hat you are wearing" during feedback to be especially effective, for both yourself and others. For example, are you there as an evaluator, or as a coach? Are you asking a question off the record, or in an administrative capacity (i.e., on the record)? Understanding the answers to these questions (which can sometimes feel muddled even to feedback givers) can help to demystify the "unspoken" rules of feedback conversations and help clarify expectations.

Put even more simply, coming to some understanding of *and being transparent about* the hat you are wearing—and learning, too, what hat the other person is wearing—can support growth and development in very essential ways. While we will talk more about employing this strategy *during* feedback in the next chapter, we mention it here because establishing this kind of transparency at the outset can help take some of the guesswork out of the relationship for all involved parties. In fact, one thing that we love about this strategy is that it can be employed from any direction! If supervisees, for instance, welcome the language of different "hats" as part of your norms, don't be surprised if you're occasionally asked, "Just so we're clear—what hat are you wearing now, please?"

## Sharing Developmental Ideas

While deepening our understandings of developmental theory and ideas is inarguably very important for us as leaders and feedback givers, we have also found great value in *sharing developmental ideas* with other adults. Rather than keeping the lens in your "back pocket," openly sharing big ideas from developmental theory—especially the four different ways of knowing and the growth-oriented promise of development over time—can help you and your colleagues develop a common lens for feedback, as well as a shared understanding of the intentionality behind new practices and ideas. As one aspiring principal recently shared after completing a graduate course about leadership for adult development, "I've learned about the various stages of child development in my role as a teacher, but have had little exposure to the idea of there being stages to adult development. I am excited to bring this back to my school!"

In terms of introducing key developmental ideas to colleagues, we recommend sharing—as helpful entry points—the charts and activities offered in tables 3.1, 4.1, 4.2, and 5.1, as well as the vignettes in exhibits 3.1 and 4.1, so that colleagues can think privately and together about their own ways of knowing. However, when you are introducing developmental ideas, it is very important to offer them, as we do, as part of an *invitation* to think differently about our learning needs and those of our colleagues. It is also important to couple this introduction with a genuine appreciation for the diversity adults will bring to their work and each other, as each way of knowing has both strengths and limitations. In other words, sharing developmental ideas is *not* about assessing colleagues' meaning making or pegging them as one kind of knower or another (although, in trusting, growth-oriented contexts, we've found that adults tend to openly self-identify with particular ways of knowing as a means of communicating their hopes, needs, areas for growth, and expectations). Likewise, sharing developmental ideas is not about pushing everyone to the "highest" rung on the meaning-making ladder, as our roles demand different things of us, and what is ultimately most important is the goodness of fit between our capacities and those demands. (Could you imagine, for instance, working on a team made up entirely of self-authoring knowers, especially if they did not see eye to eye?)

Rather, we suggest teaching colleagues about adult development as a way to establish a common language for professional growth, and as a way to provide them with a particular tool set for collaboration and capacity building. After all, the more people in your school or organization who are well versed in developmental theory, the more colleagues there will be to actively contribute to a culture of feedback for growth.

Indeed, since growing and supporting adult development is very much a collaborative, interactive process in the first place, introducing your school, team, coachee, or organization to developmental ideas and principles in these ways can help maintain trust and transparency, and can help colleagues recognize and request the supports that would be most helpful and meaningful to them over time. Of course, meeting colleagues where they are developmentally is a journey that takes a continued investment of time and care. Setting the tone up front and building practices around a shared recognition of diversity and difference lets others in on your good intentions, and helps build a more growth-enhancing and reciprocal foundation for feedback.

## Building an Infrastructure for Feedback and Collaboration

Perhaps ironically, given our strong focus throughout this book on the individual, interpersonal aspects of feedback for growth, the final strategy we'd like to highlight for developing and nurturing a culture of feedback involves *building an infrastructure for feedback and collaboration* throughout a school community. No matter how highly a leader regards adult development, and no matter how well that leader wants to serve and support colleagues, he or she could never single-handedly meet the needs of all constituents or deliver the feedback needed to build organizational and human capacity for everyone. Nor should any leader have to! More and more, scholars and practitioners are recognizing collaborative leadership as essential to school improvement, and this idea seems especially relevant when we think about building a culture of feedback.[16] To truly be a "culture," after all, shared ideas need to permeate and infuse the very fabric of an organization. They need to be practiced by individuals and groups on both the macro and micro levels, and they need to inform key practices and interactions throughout our schools and systems.

*Employing four pillar practices for growth*

With these imperatives in mind, we have detailed four *pillar practices for growth*—teaming, collegial inquiry, providing leadership roles, and mentoring—that can serve as powerful structures and channels for effective feedback, as well as for developmentally oriented collaboration more generally.[17] Informed by constructive-developmental theory, these four pillar practices constitute a learning-oriented model of school leadership that can help you reframe common collaborative experiences as developmental holding environments for groups and individuals.[18] This is important because it's not just the structures we create, but also the ways we live and work within them, that make a difference for adult learners. In light of this, understanding the developmental implications and applications of the pillar practices can help us consider a wider range of collaborative processes that make sense and fit within our current system, all while paving the way for greater change and growth.

Because the pillars involve reframing—rather than adding more—avenues and structures for working and learning together in schools, they offer viable, research-based, and compelling opportunities for educators to genuinely experience and benefit from feedback for growth. In fact, longitudinal research has shown that authentically experiencing teaming, collegial inquiry, providing leadership roles, and mentoring as developmental practices can support educator learning and growth over time, and can make a positive and lasting influence on practice as well.[19] Individually and in combination, then, the pillar practices can provide safe and productive contexts in which to offer and practice meaningful, actionable feedback for growth with and for colleagues. Moving forward, we will continue to explore specific strategies for employing these pillars as dynamic components of a culture, and infrastructure, of feedback.

## CHAPTER SUMMARY AND CONCLUSION

In this chapter, we answered the question, "What has to happen *first* in order to offer the most meaningful feedback for growth and improvement?" More specifically, we highlighted the critical importance of building a culture of feedback in schools and organizations, and outlined six promising strategies for nurturing the foundational preconditions of trust, safety, and respect. In the next chapter, we expand the conversation by exploring vital "in the moment" aspects of feedback for growth, including the important distinction between constructive and inquiry-oriented feedback.

As a bridge between this chapter and those that come next, we want to leave you with the wise words of one New York City educational leader. Speaking about the interconnection of the different phases of feedback, as well as the intentional investment leaders need to make in order to build human capacity, this leader offered the following:

> Creating a positive feedback atmosphere, message, and delivery system takes time. A lot of it. We have to think about when we're going to make time to deliver the feedback, what feedback we're going to provide, how we're going to provide it, and possible actionables after the feedback is given. And often we are far too busy with our own tasks [to put in the time]. How many times have you heard yourself say, "It would take more time for me to provide feedback and train someone to do what I want them to do than if I just did it myself"? But where does this get us? In the short run, we get the task done. But in the long run, we just make more work for ourselves.

We agree that investing in a culture of feedback is akin to taking the long view—and that feedback for growth is a means for greater change rather than an end in and of itself. Yet, just as in deliberately developmental organizations, the *process* of adult growth in schools is intimately intertwined with the *outcomes* we hope to achieve (i.e., improved student learning). And the way that work is done in schools—day in and day out—is a manifestation and a reflection of "the way the developmental principles of the organization are given life."[20] *That* is the work we need to do, and the promise we can make with and for each other.

## REFLECTIVE QUESTIONS

Please take a moment to consider the following questions, which can be used for independent reflection and group conversation. You may find it useful to reflect in writing privately first and then to engage in discussion with a colleague or team. These questions are intended to help you and your colleagues consider the ideas discussed in this chapter and how they might inform your practice of giving feedback.

+ After reading this chapter, what are two of your biggest takeaways?
+ After reading this chapter, what are one or two things you would like to do to enhance your approach to building trust, safety, and respect as preconditions to feedback for growth?
+ What feels most exciting to you about building a culture of feedback? Most challenging? What kinds of supports might you need to enhance the culture of feedback in your school or on your team?

CHAPTER 7

# Framing Constructive and Inquiry-Oriented Feedback

*Effective communication makes the world go 'round.*

—JAHIRA, first-year teacher

Now that we've carefully considered the theoretical and practical foundations of feedback for growth, it's time to dive even deeper into the quintessential *who*, *what*, and *why* of giving effective, developmental feedback in the moment (we will pick up on the *when*, *where*, and *how* in chapter 8). In particular, we highlight the promise of understanding feedback for growth as existing on a continuum, and describe two distinct but related kinds of feedback interactions, which we conceptualize as *constructive* and *inquiry-oriented*, respectively. As you will see, our conceptualizations build upon and extend key ideas from prior chapters and the feedback literature, and champion the rather radical notion that the most meaningful, growth-enhancing feedback involves listening just as much as telling.

While you can employ the ideas in this chapter when giving feedback in almost any format (verbal/written, formative/summative, formal/informal, horizontal/vertical, etc.), it is essential to hold in heart and mind—throughout the feedback process—the vital importance of the qualitatively different ways all participants will orient to and make meaning of the experience. Accordingly, we begin our discussion of giving effective feedback by revisiting the powerful centrality of who is involved, both as givers and receivers.

## KEEPING THE "WHO" AT THE FOREFRONT OF FEEDBACK

As we have explored in prior chapters, feedback needs to begin with the *people* participating in the process. The developmental capacities we bring to our work and conversations, the hopes and expectations we hold, and the relationships we develop *all* matter tremendously in this important work. As you may even recall from chapter 2, the very first item on the list of the "top ten" feedback strategies that we derived from our literature review involved individualizing feedback for the receiver. (Since we will be referencing and expanding upon many of these strategies in this chapter and the two that follow, you may find it helpful to refer back to table 2.1 for the full list.)

As we also considered extensively in previous chapters, effectively employing this strategy of individualization (as well as the other strategies on the list) requires a working knowledge of developmental theory, as well as an intentional "tuning in" to the ways of knowing of all participants involved in the feedback process (i.e., not just the recipients'). With this important truth in mind, we offer in table 7.1 a concise overview of what would feel like a "positive" feedback experience to adults with different ways of knowing, from the perspective of both feedback giver and receiver. This table also includes a "growing edge" that could apply equally to adults in both roles.

A synthesis of discussions and tables from prior chapters, table 7.1 illuminates just some of the ways that the "who" and the "you" of your feedback and leadership are always critically important. We will continue to unpack the practical implications of this developmental truth in the sections that follow.

## CONSIDERING THE "WHAT" AND THE "WHY" WHEN FRAMING FEEDBACK

In addition to carefully considering the "who" of feedback, it is very important to enter into feedback for growth processes with a clear understanding of the "what" and the "why" of your delivery. In other words, having a clear understanding of the purpose of your feedback—as well as your central intentions for the exchange—can help you frame and navigate the conversation in the most meaningful and effective ways, especially when feedback calls for continued growth. Making these explicit *before* offering feedback (as we considered in the last chapter) and *during* the feedback process (as we'll discuss here) is, without question, essential.

People often wonder, for instance, "How can I most effectively move my colleagues from point A to point B?" To really do this well, we have found, leaders of all kinds need to think carefully and caringly about *what* they most want and need to say to colleagues, and *why* they are offering the

TABLE 7.1

## Elements of a positive feedback experience for adults with different ways of knowing

| Way of knowing | What feels supportive when receiving feedback | What feels most comfortable when giving feedback | Growing edge |
|---|---|---|---|
| *Instrumental* | • Exploring concrete suggestions, models, and examples. Recognizing what went right and wrong. | • Assessing what colleagues have done "right" and "wrong." Offering concrete directions. | • Looking beyond "right" solutions for teaching and leading.<br>• Making abstract connections. |
| *Socializing* | • Feeling appreciated for effort and contributions. Receiving acknowledgments of personhood (care for personal qualities) and validation of progress and hard work. | • Offering authentic praise and "glows." Recognizing colleagues' successes, hopes, and feelings. | • Expressing own thoughts and feelings.<br>• Engaging in conflict or difficult conversations. |
| *Self-authoring* | • Being recognized for competence and expertise.<br>• Engaging in opportunities to discuss own ideas, develop own goals, and critique and design initiatives. | • Sharing assessments and suggestions that align with own beliefs and visions for improvement. | • Looking beyond one's own values, ideas, beliefs, and theories about leading, teaching, and instructional practice.<br>• Recognizing possibility in seemingly opposing viewpoints. |
| *Self-transforming* | • Co-creating a context and explicitly naming/creating opportunities to collaboratively reflect on practice and explore alternatives, contradictions, and paradoxes (internal and systemic). | • Engaging in mutual reflections and open-ended discussions to co-construct meaning and next steps. | • Managing and appreciating the sometimes slow pace of change. Recognizing when others may not be open to change or collaboration. |

feedback in the first place. Is the feedback aimed at supporting a particular skill or correcting a particular behavior? Or is it more exploratory in nature (i.e., are you trying to learn about a person's sense making, a sequence of events, or an unfolding solution to a problem)? Is it stemming from a professional or personal concern (e.g., an expression of care for an individual, an effort to scaffold a colleague's improved professional practice)? And/or is it being offered as part of a larger, required process (e.g., a professional coaching relationship or formal observation/evaluation cycle)?

While we realize that the answers to these questions may change depending upon circumstances and situations (and also that these questions are not mutually exclusive), we have found it extremely helpful to put a name to two key types of feedback, as a way to think even more clearly about the purposes and potentialities of our communications. Just as learning about constructive-developmental theory and ways of knowing can help us understand more about ourselves and others, deconstructing and explicitly naming different kinds of feedback moves can help us be even more purposeful and intentional in their applications. The two types of feedback we focus on here—constructive and inquiry-oriented—are both essential components of feedback for growth, and can be employed independently and together to support adults with different ways of knowing across diverse contexts.

## Constructive Feedback: Illuminating Needs for Improvement

Usually, when people talk or think about feedback, there is a presumption that the feedback giver has the authority and the knowledge to offer concrete suggestions to the receiving party. Indeed, a central premise of this book is that, with developmental intentionality, we can engage in these important kinds of conversations in ways that receivers can best "hear," and in ways that support adults' internal and professional growth over time. We hope it goes without saying, then, that we recognize feedback of this kind as a vital part of any leader's work, and as a key component of individual and organizational capacity building. After all, no one can see his or her self in its entirety (we need others to help us see ourselves and our actions more clearly), and growth requires an ongoing opening up and a shedding, at least at times, of that comforting sense that what we're doing is already "good enough." While the pantheon of leadership communications inarguably has room for multiple and many types of feedback (all of which are important), we focus in this section on constructive feedback, as it is the kind of feedback leaders most frequently name as a pressing challenge and a part of their practice they urgently want to grow.

By *constructive* feedback, we mean feedback that is expressly intended to point out—with and for someone else—something that may feel problematic, did not go as hoped, or may need to change in support to ongoing improvement. As Andrés, a principal of a large, urban elementary school whom we met in chapter 4, recently described it, constructive feedback is "about painting a picture of how something *is* versus how you want it to be." As Andrés's characterization implies, constructive feedback is grounded in the premise that the feedback giver (due to positional authority or expertise) *has something of consequence to communicate to the recipient*, such as a suggestion or directive for improvement. As another school leader recently put it, "Telling people how to get better is the work I do!"

As you may have noticed, many of the "top ten" feedback strategies we've derived from the wider feedback literature in business and education (see table 2.1) are likewise geared toward directional, constructive feedback. Many feedback scholars, for instance, recognize that it is important to "offer specific, focused feedback" to recipients (#2) and to "be consistent" in the message you are trying to convey (#7). Likewise, our construction of "telling people so they can hear" itself presumes both a "teller" and a "listener," a "giver" and a "receiver." Arguably, the directionality implicit in most conceptualizations of feedback is no surprise, given the fact that there are many, many times when constructive feedback (as hard as it may sometimes be to deliver and/or take in) is just what the doctor ordered. Our research and work with educators of all kinds, for instance, has taught us that they *crave* concrete and constructive feedback on things like:

- classroom management techniques;
- lesson/unit planning;
- data analysis and application;
- teaching methods/best-practice models;
- content delivery;
- use of wait time; and
- differentiation strategies.

Having a leader or colleague who is willing and able, then, to deliver constructive feedback in meaningful ways can be a very powerful and essential support to growth and improved performance.

### Constructive feedback: Directive and suggestive

Pulling back yet another layer on the what and the why of feedback, and the importance of clearly framing the purpose of your communications (for both yourself and the feedback receiver), we want to also recognize that constructive feedback can be directive and/or suggestive. By *directive*, we mean feedback that involves a specific instruction, often about things that are non-negotiable or that involve a clearly articulated vision or action. There may be times, for instance, when you need to tell a colleague about something that simply needs to be done—perhaps because such directness is what the person needs in order to best learn and grow, or perhaps because of larger compliance/accountability mandates or the dictates of a larger goal. *Suggestive* feedback, on the other hand, is more about offering one's best thinking for another's consideration and/or exploration. While both kinds of constructive feedback involve the directionality just described (i.e., from the feedback giver to the receiver), they can be powerful components of feedback for growth when offered, together and separately, with developmental intentionality.

For example, instrumental knowers will often experience clear, directive feedback as a positive support. And sprinkling your feedback with a few suggestive, open-ended comments (or asking something along the lines of "How would you feel about trying X?" or "Have you considered Y?") can help you stand in good company with these knowers as they stretch the edges of their thinking. When you are offering constructive feedback to socializing knowers, it is important to remain mindful of the fact that they will experience directive *and* suggestive feedback from supervisors as indicative of the "best" ways to think or act. While socializing adults will do their best to implement feedback from valued others (no matter its form) in order to preserve important relationships and professional esteem, they generally take in and act upon constructive feedback *best* when it is coupled with authentic, positive affirmations, and when offered within the confines of a trusting relationship. In addition, you may find it helpful to strategically hold back directive suggestions to create space for adults who make meaning in this way to consider and share their own thinking and ideas (e.g., by asking "What do you think we should do about X?") before offering your ideas and suggestions. Supplementing the content of your helpful suggestions by creating this kind of stretching opportunity can help socializing educators grow developmentally as they work with you to improve practice.

On a different note, self-authoring knowers often appreciate concise, constructive feedback when it aligns well with their own estimations and assessments (in keeping with the "Give it to me straight!" approach described in chapter 5), or when it is aimed at supporting a goal they share and find valuable. Yet adults who make meaning in this way will often let you know when a directive or suggestion "doesn't work for them," and may appreciate a more suggestive approach that invites a collegial, back-and-forth dialogue during sensitive exchanges. Like self-authoring knowers, self-transforming knowers will likely also welcome constructive feedback in all its forms—provided it is offered genuinely, transparently, and with best intentions. Just as for self-authoring knowers, directives offered without explanation or acknowledgment of these adults' perspectives and contributions can leave them feeling unsupported. However, carving out space for collaborative explorations of constructive suggestions can feel to self-transforming knowers like a meaningful opportunity to reflect on practice and overarching goals.

Ultimately, when you are offering constructive feedback—directive and/or suggestive—to adults with *any* way of knowing, what matters most is finding the balance between holding them well (i.e., meeting them where they are, telling them so they can hear) and pushing them gently just beyond their comfort zone (i.e., telling them so they can grow). While walking this line takes practice, sensitivity, and an awareness of developmental diversity, it is incredibly important in terms of building individual and organizational capacity, and in light of the avoidable challenges *not* doing this can create (as we discuss next).

### Constructive versus destructive feedback

Indeed, recognizing how to balance directive and suggestive feedback, and how to offer them with respect and care for adults' different ways of knowing, can make the difference between offering *developmental* feedback (i.e., feedback for growth) and inadvertently offering what many educators, feedback scholars, and psychologists would describe as *destructive* feedback, or feedback that limits or shuts down opportunities for future improvement and communication.[1] When, for instance, feedback does not appropriately "match" a colleague's developmental orientation and capacities (e.g., when self-authoring knowers are given directives with no explanation or opportunity to respond; when socializing knowers are offered strong, constructive feedback that does not acknowledge their efforts or strengths), or when it is offered in ways that feel vague, judgmental, disingenuous, threatening, or pessimistic, an opportunity for learning and growth can easily be missed—or even destroyed.[2] As Kegan and Lahey emphatically acknowledged, "Many a relationship has been damaged and a work setting poisoned by *perfectly delivered* constructive feedback!"[3]

Related to this, it is important to remain mindful of how your *own* preferences for and orientations to giving feedback will intersect with recipients'. Feedback givers who are instrumental knowers, for instance, can employ some of the ideas and strategies outlined in this book (and other resources) as a blueprint for offering more effective feedback, but they may also require support as they work over time to more fully understand and take in the perspectives of those in their care (a critical element of intentional differentiation). Socializing knowers, too, may find it meaningful to practice offering more directive feedback, especially when supporting instrumental and self-authoring colleagues who will appreciate this communication style. Toward this end, role playing and rehearsing constructive conversations with trusted leadership advisors can be a key support for socializing adults as they build this capacity.

For self-authoring and self-transforming knowers, keeping developmental principles at the forefront can help them prepare and offer feedback to colleagues that goes beyond their "natural" or "default" inclinations (e.g., for "straight talk" without the "sugar" [self-authoring knowers], or for mutual explorations of practice [self-transforming knowers]). Because adults will want and need different things from their feedback and from you as a leader, thinking carefully about the kind of constructive feedback you are offering up front—and about how this aspect of your communication will align with recipients' ways of knowing—can help you more strategically and caringly frame feedback so that others can best hear it and take it in as they journey "from point A to point B."

### Inquiry-Oriented Feedback: Learning More About Complex Ideas and Challenges

When faced with complex challenges and situations, we may not, as leaders, always find it best to offer a strong answer, direction, solution, or suggestion in our feedback. We may not, for instance, be clear about the "point A" from which we or others are beginning, and we may not even have a specific "point B" in mind as a destination. And this is okay! Echoing our discussion of adaptive challenges in chapter 1, feedback for growth may at times need to remain open-ended or exploratory, especially as we face unprecedented challenges and demands, and as we work to build capacity in ourselves and each other.[4] After all, acknowledging that we don't have all the answers and approaching feedback with an inquiry stance can be a powerful support for growth and development—even as doing so challenges all of us in different ways (we will say more about this in just a moment).

With this important idea in mind, we now shift our focus to another kind of feedback that you can employ to navigate and address pressing matters in your school or organization: inquiry-oriented feedback. We refer to this kind of feedback as *inquiry-oriented* because it is designed to open an investigative dialogue—from both sides—about a challenging situation, observation, or conundrum (*inquiry*, after all, is literally defined as "an act of asking for information").[5] The underlying premise here is that, while the person traditionally designated as the feedback giver (e.g., the administrator, coach, or leader-colleague) may very well enter into the feedback conversation with ideas about the nature of the problem or possible next steps (as may the feedback receiver), both parties suspend certainty and judgment in favor of a deeper, collaborative exploration of the challenge itself and potential paths forward.

Sometimes when we first describe inquiry-oriented feedback to others, people wonder, "Is this really feedback? Isn't this more like collaborative problem solving?" While we readily recognize certain similarities between these powerful processes (and see them also as interconnected), just *broaching* an inquiry-oriented conversation of this nature can itself be a kind of feedback, as it conveys to the conversation partner that something is not quite right or could be better, even if you do not offer a specific directive or suggestion to address the problem. For example, you could imagine a leader or colleague initiating an inquiry-oriented discussion after observing a challenging situation with a colleague by saying, "I'm wondering if we could talk a bit more about your lesson today," or "There's something that's been on my mind that I'd really like to discuss with you"—just as he or she would initiate any feedback conversation. Yet, in addition to preparing reflections on what went wrong or what needs to be done (as might happen with a strictly constructive approach), he or she might also think carefully about how to learn more and think differently about the situation with the colleague in question. Is there more to know about what happened and when? About one's own thinking and intentions? By temporarily suspending judgments or prescriptions in favor of learning more, inquiry-oriented feedback can help enhance and augment feedback encounters of all kinds (e.g., formal and informal, summative and formative, vertical and horizontal) and can help participants on both sides of the feedback exchange examine assumptions and stretch their thinking.

As Lawrence, a former elementary school principal and current district-level professional development leader, recently explained, reflecting on the power of an inquiry-oriented approach: "I heard or read somewhere that feedback is sometimes viewed as the 'third rail' of leadership. While I would agree that conversations involving feedback are often extraordinarily complex balancing acts, replete with elements of fear, courage, and risk taking, I strongly believe that if we are able to begin these discussions within a framework of genuine curiosity, we will be able to nurture and grow powerful change." Further capturing the philosophy behind an inquiry-oriented approach "in medical terms," Lawrence continued: "[Effective feedback can] be closer to the 'discovery phase' in which the physician asks questions about symptoms, and may be at the beginning stages of diagnosis, rather than being a 'postmortem' about what went wrong."

Kegan and Lahey make a similar distinction in their book *How the Way We Talk Can Change the Way We Work*. As one part of their discussion about the power of language, they highlight what they call "deconstructive feedback," or feedback intended "neither to tear down nor to build up but instead to disassemble."[6] As they frame it, this alternative approach to feedback involves letting go of one's "vested interest" in holding "The Truth" or "The Answer" as a leader, and instead entering into feedback as "explorers, tentative with our meanings, and open to changing them when we discover new vantage points or information."[7] Kegan and Lahey explain that, when engaging in this kind of communication, "we shift from thinking about clever ways to help the person see it our way . . . to thinking about trying to understand what's been happening and whether our criticism is warranted."[8] In a similar way, our conceptualization of inquiry-oriented feedback is not just about changing other people's minds or behaviors—it's about remaining open to changing ours as well. As one leader aptly put it, "Good feedback is about exploring the questions that really need answers, not about asking questions that will lead a conversation to the place I think I want it to go."

That said, we recognize that suspending certainty in this way can be very hard to do, and that it also directly implicates our ways of knowing and internal capacities as leaders and feedback givers. Instrumental and self-authoring knowers, for example, may have a particularly hard time letting go of the "reins" or "The Truth" during feedback conversations, since they orient strongly to particular worldviews and understandings (either as representative of the "right" thing to do [instrumental knowers], or as reflections of their own value propositions [self-authoring knowers]). While an inquiry-oriented stance may feel more comfortable in some ways for socializing or self-transforming knowers, feedback givers who make meaning in these ways will have to think carefully about how their developmental propensities for holding back judgments (either in favor of those of valued others or as a show of respect and mutuality) may or may not accord with the feedback needs and preferences of those in their care.

## From Constructive to Inquiry-Oriented Feedback (and Back Again): Exploring a Continuum of Communications

With all of this in mind, we want to emphasize once again the vital importance of striving for balance in our feedback—of differentiating supports and challenges along a continuum and in accordance with needs and circumstances. Understanding the potential benefits of both constructive and inquiry-oriented feedback can help us be more intentional as we seek to shape feedback conversations as genuine holding environments for learning and growth, and as we challenge ourselves and each other to do and be more as leaders and educators. Put another way, while constructive and inquiry-oriented feedback can both be oriented toward growth and improved performance—and while we see them as mutually reinforcing parts of a larger whole—the distinction can help us more clearly conceptualize and articulate the *what* and the *why* of our feedback, and how it can best be used as a professional and developmental support and challenge. Figure 7.1 offers a loose visualization of this continuum connecting constructive and inquiry-oriented feedback. We hope you find it useful.

As figure 7.1 shows, constructive and inquiry-oriented feedback are both very important and can filter into and out of any feedback conversation. However, they differ in relation to: (a) directionality (i.e., who is guiding/directing the feedback process), (b) orientation (i.e., whether the

**FIGURE 7.1**

### Feedback continuum: Constructive and inquiry-oriented conversations

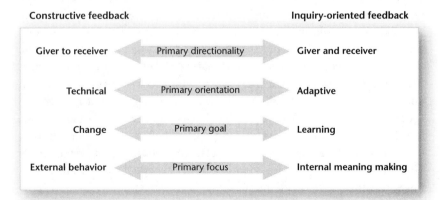

*Note:* This visual was informed and inspired by foundational ideas from Kegan and Lahey (2001), p. 134–135.

feedback is primarily technical, with an assumption of a clear answer and/ or problem, or adaptive, with a more exploratory approach), (c) the goal or purpose of the feedback (i.e., whether it is intended to facilitate a specific change in thinking or acting, or to support learning over time), and (d) the focus of feedback (i.e., whether it addresses external behavior or internal meaning making). As mentioned earlier, both conceptualizations of feedback exist on a continuum, so it is important to recognize that, in any given moment, our feedback most likely falls somewhere on this sliding scale. In other words, constructive and inquiry-oriented feedback are not either/or constructions, as we may draw from elements of both in practice rather than from only one in its purest form.

For example, when you are offering constructive feedback, there may be the assumption that you know what is wrong and that there is a prescription for resolving it. In contrast, in the case of inquiry-oriented feedback, you can have an idea of what needs to be addressed, but you suspend judgment or assessment in favor of understanding what is happening for the other person and how he or she is making sense of it. In practice we may do a little of both as we strive to meet diverse adults where they are developmentally, so understanding and being purposeful about the distinction can make a big difference.

## CHAPTER SUMMARY AND CONCLUSION

As we look back over the ideas and considerations presented in this chapter, including the vital distinction between constructive and inquiry-oriented feedback, one of the most important takeaways is the importance of balance. We mean this in three distinct but related ways: (1) the balance between your own agenda and the hopes and needs of feedback recipients, (2) the balance between inquiry and advocacy (i.e., between arguing for your own position and seeking to better understand the disagreement itself), and (3) the balance between listening and sharing. While intuiting and walking these complex lines day in and day out requires a certain degree of practice and developmental capacity, there is something magical that happens in those moments when we find ourselves balanced just right, and something that leaves us (and/or others) wanting more when we lean too far in one direction or another. As Carl Rogers explained, reflecting on these different outcomes of exchanging ideas: "[S]ome of my experiences in communicating with others have made me feel expanded, larger, enriched, and have accelerated my own growth. Very often in these experiences I feel that the other person has had similar reactions and that he too has been enriched, that his development and his functioning have moved forward. Then there have been other occasions in which the growth or development of each of us has been diminished or stopped or even reversed . . . I should like to avoid those communication experiences in which both I and the other person feel diminished."[9] While, like Rogers, no one wants to experience or feel responsible for facilitating the second, diminishing kind of communication described in this passage, we do think it's important to remember that feedback for growth is itself a *process*. No matter how good our intentions, our in-the-moment feedback may not always fully align with a recipient's hopes, needs, experiences, and ways of knowing—and this is okay. The idea, then, becomes celebrating the increasing number of moments in which we can truly join *with* others in the spirit of progress and improvement, while acknowledging with courage and transparency those instances that propel us to do more, to do better. The inevitable bumps in the road are part of what growth *feels* like, and navigating them with colleagues helps us to generate—together—the collective stories of our working and becoming. For better or for worse, and from moment to moment, growth is all around us, and we are always in it. That is the challenge and the gift of this work.

In the next chapter, we will highlight additional strategies you can use to help deepen your practice of in-the-moment feedback for growth in order to even more effectively meet others where they are developmentally.

## REFLECTIVE QUESTIONS

As is now our custom, we invite you here to consider the following questions, which can be used for independent reflection and/or group conversation. These questions are intended to help you and your colleagues consider the ideas discussed in this chapter and how they might inform your practice of giving feedback in the moment. You may find it useful to reflect in writing privately first and then to engage in discussion with a colleague or team.

+ After reading this chapter, what are two of your biggest takeaways?
+ In what kinds of circumstances/contexts do you think a more constructive approach to feedback would be most effective? When, from your view, might a more inquiry-oriented approach be preferable? Can you think of times when a blend might be in order?
+ What kinds of supports might help you grow your practice of offering both constructive and inquiry-oriented feedback?

# CHAPTER 8

## Giving Feedback in the Moment

*I don't care what you say to me. I care*
*what you share with me.*

—SANTOSH KALWAR

This chapter offers guidance for deepening your feedback conversations with colleagues, all while taking recipients' (and your own) developmental orientations into account. In particular, we turn our attention to key logistical decisions about the *when* and *where* of feedback, as well as seven in-the-moment strategies (i.e., the *how*) for deepening and enhancing the feedback you offer to others. While, in many ways, these strategies are relevant regardless of an adult's way of knowing, we recognize them as foundational to feedback for growth, as they reflect and help make tangible the essential preconditions of trust, safety, and respect.

### WHEN SHOULD YOU OFFER FEEDBACK?

We know that it is important to offer feedback "in a timely manner" (#8 in our "top ten" list in table 2.1). Yet, as we shared in chapter 2, this knowledge begs the question of what "timely" will mean for the different parties involved. Take, for example, the increasingly popular Real Time Teacher Coaching model.[1]

In this innovative approach to professional development, teachers wear an earpiece while delivering an actual lesson and receive feedback, suggestions, and tips from an observer *while they are teaching*. In talking with educators of all kinds, we have heard many enthusiastic testimonials about Real Time Teacher Coaching, as well as contrasting stories about feeling overwhelmed and distracted by such "in the moment" (and literally "in your ear") feedback. While we can envision a type of real-time coaching that takes into account developmental diversity and the importance of the preconditions discussed earlier (i.e., safety, trust, and respect), this kind of mixed response makes perfect sense given what we know about adult development, as well as many conventional understandings of feedback. As we have been exploring, for instance, people will orient differently to authority, taking direction, collaboration, and directional feedback. Another big takeaway here is that individuals will need different amounts of time and space to process and make sense of feedback.

While, unfortunately, there is no hard-and-fast developmental rule for calculating the "right" time to open or offer a feedback conversation, we have found that thinking intentionally about when to wait—and when to initiate—can be an important support to growth. Especially when feedback may have a critical edge, carefully considering the other person's (and your own) readiness to talk can make a big difference. Are emotions running too high? Could the person really take in your message if you shared it immediately? Would waiting allow time for reflection, or would it create undue consequences and/or stress for the recipient or others? Again, your answers to these questions will depend largely on the people involved, as well as the particular circumstances and relationships that contextualize the situation. That said, in table 8.1 we offer a list of guiding factors that can help you even more intentionally think about when to push forward and when to hold back when contemplating the timing of feedback.

**TABLE 8.1**

### Factors that inform the "when" of feedback

| | |
|---|---|
| **When to wait** | • Time and space are needed for independent reflection (for you or others). |
| | • Emotions are running too high (for you or others). |
| | • Waiting would not unduly risk individual or organizational well-being. |
| | • Delaying feedback feels like a developmental support and/or challenge for growth. |
| | • The moment is not right (e.g., others are present, no private space is available, a needed participant is busy with other pressing matters, interpersonal chemistry is temporarily "off"). |
| **When to initiate** | • You have thought carefully about the "what," "why," and "who" of your feedback. |
| | • The other person seems ready and available to participate. |
| | • Sharing feedback feels like a developmental support and/or challenge for growth. |
| | • There is a warranted sense of urgency. |
| | • There is an appropriate mechanism for delivery (e.g., a place for private conversation; a trusting, relational context). |

As noted, we realize that there are other contextual and relational variables that can influence your decisions about when to give feedback and when to wait. We offer table 8.1 as a complement to strategies and conditions that you already care for and about in your feedback practice.

## WHERE SHOULD YOU OFFER FEEDBACK?

As some of the factors in table 8.1 suggest, the timing of feedback can depend on the technical aspects of place just as much as the developmental aspects of personhood. For instance, we have learned that *where* we offer feedback can be an expression—for better or worse—of power dynamics and/or our feedback philosophies. Especially when initiated by leaders, the physical setting of feedback conversations (e.g., in your office, in a teacher's classroom, publicly in a group, or even over the phone) and how we position ourselves in the setting (e.g., who is standing, whether we are sitting behind a desk or at a round table, or simply sitting next to each other) can convey messages about authority, respect, confidentiality, and transparency.

Take, for example, the common practice of publicly reviewing student performance data in schools. While, just as with Real Time Teacher Coaching, we could imagine scenarios in which this practice could safely and transparently support professional growth and development (particularly in the context of a deliberately developmental school or organization), we are also mindful that, without careful framing and practice, these times could feel more like "gotcha" moments or even examples of "data shaming." Imagine, for instance, the real-life example of a school principal who presented student behavior data (aggregated by classroom teacher) during every full faculty meeting, as this was a key focus for school improvement. While the principal's charts and graphs were offered with good intentions, his focus on particular teachers—rather than, say, individual students or the time of day certain kinds of incidents occurred—made many teachers feel like he was purposefully celebrating "good" teachers (i.e., those who kept behavioral disruptions to a minimum, at least on paper) and calling out the "bad" ones (i.e., those who reported problems in their classrooms). As one newer, struggling teacher in this school explained, "I felt increasingly humiliated at every staff meeting, but never got a single piece of feedback that would help me improve. How is embarrassment, in and of itself, supposed to make me a better teacher? I mean, I'm really trying here!" Moreover, because this teacher self-identified as a self-authoring knower, the issue wasn't about her internalizing her principal's negative feedback as her own, or even about her willingness to take in constructive criticism more generally. Rather, the issue involved her resenting her principal's feedback because of the place in which it was delivered.

As the focus in schools increasingly shifts to student performance outcomes and high-stakes accountability practices, the challenge of publicly presenting data in safe and productive ways remains front and center. In light of reform initiatives that operationalize the underlying (and often flawed) assumption that teachers already know how to do a good job but just need more pressure to push things into high gear, we emphasize the importance of remaining continually mindful of how our actions, as leaders and colleagues, align with and communicate our hopes and commitments.[2] Ultimately, this means reflecting carefully and thoughtfully on how the ways our feedback choices—even the logistical ones—will feel to and affect others involved in the process.

While public feedback can be a wonderful opportunity to learn and grow together, and to celebrate individual and collective success, we nonetheless recognize the central role that private conversations continue to play in feedback for growth. As one school principal recently shared, reflecting on her use of a popular new teacher evaluation system, "We use the system, but what I *really* value are my private conversations with teachers. These are my real opportunities to ask them what they need help with, and how I can help them."

In the next section, we describe a number of in-the-moment strategies that you can use to help infuse your private feedback conversations with developmental intentions. While we frame these promising elements of feedback for growth in the one-on-one context (as the most common starting place for transformational feedback), we want to also acknowledge and highlight their transferability to other contexts and settings (public, group, written, etc.). In addition, we want to emphasize that these in-the-moment strategies can be employed whether you are a supervisor or colleague, and they can be used in one-on-one conversations, coaching relationships, teams, and professional learning communities more broadly.

## HOW CAN YOU OFFER EVEN MORE EFFECTIVE FEEDBACK?

Next, we share seven in-the-moment strategies that can guide effective feedback conversations with and for those in your care. These strategies stem from our research, practice, and work with educators of all kinds in university courses, workshops offered to districts and schools, institutes, and other professional learning initiatives. Promisingly, whether your feedback is formal or informal, formative or summative, or constructive or inquiry-oriented (or any combination thereof), the seven strategies described here can help you engage in feedback conversations that more genuinely feel like and serve as holding environments for authentic growth and improved performance. Importantly, they can also be adapted to support adults with any way of knowing. In addition, as you will see, they call to mind more universal dimensions of genuine respect and authentic regard for personhood. Because these seven strategies loosely reflect a chronological process, we present them next in a numbered sequence (although, as you might imagine, responsiveness presupposes room for variation):

1. Preparing carefully
2. Asking permission
3. Being transparent
4. Checking in
5. Really listening
6. Giving and getting energy
7. Checking out by checking back in

## Strategy 1: Preparing Carefully

No matter how we make meaning, no matter our age, rank, or level of accomplishment, there is something precious that happens when another person invests his or her heart and mind into our lives, into our well-being. Especially as the world whips around us (and we around it) like a high-speed car chase in a big-budget action film, knowing that someone else has invested time and self into caring for *us* can make a big difference. Decades ago, Kegan dubbed this gift "the hidden treasure of paid attention," and before him, philosopher Simone Weil argued that "attention is the rarest and purest form of generosity."[3] More recently, Linda Stone, author and former Microsoft executive, went so far as to predict that "full attention will be the aphrodisiac of the future."[4]

As these quotes might suggest, *preparing carefully* for feedback conversations is one way to convey to those in your care that your attention is firmly and fully with and for them. Of course, adults with different ways of knowing may recognize preparation (and paid attention) in different ways (e.g., in the concrete gestures you make or the amount of time you commit to a conversation, in the more subtle ways you recognize *who they are* and *what they care about* in your feedback and conversation). Whether you bring copious notes, thoughtful and individually tailored questions, elegantly prepared write-ups, or simply your undivided care and attention, thinking deeply about the situation and the person and his or her way of knowing *before* engaging in feedback can communicate the depth of your investment in your colleague as both a person and as a professional, and can underscore the value you place on the feedback exchange itself.

From our perspective, the person with whom one engages in a feedback conversation *knows* when the other person has prepared for it. He or she can feel and sense it. Ultimately, as Eleanor Duckworth has found in her decades of research, what we pay attention to (and paying attention to another person's thinking) matters, as the act of paying attention in and of itself has been shown to support development.[5]

## Strategy 2: Asking Permission

While we understand the expectation that leaders, especially those with positional authority, must offer feedback as part of their jobs, we have nonetheless learned from others and from our own experiences that there is great value in broaching feedback conversations by *asking permission* to share. More specifically, leading with a question like "Would it be okay if I offer you some feedback?" can help the other person understand what he or she is getting into (especially if the feedback is unsolicited) and can also help you gauge whether or not the timing is right. Even if, in the worst-case scenario, someone were to directly answer "No" (which, in our experience, is a rare response), this answer would be an important signal that something else is going on for the other person, whether it's just not a good time or there's an underlying concern you may not have been aware of (all of which are important data points).

Take, for example, the experience of Reynold, an assistant principal of a large K–12 charter school. At the time of this example, Reynold was in the transition between a socializing and a self-authoring way of knowing, and had set a personal improvement goal of sharing more about what he was really thinking and feeling with colleagues. So, when Joe (a colleague who was more firmly self-authoring in his meaning making) openly challenged Reynold during a staff meeting, Reynold felt disappointed that he did not handle the confrontation as well as he would have liked. That evening, Reynold went home and thought carefully about all the things he needed and wanted to say to Joe (and also about all the things he wished he'd shared in the moment), including how Joe's comment made him feel, how it might really help if Joe could think differently about the situation, and more. The next morning, with a great sense of urgency, Reynold walked directly into Joe's classroom and began to detail how he was feeling about Joe's behavior in the meeting and how he thought they might resolve the situation. Listening respectfully, Joe finally responded, "Thanks so much for bringing this to me, Reynold. You've got some really good points and I'm really sorry if you felt I was disrespectful during the meeting. Actually, I'd really love to talk with you more about all of this, but I have to be at an IEP meeting in about five minutes. Would it be okay if we checked in later or after school?"

While, fortunately, Reynold and Joe *were* able to have a meaningful conversation that afternoon, Reynold's feedback "bombshell" (as he called it) helped him realize that he'd skipped an important step. Because he was so focused on meeting his own goals and timeline for the conversation, he neglected to ask Joe's permission to share the feedback—a simple but profoundly important in-the-moment strategy.

## Strategy 3: Being Transparent

Related to asking permission, we have also found in our research and experience that it can be incredibly powerful to be *transparent* about the kind of feedback you're going to offer, how you're going to offer it, and, as we shared earlier, the "hat" that you will be wearing. There are few things more unsettling, for example, than receiving an e-mail, a note in your mailbox, or a voicemail with an ambiguous request for a check-in. While "Can we talk?" sends a clear message that you'd like some of a person's time, it offers little else in terms of clarity. How much time? What is this proposed conversation about? Is it good or bad or both? While this may seem like a small thing, being transparent about a feedback request can relieve undue anxiety and help to maintain trust and respect—for adults with all ways of knowing. After all, even if it is not intended this way, withholding information can feel to others like an attempt to maintain the upper hand, or even like a push to create or emphasize an imbalance of power.

That being the case, whenever possible, we recommend sharing something specific in your requests for feedback. Even a slight shift from "Can we talk?" to "Can we talk about X?" can make a big difference. For example, we often smile at the lighthearted story of Nan, who needed to stage an "intervention" with her principal, Cliff, about the way he sent her text messages. After feeling flooded by adrenaline (more than once) after checking her phone and seeing a message from Cliff that simply read, "Call me," Nan explained to him that these messages made her anxious and worried, especially when she could not immediately reach him by phone. While, according to Nan, Cliff still doesn't offer many specifics in his texts, he *has* started adding smiley face icons to communicate that all is well. (His texts now read something like, "Call me ☺ ☺ ☺." A big improvement, from Nan's perspective, as these new messages make her laugh instead of worry.)

Of course, sometimes we *do* have difficult news or feedback to deliver, and we have learned that transparency is of the utmost importance during these instances as well. In particular, acknowledging the mutual challenge of engaging in difficult feedback conversations—particularly those that are more constructive in nature—can help bring the relational components of feedback to the foreground. For example, saying something about how *you* are feeling about the conversation (e.g., "I'm feeling sad/nervous/bad about sharing this with you, but . . .") can help humanize the feedback, and also remind the recipient that your feedback is coming from a place of genuine care.

Again, while being transparent can feel supportive to adults regardless of how they make meaning, sharing this aspect of one's own thinking and feeling as a leader and feedback giver may be a developmental stretch for adults who are more instrumental or self-authoring in their ways of knowing. Similarly, it can be very helpful to consider how adults with different ways of knowing might experience and interpret transparency on the receiving end. Instrumental knowers, for example, will appreciate understanding the reasoning behind your transparency, while socializing knowers will want to feel sure that your transparency is connected to your care and concern for them as individuals. For adults who make meaning primarily with a self-authoring way of knowing, linking your transparency to your respect for *their* competencies and highlighting authentic appreciation for their reciprocal transparency can be a helpful entrée into a difficult feedback conversation.

Looking ahead a bit further in the process, transparency about the "little things" you do *during* feedback meetings can be equally critical. Are you looking at your computer? Are you taking notes? Are you asking a lot of questions? It can be very helpful to the other person in the conversation if you share your rationale for doing what you are doing while or even before you do it. For example, it can help to say something like, "While we're talking I am going to _____ because _____. Will this be okay with you?" Because adults will experience and interpret our outwardly observable actions differently, it is important to make our intentions clear—and also to understand how our behaviors feel to others involved.

Take, for example, a real-life misunderstanding that inadvertently muddled one school head's performance review with a principal. As the head of a large, K–12 urban charter school, Jonah, whom we met in chapter 5, adopted the practice of taking detailed notes during feedback meetings with colleagues *as a show of support*. As he explained, he took notes during feedback conversations with everyone—teachers as well as members of his leadership team (i.e., principals and assistant principals who served in the different divisions of his school)—and thought it was "a powerful way" to show how much he "valued the other person's thoughts." Moreover, Jonah shared, his notes also helped him "to track a person's thinking and feelings and questions" so he "could be more present in the moment and also refer back to the notes later to be of best support to the person." Despite these good and caring intentions, one principal at his school responded to Jonah's note taking in a surprising and painful way: with tears. "Can you please stop taking notes?" this principal asked, clearly distressed. "Are you even listening to me?" As it turned out, what this principal really wanted and needed was *eye contact*, so Jonah's earnest effort to show support through writing (while looking down) felt like something else entirely.

While this example underscores the vital importance of being transparent about your intentions and actions as a feedback giver, it also previews the power of our next strategy: checking in with the others involved to see what would feel helpful and supportive to them in the moment.

## Strategy 4: Checking In

As shared in chapter 6, checking in is an integral part of building community, trust, and connection in teams and other kinds of professional relationships. In one-on-one and other kinds of feedback conversations, checking in at the opening—by asking how the other person is feeling about things (or about our own practices, such as taking notes)—can similarly help set a safe and productive tone for sharing. Moreover, checking in is not just about sharing feelings per se. Clearly understanding another person's hopes and worries for a conversation can help us better meet that colleague where he or she is in the moment—and starting from more common ground can actually help us get better results! After all, acknowledging and understanding another person's feeling honors the deep interconnection of emotion and cognition, since how we *feel* inevitably influences how we *think*. Of course, and as you will recall from previous chapters, not all colleagues will feel equally comfortable sharing with you up front and out loud (e.g., socializing knowers), so differentiating check-in questions and/or even offering a brief moment for private reflection or writing can help adults with different ways of knowing begin the feedback session in ways that feel most comfortable and meaningful to them. While there are many ways to do this, in table 8.2 we offer a few possible ideas for differentiated, developmentally oriented check-in prompts that can help you meet feedback recipients where they are.

**TABLE 8.2**

## Feedback check-in strategies for adults with different ways of knowing

| Way of knowing | Primary orientation for checking in with this kind of knower | Opening check-in prompts for feedback conversations |
|---|---|---|
| *Instrumental* | Ask questions about knower's needs, wants, and hopes. | • Is there anything you need before we begin?<br>• What is your biggest hope in terms of our conversation today? If there's one thing you really want to walk away with, can you help me understand what that is for you?<br>• Do you have any questions about the process or purpose of this meeting? Is there anything you want to add?<br>• What would you like to accomplish during our time together? |
| *Socializing* | Begin by acknowledging knower's contributions, efforts, and personal qualities; ask questions about knower's feelings and experiences. | • How are you feeling?<br>• How do you feel about the (lesson, situation, challenge, etc.)? What do you feel good about?<br>• What kinds of feedback would feel supportive and helpful to you right now? Is there anything in particular that you want to share with me? |
| *Self-authoring* | Ask questions about knower's ideas and goals for the meeting. | • How do you think the (lesson, situation, challenge, etc.) went?<br>• Are there ways that you'd like to proceed in this conversation?<br>• What kinds of feedback do you think would be most helpful right now?<br>• Before we begin, do you want to share any reflections on the (lesson, situation, challenge, etc.)? Before getting started, do you have any feedback for me about the process thus far? |
| *Self-transforming* | Ask questions about knower's current thinking and hopes for learning. | • How are you feeling about our meeting today?<br>• How have you been thinking about the (lesson, situation, challenge, etc.)?<br>• How would you like to think and talk together about this?<br>• In what ways do you think we can be most helpful to each other during this conversation? |

More specifically, while we realize you may pull from different question sets outlined in table 8.2 in order to differentiate the kinds of check-in questions you ask (particularly if you are unfamiliar with a colleague's way of knowing), instrumental knowers will feel supported by questions that attend to their needs, wants, desires, and hopes. Socializing knowers will want to feel acknowledged and valued during check-ins, and will appreciate questions that illuminate their feelings and experiences. Self-authoring knowers will often respond well to questions that invite their thinking about and contributions to the process, and self-transforming knowers, too, will welcome opportunities to collaboratively discuss goals and hopes for the meeting. As table 8.2 shows, our check-in questions can actually help us to meet adults where they are in order to set the stage for even more powerful and effective feedback conversations.

### Strategy 5: Really Listening

The fifth in-the-moment strategy on our list—to really listen—may sound counterintuitive in the context of feedback, at least at first. After all, as we shared earlier in our discussion of feedback directionality, people often think of feedback as something you give or say *to* another person. Yet the fact that listening isn't always one's first instinct during feedback makes it all the more important to highlight it here as a promising and growth-enhancing approach. We know, for instance, that the quality of our listening is a developmental support, and that listening is one of the most effective ways to really join another person in his or her meaning making and experiences.[6] Still, listening—really, *really* listening—is not an easy thing to do.

For example, many leaders share that they strive to get better at this aspect of their work, but feel pressured both to get things done and to demonstrate competency in doing so. "I *want* to listen to my teachers," one principal explained, "but sometimes, when someone is talking to me, I find myself thinking about what I want to say next instead of taking in what they're trying to say." Just as when you're talking on the phone and—because the other person has put you on "speaker" or because of a bad connection—you suddenly hear your own voice echoing back at you, this kind of self-talk and internal monologue can be incredibly distracting, and can also prohibit deep engagement with colleagues. Ironically, missing out on such genuine moments of mutuality (because we are caring so much for our own words, thoughts, worries, agendas, and/or performances) can limit growth and development. As Alan Briskin, Sheryl Erickson, Tom Callanan, and John Ott wisely wrote, "Real change comes from an awareness of our deep connectedness."[7]

The quality of our listening, however, is intimately tied to our inter- and intrapersonal capacities for connection and to our orientations toward feedback. As we have discussed, instrumental knowers have not yet developed the capacity to fully take another's perspective, socializing knowers cannot yet fully disentangle valued others' assessments and feelings from their own, and self-authoring knowers can have a hard time opening themselves up to perspectives that do not align with their own current ways of thinking or seeing. Yet, despite these and other potential barriers to deep listening, we have found that intentionally carving out some space for purposeful listening (during check-ins and throughout feedback conversations) can help adults who make meaning in any of these ways stretch their own limits and capacities, while inviting a more dialogical approach to learning and improvement that can support the growth of all participants.

Describing the integral role listening can play in effective feedback from another angle, one very experienced and accomplished school leader recently shared that "Feedback, as we usually think of it, can feel very one-sided." As she continued, "The best feedback actually involves structuring conversations so that others can explore their own practice and assumptions. If you invite people to talk in just the right ways, you can learn what they really need to push things forward." In the spirit of diving deeper into this promising and powerful idea, we now introduce a framing on listening that is more frequently associated with developmental coaching than with performance feedback: empathic listening.[8] From an empathic listening perspective, listening is really about *entering into and striving to understand* another's experience, and is conceptualized as a distinct and essential part of engaging with and truly joining another person. More specifically, building on Kegan's ideas about the different levels of listening, which in turn has roots in Carl Rogers's humanistic approach to psychology, we next highlight how these five different levels of listening correspond to degrees of empathic engagement (e.g., levels 1 and 2 most directly relate to the experiences of the listener, while levels 4 and 5 are more about the person being listened to and accordingly reflect a higher level of empathic engagement). Because we have found these levels to be incredibly helpful when thinking about the quality of our own and others' listening, we offer them in table 8.3 as another way of thinking even more deeply and intentionally about the different kinds of listening and the ongoing process of developing the capacity to listen genuinely and authentically.

TABLE 8.3

### Five levels of empathic listening

| Level of listening | Qualities |
|---|---|
| Level 1 | Level 1 involves recognizing, but not joining, in the feelings of the person who is being listened to. For example, a listener at this level might say something like, "I don't feel the same way that you do about X" (e.g., an event, a relationship, an idea, or a feeling). |
| Level 2 | Listening at level 2 involves trying to *solve or fix the perceived problem* of the person who is sharing and who is being listened to (even if this was not specifically requested or otherwise indicated). |
| Level 3 | Effectively, level 3 listening is a neutral affair. It primarily involves *asking questions*, but depending upon the purposes behind those questions, the listener could move back down to level 1 or 2, or up to level 4 or 5. |
| Level 4 | Empathic listening at level 4 strives to connect and to join with the *feelings* that underlie ideas and perspectives expressed by the speaker. In essence, it is an attempt to join and be with the other person. |
| Level 5 | Empathic listening at level 5 strives to intuit the bigger narrative or wider set of feelings being experienced by the other person. In other words, listening at this level involves seeking to understand *what is at stake* for the other person. |

*Note:* Adapted from notes taken during lecture. Robert Kegan, "Empathic Listening" (lecture, Minds at Work [MAW] Coach Certification Program [CCP] residency, Cambridge, MA, October 15, 2014).

## Strategy 6: Giving and Getting Energy

Yes, we realize that the name of our sixth in-the-moment strategy—giving and getting energy—may sound a bit unusual at first. Actually, we first heard this particular phrase from Jonathan, an educator who currently serves as a professional learning leader in a prominent alternative teacher certification program. Jonathan coined the phrase when describing the written developmental feedback he received on an important project, in reference to the clear, constructive ideas and genuine encouragement he felt were offered simultaneously (and to powerful effect). In other words, he appreciated how the feedback he received was intended to deliberately fuel his progress and confidence on the one hand (i.e., *give* him energy), and constructively guide his work in light of the feedback giver's expertise and direction on the other hand (i.e., allow the feedback giver to *get* some energy and thinking from him in return). Quite succinctly, the phrase "giving and getting energy" brings together and encapsulates two ideas frequently mentioned in the feedback literature: namely, offering specific, focused feedback (#2 on our top ten list), and maintaining a positive, compassionate focus (#4). Indeed, because the intentional balance of supportive and challenging feedback worked so well for Jonathan—and because it was so clearly evident on the written document he received—he decided to share copies of the highly valued feedback with his team as an example of effectively blending positive and constructive feedback in developmental ways to help them learn from it. As he pointed out, "Offering genuine appreciations alongside critical suggestions doesn't take away from the constructive feedback. If anything, it makes it easier to take in!"

As this example suggests, *giving and getting energy* is a strategy that can work across feedback formats (written, verbal, one-on-one, group, etc.). And, with practice, it can even infuse the larger feedback culture of your school, team, or organization. We have often been honored and inspired, for instance, when the individuals and groups we've had the privilege of working with (and modeling this strategy for) begin to adopt such a stance in their communications and feedback. The truth is, feeling well held is contagious, regardless of our ways of knowing, and something that most people want to hold on to and pay forward to others in their care. Understanding, then, the developmental underpinnings of meaning making (others' and our own) can guide us in even more effectively balancing the supports and challenges we offer, and in facilitating meaningful feedback that colleagues can truly hear, take in, learn from, and act on. In the end, *giving and getting energy* is really is about individualizing and "developmentalizing" this balance. Indeed, as another school leader aptly pointed out, too much support or too much challenge can each be debilitating in different ways. As he explained:

> I think the balance between praise and criticism is very tough. I had a manager who offered so much praise that it all came to feel very empty and almost exhausting. I kept yearning for a more focused delivery of the advice that would improve my practice. My next manager was the exact opposite—very little praise, and a lot of direct, unfettered criticism. I appreciated that she had the courage to be honest with me and truly, genuinely push me as a teacher. But at the same time, I became so directed toward my deficits that I lost sight of some of my strengths, and I really began to unravel a bit after a while—not so much because someone was being "mean" to me, but because I was forgetting who I was in an attempt to meet the demands of someone else. So I think praise in excess and criticism in excess are both very dangerous.

As you think about ways to give and get energy in your own context, you may find it helpful to revisit table 7.1 as a handy synopsis of the kinds of things that will feel energizing and challenging about feedback to adults with different ways of knowing.

### Strategy 7: Checking Out by Checking Back In

As the last example about balancing supports and challenges illustrates, the importance of understanding how your feedback partners are feeling about your exchange cannot be overemphasized. Once again, we suggest the simple yet powerful strategy of *asking* people about their experiences as part of the process of closing—or checking out of—a feedback conversation. How, for instance, is someone feeling? Is there something the other person would like to add? Do things feel clear? What questions does he or she still have? Is there anything else you could do to help? What's the next step—for the person *and* the primary feedback giver? How did the person experience you and what you shared in the feedback process? Part of this, of course, is about ensuring clarity (on both sides) and revisiting hopes and understandings. After all, feedback conversations should never leave people feeling like they're swinging blindly at the piñata of others' expectations, just hoping to make contact. That sort of uncertainty, we've found, is much more enjoyable when it eventually comes with a heaping side of candy!

That said, checking out is also about ending well and laying the groundwork for forward momentum and future results. As a school principal once shared, without this kind of purposeful closing, feedback conversations "can get stuck in that moment—even if the conversation is incredible." In the next chapter, we will offer more in relation to strategies for following up on feedback. For now, though, we want to end our discussion of in-the-moment strategies by highlighting the quiet power of pausing, together, to look back and ahead before returning to the burning bustle of the everyday.

### CHAPTER SUMMARY AND CONCLUSION

In this chapter, we explored key developmental aspects of the *when*, *where*, and *how* of in-the-moment feedback for growth, and outlined a number of promising strategies for making your feedback even more effective and intentional, including:

1. Preparing carefully
2. Asking permission
3. Being transparent

4. Checking in
5. Really listening
6. Giving and getting energy
7. Checking out by checking back in

As we've discussed, each of these strategies can be employed with developmental intentionality across a variety of contexts and relationships, and can help you even more effectively deliver feedback that others can "hear." In the next chapter, we turn to the power and promise of following up on feedback; first, though, we invite you to consider the following reflective questions designed to help you connect the ideas in this chapter to your own experiences.

## REFLECTIVE QUESTIONS

Please consider the following questions, which can be used for independent reflection and/or group conversation. As always, these questions are intended to help you and your colleagues consider the ideas discussed in this chapter and how they might inform your practice of giving feedback in the moment. You may find it useful to reflect in writing privately first and then to engage in discussion with a colleague or team.

+ After reading this chapter, what are two of your biggest takeaways?
+ What are one or two in-the-moment strategies you would like to use to enhance your approach to giving feedback?
+ What kinds of supports might help you grow your practice in the important ways you identified in question 2?

# CHAPTER 9

---

# Bridging Feedback and Action

---

*We do not grow absolutely, chronologically. We grow sometimes in one dimension, and not in another; unevenly. We grow partially. We are relative . . . The past, present, and future mingle and pull us backward, forward, or fix us in the present. We are made up of layers, cells, constellations.*

—ANAÏS NIN

In this chapter, we highlight promising approaches for bridging feedback and action—or, in other words, for helping adults to *use* and *apply* the feedback they've received in meaningful ways. More specifically, we explore how to further scaffold feedback by collaboratively planning for next steps and following up with developmental supports and challenges. As we will explain, effective *follow-through* by others often requires effective *follow-up* on the part of the leader or feedback giver. Feedback alone is not always enough; in many cases, there needs to be ongoing support and communication that intentionally attends to all participants' thoughts, feelings, and meaning making, including the feedback giver's.

To help with this, we deepen our discussion of "checking out" with another person at the close of a feedback conversation that we began in chapter 8. We also highlight strategies and reflective questions that can guide key follow-up processes, and we illustrate how the type and nature of the feedback we offer to others can and should change over time as all parties learn and grow. In these ways, this chapter extends our "developmentalization" of key feedback strategies that we began in chapter 2, particularly #9 ("Follow up on feedback") and #10 ("Provide feedback recipients with opportunities to respond, reflect, and contribute"). Promisingly, and as you will see, following up on feedback for growth with such developmental intentionality can help participants grow and learn, as we stretch and build our capacities as feedback givers and feedback receivers alike.

## PAUSING—AND CONTINUING—FEEDBACK CONVERSATIONS WITH AN EYE TOWARD GROWTH AND ACTION

In chapter 8, we explored seven in-the-moment strategies for giving feedback for growth, ending with the importance of "checking out" of feedback conversations with other adults to ensure clarity (on both sides), revisit hopes and expectations, and lay the groundwork for forward momentum. While, in some cases, checking out can be a relatively quick pause to explore the kinds of questions we mentioned in that chapter, it can also be a launch pad to action and improvement, and to further conversations. As we will describe next, this can involve caring for the interpersonal, emotional aspects of life after feedback, and/or diving deeper into action planning. Each of these important follow-up strategies plays an important role in building individual and collective capacity, and in enhancing the culture of feedback in your school or organization.

### Acknowledging Emotion in Feedback

As we have discussed throughout this book, there are few things more personal than feedback. While we are often encouraged "not to take it personally" or to "remain objective," it nonetheless matters deeply to most of us when someone finds value in our work, or when something doesn't go as well as we would have hoped. After all, educators often feel like their work is part of who they are, not just something they do. You may, for instance, be familiar with the phase coined by John W. Gardner, "We teach who we are." Teaching and leading are indeed personal ventures and require that we bring ourselves to each task. As we have discussed, building capacity in adults through our feedback—before, during, and after—requires an understanding of who they are as people, and as developing, developmental makers of meaning. As we've also considered, feedback for growth involves finding just the right balance between support and challenge for individuals. We really do need both to take in and grow beyond feedback.

For example, instrumental knowers will feel well supported and well held after feedback when given concrete steps and takeaways, but may initially feel unsettled or uneasy about feedback that nudged gently at their growing edge (e.g., if a leader, coach, or colleague in a PLC challenged them to look beyond what they felt was the "right" solution). Socializing knowers may at first feel deflated by difficult feedback if it is not scaffolded by caring, genuine support and appreciation for them as a person, and self-authoring knowers may struggle to balance their own ideas with the suggestions made by others, whether they are colleagues on their team or supervisors. Yet, for adults with all ways of knowing, it is the subtle discomfort (or developmental stretching) of carefully offered challenges that helps us to see things and ourselves anew, and to develop new capacities for teaching, learning, leading, and living.

Still, even knowing the power and promise of such caring, intentional stretching, it can sometimes be hard to tell how well (or not) you've struck the support/challenge balance with your feedback, so asking about others' experiences, feelings, and reactions can help you understand even more deeply what they need to effectively act on feedback and implement next steps. We have found that having these kinds of conversations is also a powerful way to signal to colleagues that you care, and can deepen the essential preconditions of trust, safety, and respect. While it is very important to gauge and understand how others are feeling after feedback as a support to them, checking out in this way can also provide you, as feedback giver, with a chance to consider your own feelings and emotions. You might want to think about this as an internal check-in or temperature taking. Just as *getting* feedback can be intensely personal, *giving* feedback can conjure a full spectrum of internal reactions and experiences, and sharing these with the receiver—at least in part—can help to enhance the holding environment for everyone. Just as it is vital to be transparent when offering feedback for growth (the third in-the-moment strategy we described in chapter 8), acknowledging the emotional dimensions of feedback for all involved can help foreground the human element of this important work and draw attention to the implicit connections between feedback, authentic care, and systemwide capacity building.

For example, you might share something like, "Wow, I'm feeling so great about our meeting and the conversation we were able to have together. I hope it's okay to ask, how are you feeling?" Or, "I trust you know that some of what I shared with you was really hard for me, and that all I offered was offered in the spirit of care and respect." Or even, "I'm feeling very fortunate that we have the kind of relationship where we can speak so honestly with each other." Regardless, the idea is to honor the deep emotional weight of feedback for adults on both sides of the proverbial table, and to acknowledge the simultaneous beauty *and* challenge of accompanying others in their growth.

### The courage to continue

Related to acknowledging the emotional components of feedback for growth (and any kind of feedback for that matter), it's essential to recognize the great courage it takes to continue feedback conversations—and sometimes even collegial relationships—after and beyond an initial feedback meeting. As a feedback giver, it takes courage to offer authentic feedback for growth, and to support adults through and beyond its initial delivery. Likewise, it takes great courage on the part of a feedback receiver to really hear, consider, and act upon feedback that's been offered, especially when it pushes gently at that person's growing edge. Ultimately, no matter one's role or way of knowing, critical feedback can cause anxiety in us because we care deeply for the other person, his or her growth, and instructional improvement. Nevertheless, it is vital that we work through and beyond these moments with an eye toward growth.

In our research with and practice of teaching educators, coaches, and leaders of all kinds, we have learned that adults sometimes spend so much time preparing for the *delivery* of feedback that it can be hard to anticipate what happens next, especially when the feedback being planned for feels challenging for us and/or the other person. Yet, as the following example from the field illustrates, we need to think *beyond* an initial conversation if we want to infuse our feedback with a true growth orientation. Sometimes, we may not be ready for this kind of continuing in the moment (especially when it is heavily emotionally laden), but we have found the great power of this work is that there is always room to pick up where we left off, or to try something new and different the next day.

### Building up to feedback as a team leader

Take, for example, the experience of Alice, an elementary school teacher leader who was struggling to work with and support Bridget, a fellow teacher and a member of her grade-level team. As the newly appointed team leader, Alice found herself increasingly frustrated by Bridget, who was falling behind on curriculum mapping deadlines agreed upon by the group. Yet, as a socializing knower, Alice was hesitant to bring her concerns directly to Bridget (whom she did not know well or have a strong relationship with), and felt especially uncomfortable broaching the topic at this point since she had "let things slide" the first few times Bridget came to the meetings unprepared. To make things even more complex, Alice's decision to "keep her frustrations quiet and hold them in her back pocket for a while" was further reinforced by the advice of a few trusted colleagues, who warned Alice about Bridget's reputation for being "stubborn" and "unpredictable."

Truth be told, Bridget was a well-respected teacher who had a lot of clout in the building, and Alice was loath to get on her "bad" side.

After struggling internally with the situation for some time, however, Alice realized that she *needed* to talk to Bridget about her performance, and to articulate how things needed to improve moving forward. As you might suspect, Alice (like other adults who make meaning in a more socializing way) felt a great deal of anxiety about offering this kind of direct, critical feedback, but ultimately decided to talk with Bridget about her late submissions and how they were affecting the team and their collective progress. In keeping with the inquiry stance we described in chapter 7, Alice also decided to ask Bridget about *her* experiences of their teamwork so far, and to hold out the possibility that Bridget wasn't missing deadlines deliberately or with any ill will. This seemed particularly important since, at the time of the conversation, Alice was unsure about Bridget's feelings, circumstances, and meaning making about the situation (developmental or otherwise).

So, when the moment seemed right, Alice mustered the courage to ask Bridget for a conversation. She pulled Bridget aside and said, "I wonder if you might have a few minutes to talk with me, please? I want to check in with you about the curriculum mapping, and I'd really appreciate the chance to talk with you about how you think it's going." When Bridget agreed, Alice felt a great sense of relief that she'd finally be able to address what was beginning to feel like the "elephant in the room" during grade-level meetings. While, admittedly, Alice was nervous at the start of the conversation, she was proud that she was able to share what she was really thinking and feeling with Bridget, and felt that just inviting her to talk was a big growth move in her leadership. Moreover, when Bridget responded with what seemed like a sincere apology and a promise to do better, Alice was incredibly relieved and optimistic. As she explained: "I really surprised myself. Having the conversation felt like a big step for me, and I feel like it's going to help a lot. I didn't feel like I had to hide how I felt or completely avoid Bridget or stop talking with her—like I usually do in situations like this. I'm so much less frustrated and angry with her. [Pause.] And, honestly, I'm really proud of myself. While it was hard and very scary, I was able to be honest. I don't have to hold it in the same way any longer."

While, inarguably, just getting to the conversation was a developmental achievement for Alice (and we're also delighted to point out how thoughtful and intentional Alice was in her feedback approach), she soon realized that she would need to do something *more* to follow up. Despite their conversation, Bridget continued to lag behind promised deadlines, and even seemed to be giving Alice "the silent treatment" in the hallways. We mention this here not to undermine the hard work that Alice put into the feedback conversation or the effectiveness of her thoughtful framing, but to really underscore the fact that feedback—especially hard feedback—isn't usually a one-off endeavor, even when you do lots of things "right" and with great care. As leaders and feedback givers of all kinds and with all ways of knowing, we need both the courage and the capacity to continue forward with and for others. We will circle back to particular strategies you can use to do this later in this chapter.

For now, though, we think it's important to emphasize the fact that, all too often, teachers and other educators, like Bridget, are expected to improve in areas that need improvement and to excel in areas of strength without a blueprint or process for "after feedback." In our experience, this inadvertent oversight finds root in the pervasive assumption that adults, as professionals and proper "grown-ups," have (or at least should have) already developed the capacity for self-direction or self-authorship. For example, because Alice perceived Bridget as smart, strong, and independent, she assumed that Bridget *already* had the capacity to turn in her curriculum maps on time, as long as she wanted to. So when Alice first noticed Bridget falling behind again, her first reaction was one of resentment and defensiveness. "Why," she wondered, "wasn't Bridget doing what she promised?!"

*Developmental extensions and takeaways*

As you now know, a developmental perspective helps us to see that—as living, growing human beings—most of us will need something more than isolated feedback suggestions or requests as we strive to grow ourselves and our practice, even when we really *want* to improve. Indeed, a deeper understanding of constructive-developmental theory sheds light on the fact that, for most of us, feedback needs to be part of a larger constellation of ongoing supports and challenges, rather than an end in and of itself. Feedback cannot, for instance, be something that we simply "drop off" or "turn over" to others, along with the responsibility for change. Ultimately, as Alice's example helps to show, *not* thinking carefully about next steps before, during, and/or after feedback conversations—and not considering the very real possibility that a colleague may not yet be ready or willing to hear or act upon your feedback—can lead to undue tension or offense on both sides, or what David Garvin and Joshua Margolis (2015) describe as the lost opportunity of "mishandling the aftermath."[1]

So what does this all mean? Why are we sharing Alice's story with you? As Alice's example shows, just *getting to* the feedback can take both fortitude and forethought, and delivering it can feel like a great exhale, triumph, or even catharsis, no matter the outcome. As another school leader recently shared with us after speaking his mind to a difficult colleague, "For a minute there, I felt like I finally won!" Still, it takes another kind of courage to acknowledge and attend to the complications of life and work after feedback, and to use feedback as an opportunity to deepen and expand our connections with others (rather than mishandle the aftermath and unintentionally truncate them or cause a rift).[2] While effective follow-up, especially after challenging or disappointing feedback encounters, will mean different things to different people, it seems clear that a deep sensitivity to both the emotional and developmental dimensions of feedback can help pave the way for even more effective communications and outcomes.

Instrumental knowers, for instance, will likely need support or encouragement to move beyond the "right" and "wrong" of a challenging feedback encounter, and to refocus on the larger mission of the school, team, or district. For adults who make meaning in this way, coming to some agreement about the particulars and deliverables of change—including concrete steps and supports for forward momentum—can help them recommit to a collaboration or endeavor. Reconnecting after a difficult feedback conversation can likewise feel formidable for socializing knowers like Alice, who tend to experience conflict as a palpable threat. Sometimes, adults who make meaning in this way may even opt to retreat from a relationship rather than address the interpersonal fallout head on. As a feedback giver or partner to a socializing knower it can be incredibly supportive for you to say out loud that your relationship will continue after feedback, and to make a point of emphasizing that you really mean it. Self-authoring knowers, too, can benefit from feedback encounters that reintroduce the well-intentioned, growing individuals behind carefully honed arguments—not necessarily to build consensus with alternative-minded others, but to open, at least, the possibility of greater common ground and mutual growth. In other words, stepping back from the larger "argument" and connecting with self-authoring adults as a human being they like and respect (rather than, say, as the embodiment of a particular ideology or value system that differs from their own) can help make the work of growing through and from feedback more palatable and possible for them. Finally, self-transforming knowers, who tend to seek harmony in relationships and orient more naturally to whole-person follow-ups, will likely yearn for this kind of after-feedback bridge building, so *not* continuing or following up on feedback could feel like a frustration or disappointment to them.

## Considering Next Steps: A Guide to Action Planning

As part of following up on feedback and effectively bridging feedback and action, it is of course vitally important to consider and plan for practical, actionable next steps and to involve feedback receivers in this process. This was another important and inspiring lesson that Alice learned in her evolving work with Bridget. Specifically, after two grade-level meetings passed without a curriculum submission from Bridget, Alice decided they needed to check back in about the situation at hand. "Bridget," she asked after the close of the second meeting, "do you have a few minutes, please? I was hoping we could talk about the maps." When Bridget answered, "I guess so" in a monotone voice, Alice could feel her anxiety rising, but braced herself for the conversation. Soon after they began, however, it became clear—and this was a profound realization for Alice—that what Bridget *really* needed was more support with her curriculum work.

"Alice, I'm really trying," Bridget confided. "I mean, do you know how hard this is for me? I'm the most senior teacher on our team, but I'm drowning in this Common Core mapping. I want to help, but all of my teaching materials—and I've been developing and using these for *years*—are aligned with our old state standards. I pretty much feel like the rug's being pulled out from under me, and I don't think anyone gets that."

Seeing how upset Bridget was, and how genuinely she wanted to help and contribute, Alice realized that she, as the team leader, needed to learn more about the specific supports that would feel helpful to Bridget, and that could enable her to succeed. "What can I do to help you?" Alice asked with genuine interest. "How could we make this feel more meaningful and manageable for you?" While, fortunately, Alice and Bridget were able to talk through and follow through on some specific supports for Bridget (including exemplar curriculum maps, more explicit directions about what to include in the documents, and partnering with Daisy, another teacher on the team who had more experience with curriculum sequencing), we want to emphasize that this positive outcome was precipitated first and foremost by Alice's willingness to ask and to listen, and by Bridget's courage to share what she truly needed—even though things did not initially go as well as either had hoped. This vital kind of *coming together* is essential because action planning—like feedback itself—needs to be differentiated and adaptable in order to find and meet adults where they are. A developmental lens can help us see even deeper into each other and ourselves so we can best implement feedback *and* learn and grow from the experience.

For instance, instrumental knowers tend to favor explicitly outlined steps and transparent, concrete explanations of what they "need" to do and how they need to do it. Models of best practices will enable them, just as they did for Bridget, to feel well held and supported. Nevertheless, it can sometimes also be a developmental challenge (and support) to gently encourage adults with this way of knowing to consider and eventually recognize that growth and change—and the successful implementation of feedback—can require more than "doing" a series of particular things in a particular sequence. Especially when working to manage adaptive challenges, you can encourage adults with an instrumental way of knowing to look beyond technical goals and solutions to softly push at the edges of their thinking and meaning making. Explaining your rationale for encouraging them to consider this will feel supportive to instrumental knowers and will help them to try on or test out what you are inviting them to consider and do.

Socializing knowers will often look to you, as the feedback giver, for the "best" response to feedback and for what you think would be good for them to do as a next step, so encouraging and helping them to steer at least *some* of the follow-up planning—while explicitly recognizing what they've already done well and offering your best thinking and support—can help them to build internal capacity while implementing and learning from feedback. It can also be helpful to provide socializing knowers time and space to take in and reflect on feedback, and to consider the kinds of things that would feel supportive to them as they navigate a path forward. As mentioned earlier, time to think and gain perspective can be a powerful developmental support before and after feedback, especially for adults who may feel less comfortable sharing their internally generated ideas. As one teacher explained of the luxury of reflective space, "Everything's usually just so in-the-moment, and I think there's a place for that. But waiting a little bit—that really helps me."

When it comes to action planning, self-authoring knowers tend to feel most comfortable when invited to reflect on their own performance, and to author their own goals and next steps. Yet gently encouraging them to consider alternatives, and to remain open to feedback as a process of inquiry and dialogue, can support growth and perspective broadening over time. It can also help them to consider ideas and ideologies about instructional practice and/or instructional leadership that initially may have seemed to be diametrically opposed to their own.

Finally, action planning for self-transforming knowers needs to honor and acknowledge these adults' value of synthesis, inquiry, self-discernment, and interconnection. While adults with this way of knowing would likely feel supported by a mutual, peerlike exchange with you as the feedback giver, they may also want the time and space to seek out feedback from others, and to experiment with implementation and next steps. Acknowledging the challenge of the more top-down components of feedback for these adults, and—in some cases—helping them to pin down a specific, actionable area of focus (as many areas might seem important and valuable to them) can also help them grow and learn from feedback in meaningful ways.

In table 9.1, we summarize these key supports and challenges for action planning with adults with each way of knowing, including developmentally oriented guiding questions that you can use to help structure and facilitate this phase of feedback for growth. You might want to think about these questions as a way to further calibrate or differentiate your feedback, as well as the accompanying strategies you implement for collaborative action planning. Thinking back to Alice's example, you may also find it helpful to include follow-up questions of this nature in your feedback as a way to keep the door open for future conversations. Since growth and change take time, and since working up the courage to deliver feedback isn't always enough to make a sustainable difference with and for colleagues (as Alice learned), deliberately carving out a space for future check-ins can take some of the potential awkwardness or uncertainty out of revisiting or rebroaching important feedback conversations.

In addition to helping adults select goals and next steps after feedback, the questions, supports, and challenges presented in table 9.1 can help you infuse follow-up action plans with developmental intentionality. For example, after collaboratively exploring feedback and considering possible next steps with feedback receivers, you may find it helpful to invite adults to complete the work sheet in table 9.2. This action planning sheet, which could be used both formally and informally, includes spaces for individual action steps, as well as a proposed timeline, progress markers, and requested supports and challenges for each.

Importantly, depending upon the needs and developmental orientation of the feedback receiver, the action steps can be collaboratively determined and/or self-generated by the implementer, and they can likewise fall on different points of the spectrum of technical and adaptive (as well as professional and personal). Similarly, the work sheet can be completed within the context of a feedback meeting and/or submitted within a designated timeframe afterward if that would feel more helpful to the feedback receiver. For example, as mentioned earlier, instrumental knowers will appreciate your guidance about the "right" action steps needed to achieve their ends, and will likely prefer to focus on more tangible, concrete deliverables. Socializing knowers may want to understand *your* vision for next

TABLE 9.1

## Strategies for action planning, by way of knowing

### Guiding questions for action planning
*(These kinds of questions can be helpful for adults who make meaning with any way of knowing.)*
- How would you go about doing that?
- How would you figure it out?
- What kinds of supports would help you with acting on feedback? How can I help you with securing them?
- What would you do?
- Why would you do that?
- What challenges do you anticipate?
- In what ways can I be helpful to you as we move forward?

| Way of knowing | Developmental supports | Challenges (stretches) for growth |
|---|---|---|
| *Instrumental* | • Offer concrete steps and specific deliverables.<br>• Invite adult to outline what he or she sees as most important.<br>• Establish timeline. | • Introduce a goal or action step that feels less tangible or technical.<br>• Encourage adult to make connections between feedback in different domains.<br>• Introduce the idea that timeline *may* need to be adjusted. |
| *Socializing* | • Explicitly recognize adult's progress and potential at the outset of goal setting process.<br>• Offer your best thinking and ideas in relationship to goals and action steps.<br>• Provide time and space for adult to reflect privately before committing to goals.<br>• Check in regularly to follow up and offer guidance and support. | • Encourage adult to voice own views, feelings, needs, and perspectives.<br>• Invite adult to consider and ask for supports that would help him or her with implementation. |
| *Self-authoring* | • Recognize adult's accomplishments, value, and competencies.<br>• Acknowledge ways to build upon adult's competencies and expertise.<br>• Invite adult to reflect on own performance and self-select goals and next steps. | • Approach goal setting/action planning as a dialogue and mutual exchange of ideas.<br>• Challenge adult to see value in goals and ideas that may not directly align with (and/or seem diametrically opposed to) his or her own. |
| *Self-transforming* | • Honor and acknowledge adult's value of synthesis, inquiry, and interconnection.<br>• Approach feedback goal setting as a mutual, peerlike exchange of ideas.<br>• Engage with adult as colleague/companion in experience. | • Recognize the challenge of the more top-down components of feedback.<br>• Help adult pick from an array of important goals and meaningful next steps. |

**TABLE 9.2**

## Work sheet for your action planning

| Action step | Timeline | Progress markers | Supports |
| --- | --- | --- | --- |
| *What action steps will you focus on? (Item(s) listed should be important to you **and** specific enough to be actionable.)* | *When will you begin work on each step? Are there intermediate milestones or deadlines that would be helpful? When would you like to check back in about our progress?* | *How will you assess how things are going? How will you reflect on your progress?* | *What resources, check-ins, colleagues, or other supports do you think could be helpful? (You may want to consider anticipated challenges, if any, when shaping this list.)* |
| 1. | Start:<br><br>Checkpoint(s): | | |
| 2. | Start:<br><br>Checkpoint(s): | | |
| 3. | Start:<br><br>Checkpoint(s): | | |

steps before completing the chart, so they could benefit from additional time and/or reflective space to more deeply consider their own ideas. On a different note, self-authoring knowers may need some gentle nudging to address important action steps that fall outside of their own hopes or plans for improvement—although they will likely still enjoy the room for autonomy embedded in the process. Regardless of an adult's way of knowing, however, the idea is that the pinpointed action steps balance supports and challenges, and that they feel and *are* important to the implementer.

While adults may orient to this kind of planning differently (and, by design, the process can be flexibly employed), there is something quite powerful and compelling, from our view, about committing one's thinking and ideas to paper, even if that paper does not necessarily become an "official" document or part of the feedback record. For example, educators often share that writing down their goals helps them to see them more objectively and also commit to them. Moreover, as we emphasized earlier, inviting adults to consider specific steps and supports could help you, as feedback giver, better understand and meet them where they are—and it can also help you expand the circle of support for feedback receivers. Are there, for instance, groups or individuals a person would like to work with in relation to the plan? Are other colleagues working on similar or related goals? Might a group of individuals benefit from a similar pool of resources or experiences? Following up on individuals' requests for additional supports and collaboration can be one promising way to expand the circle of support for individuals while building a larger culture and community of feedback in your school or organization. After all, carefully attending to how we offer feedback—and how we support its application in practice— rests at the heart of instructional and systemic improvement.[3]

## AN EVOLVING FEEDBACK JOURNEY: MEETING ADULTS WHERE THEY ARE OVER TIME

Throughout this book, we have emphasized the profound importance of meeting adults where they are developmentally in your feedback and leadership. As true and as powerful as this is, it is also vital to recognize that the kinds of supports and challenges we give to each other during feedback will of necessity change over time. In fact, this is the hope. In other words, as a person grows (both in terms of improving practice and/or leadership and in terms of increasing internal capacities), he or she will need different forms of support and challenge to feel well held in general, and in the context of feedback relationships more specifically. Similarly, as we ourselves grow as feedback givers, our preferences and capacities for giving feedback will likely evolve too—and all of this is a good and wonderful thing.

For example, with the right supports and challenges, those who make meaning primarily with an instrumental way of knowing can develop greater internal capacities for perspective taking and reflection. Accordingly, when they receive feedback, their needs may shift from desiring the "right" answers or solutions to wanting greater acknowledgment of their feelings and internal experiences. They may focus more on wanting and needing your approval and looking to you to help them identify a "good" path for improvement, instead of a "right" one. Likewise, feedback givers with a socializing way of knowing—who previously struggled to give hard or constructive feedback to valued others—may develop a greater facility for such honest exchanges over time with practice and intentional support. This kind of sea change, which can inch forward gradually and powerfully for adults across the developmental spectrum, serves both as a product and driving force of effective holding environments, which are flexible yet stable enough to grow with and for the new, bigger selves of those within.

### Overcoming Feedback That Feels "Stuck" and Maintaining Hope

Of course, not all feedback experiences will yield immediately measurable transformation, and some may even feel increasingly "stuck in place" despite one's best (and most developmental) efforts. Yet it is during our most difficult feedback moments that we bear the greatest responsibility for carrying the work forward, and for caring deeply for the person before us while simultaneously holding the collective best interest in heart. What, for example, is best for the person in question? For the larger team? For our students, school, or organization? And how can we achieve this together?

As we highlighted with our earlier example about Alice and Bridget, it is not always easy to move forward with another person when things feel upsetting or unsettled. This feeling only grows when you begin to suspect—after repeated and increasing attempts to meet someone where he or she is with your care and feedback—that moving forward at this given point in time may not be in the best interests of all. How, for instance, can you give someone the hardest kind of feedback (e.g., that things are not working out)? Ultimately, we have found, offering feedback for growth is like an invitation, and depends largely on the mutual co-construction of experience. We can only do our best to set the conditions for growth, and hope that we've been welcoming, genuine, and thoughtful enough in our feedback that others will "RSVP" to our invitation in the affirmative. Sometimes, however, for one reason or another, a person may not be ready, able, or willing to perform at the levels needed, or to take the necessary steps to make satisfactory progress. In our increasingly high-stakes educational context, and amidst a growing chorus of voices demanding that folks "get with the program" or "get off the bus," we think it's important to explicitly recognize the role that growth-oriented feedback can play in informing and reframing the toughest kinds of personnel decisions.

While we wish we could offer a firm set of criteria for knowing when "enough is enough" in terms of supporting another person's unsuccessful improvement efforts, the fact of the matter is that there are many factors— legal, moral, developmental, personal, and otherwise—that can and must influence such a decision, depending upon circumstance and context. In our own experience, however, and barring any other immediate exigencies, we tend to follow Jiminy Cricket's simple yet sage advice to "always let your conscience be your guide." When you know, for instance, that you have truly done everything that you can for another person, but it's still not working out, it's time to explore more serious options.

For example, people are sometimes shocked to learn that we have, in essence, "fired" people. "You?" they ask. "But you guys are all about growth." While we humbly agree that this is the case, it is also true that a growth orientation isn't isolated from high expectations. In fact, we see them as synergistically reinforcing. That said, while it is always very painful to make a hard decision about someone's place on our teams or projects, approaching that decision in a way that provides the other person every opportunity to improve, to clearly understand what's at stake, and to reflect about what would truly be best for him or her can help to shape even these most difficult conversations as holding environments for growth. Sometimes, meeting people where they are means letting go with love.

By way of illustration, we'd like to share the challenging but hopeful story of our work with Constance. Years ago, we were excited to invite Constance, a teacher leader who was a former student in a graduate course, to help us with an important project. Constance, on her end, accepted our invitation with characteristic interest and enthusiasm, and things seemed off to a great start. From the outset, she was a fantastic and giving team member. She was caring, responsible, collaborative, and eager to learn and do well. After a few weeks on the team, however, it became clear that Constance was struggling to keep up with the workload. As a full-time teacher, she was juggling her work on the project with her care for her students, and we began to suspect that she was burning the candle at both ends, so to speak. We escalated our level of support, and repeatedly offered to help in new and different ways, so when Constance assured us that she could (and still wanted to) meet her project deadlines, we were moved by her confidence and agreed to proceed. Unfortunately, it was a very painful experience for all of us when, the day before a major deliverable was due, Constance let us know that she was far, far behind in the work she had promised, and that we would miss our deadline despite all of our best efforts.

Recognizing and empathizing with Constance's deep sense of failure and embarrassment at this mishap—all while scrambling to make good on the deadline that had just passed—we knew that the fit and the timing just wasn't right, but wanted to deliver this painful news to Constance in a way that honored her as a person and left open the possibility for healing. Like the feedback we offered to her throughout, we framed this harder conversation around our great esteem for her and her contributions. We acknowledged her challenging experiences managing such a full plate, and we invited her to share her own thinking, feeling, and sense making about what happened. Out of respect and care, we also shared with Constance what we saw as some of her possible missteps, and how she, and we, might have handled things better or differently. Ultimately, after learning more about Constance's struggles to balance the many aspects of her work and life, and after hearing the genuine exhaustion and deflation in her voice, we gently encouraged her to consider resigning, and let her know that doing so would be okay. After all, *she* was more important to us than the work, and always would be.

From a developmental perspective, it was becoming increasingly clear to us that Constance did not, at the time, have the capacity to tell us how much she was struggling, or to accept that, all things considered, it would probably be best for her to withdraw from the project. As a socializing knower, she did not want to disappoint us, and so was working around the clock to avoid "quitting" (which, from her view, would be tantamount to destroying her connection to us). Because of this, *we* needed to gently help Constance make the decision that was best for her and all, as she was not able to make it on her own. We encouraged her—strongly—to resign, and left open the possibility for future work together should the circumstances change. Most importantly, though, we reassured her that we cared deeply for her as a person, and that a decision to leave the team would not change that.

On her end, while feeling embarrassed and disappointed about what had transpired, Constance was able to hear and take in even this very painful feedback, and to accept it as it was intended: as a support for her, and her growth and well-being. Courageously, she said as much in a beautiful follow-up e-mail, an excerpt of which we share now with you: "I am learning a lot about myself and what I could have done and not have done through this time to have different results . . . and as hard as it is right now, I'm sure I will come to appreciate this learning experience too. So thank you so much for supporting and loving me even through my mistakes, and weak and ugly moments . . . I will always be grateful."

While not all difficult conversations end in such hopefulness, we have repeatedly found comfort in the common wisdom that it is often darkest before dawn, even if we don't quite know when the morning will arrive. At the very opening of this chapter, we presented a quote by the author Anaïs Nin, in which she spoke of the mystery and nonlinearity of our change and development: "we do not grow absolutely, chronologically" and "we grow sometimes in one dimension, and not in another." It is true that growth sometimes happens in fits and starts. And while on the one hand this might be frustrating or unsettling, on the other it leaves open the possibility of newfound beauty, and of pleasant, light-bearing surprises down the road.

Recently, Constance gave us such a moment of light when, years after the encounter we just described, she popped in after one of our workshops to reconnect and to share some goodies and some hugs. She was doing well in every aspect of her life, and felt confident that the painful decision we had made together years ago was the right one. As can happen, we had temporarily lost touch amid the busyness and bustle of life, so reconnecting with her was a great and welcome pleasure. In fact, we hold out the hope (for us and all of you!) that any other, less-resolved moments of feedback may still find such propitious resolutions, and we recognize magnificence in the fact that—no matter what came before—they always can. This truth and these hopes, we believe, exemplify the lasting power of feedback for growth, and the enduring promise of genuine human connection, maintained and strengthened over time.

## CHAPTER SUMMARY AND CONCLUSION

In this chapter, we looked closely at the importance of following up on feedback, on both the emotional and practical levels. While, as we've shared, we see feedback for growth as an ongoing, evolving, and collaborative process, we feel strongly that following up in these ways (in the short and long term) can help the adults in your care even more effectively hear, consider, learn from, and act upon feedback as they work together to build new capacities and possibilities. As Margaret Fuller once wisely said, "If you have knowledge, let others light their candles in it." In the end, successfully offering and implementing developmentally oriented feedback is really about both of these things. It is about communicating and sharing the knowledge that you bring to the table, *and* it is about equipping others to recognize and develop their *own* expertise and capacities as a result of your coming together.

In order to serve all students well and to meet the mounting adaptive challenges at our doorstep, we need to help each other grow and improve our practice, and we need to embrace the unique glow and spark that resides within each of us. While we may not all wear our competencies, our leadership, or our know-how in quite the same ways or styles, this diversity is a gift, and a resource to be nourished. As another wise woman, Edith Wharton, mused, "There are two ways of spreading light: to be the candle or the mirror that reflects it." A developmental perspective helps us to see that, to different degrees and in different combinations, each of us can be both the candle and the mirror, with and for one another, as we follow up on feedback with care.

In the next chapter, we come full circle and raise up the critical importance of seeking out feedback as a way to more deeply understand ourselves and our practice, and to grow our feedback and instructional leadership with the support of others. As we will discuss, seeking out and learning from feedback is one vital way we can bring our biggest, best selves to the urgent work ahead.

## REFLECTIVE QUESTIONS

Once again, we invite you to consider the following reflective questions, which can be used for independent thinking and/or group conversation. We hope they are helpful to you as you consider ways you might like to apply or extend the ideas in this chapter about following up on feedback to your own leadership, collaborations, and/or instructional practice. You may find it useful to first free-think or free-write privately, and then engage in discussion with a colleague or your team.

+ After reading this chapter, what are two of your biggest takeaways?
+ What are one or two things you would like to do to enhance your approach to following up on feedback?
+ How, if at all, has reading this chapter helped you to better understand—from a developmental perspective—your own and/or other people's experiences of giving and receiving feedback, as well as what may have happened afterward?

CHAPTER 10

# Seeking Out and Growing from Feedback

*The curious paradox is that when I truly accept*
*myself just as I am, then I can change.*

—CARL ROGERS, *On Becoming a Person*

Throughout this book, we have explored the power and promise of a new, developmental approach to feedback that takes into account the different developmental capacities of feedback givers as well as receivers. Before discussing how seeking out feedback can help us grow—and strategies we can employ to do just that—we thought it would be helpful to pause and highlight the terrain presented in this book so far.

We began, in chapter 1, by highlighting the growing need for this approach, which we call *feedback for growth*, in light of increasing accountability and evaluation mandates, as well as the growing number of adaptive challenges that infuse education today.[1] In chapter 2, we further situated this work within the larger feedback literature, and foreshadowed how a developmental understanding of feedback *complements, deepens, and extends* key lessons about effective feedback that we synthesized from scholarship across professional domains.

In chapters 3, 4, and 5, we explored the theoretical underpinnings of feedback for growth, and considered how constructive-developmental theory offers one helpful lens for understanding the qualitatively different ways that adults orient to and experience feedback.[2] As we've emphasized in these chapters and throughout this book, a working understanding of this theory can help us give and receive feedback that can be even more effectively heard, taken in, and acted upon. More specifically, we stressed the importance of meeting adults *where they are* in the developmental sense when offering feedback, and of remaining mindful of our *own* preferences, capacities, and orientations as feedback givers. In chapters 6, 7, 8, and 9, we took an up-close look at the practical processes that constitute feedback for growth, and highlighted key strategies for strengthening our developmental communications and collaborations before, during, and after feedback itself.

In this chapter, we come full circle and raise up the critical importance of *seeking out* feedback as a way to grow oneself, one's leadership, and one's instructional practice. This is important to consider whether you are offering feedback to colleagues as a supervisor, a peer, and/or a member of a team or a professional learning community. As Carl Rogers explained in the epigraph, it is only when we accept ourselves as we are—when we recognize and honor our limitations as well as our strengths—that we can open up authentic growing spaces in our hearts and minds for real improvement and change. Indeed, learning to seek out, grow through and from, and embrace feedback of different kinds (e.g., formal, informal) and from different sources (e.g., supervisors, colleagues, supervisees, students, families, and other stakeholders) is one of the most powerful ways to grow as an educator and human being. Put another way, accepting the need for our own continued growth and getting truly comfortable with feedback about our performance can help us gently stretch our growing edges, and thereby expand our cognitive, emotional, intrapersonal, and interpersonal capacities.

## GROWING ONESELF THROUGH FEEDBACK: STRATEGIES AND IMPERATIVES

In today's fast-paced, high-stakes educational environment, it is more important than ever that we bring our biggest, best selves to the vital work of teaching, learning, and leading. While current policy mandates and new reforms—such as the Common Core State Standards, high-stakes teacher and principal evaluation systems, and Race to the Top initiatives—place new demands on teachers and educational leaders of all kinds, these pressures (alongside the intrinsic imperatives we feel to best serve those in our care) have also heightened the critical role of effective, actionable feedback in our change and improvement efforts, for others as well as ourselves.

In fact, like leadership itself, effective feedback for growth must emanate from *and* circle back to the selves we bring to this work. It must, in other words, both "begin with and rest on" our own growth and development, so that we can even more effectively give our best to others.[3] With this urgent necessity as backdrop, we next present three strategies for seeking out and growing from feedback that you can use to enhance your noble work, leadership, and collaboration with colleagues. Importantly, each of the strategies can be employed to facilitate self-growth for adults with any of the ways of knowing we have illuminated in this book. We emphasize this here because we contextualize each strategy with an example from a different leader—and, as you will see, these leaders make meaning in qualitatively different ways. We've done this to paint a more on-the-ground picture of these strategies in action, and to help emphasize that seeking out and growing from feedback is important for all leaders and educators, regardless of one's way of knowing. So, as you read the examples that follow, please keep in mind that any of the strategies can be helpful to any leader or educator, just as they can be helpful to all of us.

### Strategy 1: Informal Surveys

Sometimes, the most effective way to learn about (and from) others' experiences of your work, leadership, and collaboration is to ask them about it. Especially when you've created a safe and respectful culture of feedback, you may be pleased by how readily people will share their ideas and perspectives to support your growth and professional development. After all, your colleagues have a vested interest in your success. Moreover, asking for feedback is a strategy that can be used in one-on-one settings, or when working with groups of varying sizes. Still, knowing what you know now about development (i.e., that, even under the best conditions, many people may not feel comfortable offering direct, honest feedback out loud and in your presence, especially if you are in a supervisory role), it can be helpful to invite adults to share their feedback in ways that simultaneously honor their ways of knowing and feel safe in light of any organizational, power, or intra- and interpersonal dynamics that may complicate a more direct exchange.

Toward this end, we often find it valuable to invite adults to complete an informal survey when seeking to further improve our work and/or professional initiatives (courses, workshops, seminars, teamwork, professional learning experiences, etc.). While, in some ways, sending out such a survey demands a certain amount of vulnerability (after all, you never quite know what information will come back to you), openly asking for feedback in this form is a great way to learn. It also models an authentic commitment to caring for others' experiences, and an understanding of feedback as something valuable and necessary for everyone, no matter one's role or hierarchical position.

There are two key points about using such a survey (which you could distribute via paper, e-mail, or other online survey administration tool) that we want to underscore here. The first is that including an option for anonymity is very important. The opportunity to leave one's name off a feedback form, for instance, can in some cases open a safer space for new and different kinds of feedback. Plus, adults always have the option of self-identifying if they choose to do so. Sometimes adults *want* to put their name on these kinds of surveys for a variety of reasons—including but not limited to having something they would like to share on the record or want to address more directly.

The other point is about the power of doing this informally. While a survey can be a valuable part of more formal evaluations, giving people a chance to formatively share in a "just between you and me" manner can similarly help you learn from ideas and feedback that might not otherwise come up. Sticking for a moment with our own example of seeking out feedback from participants when teaching in university settings, you could imagine, for instance, the difference between what professors might learn from informal, mid-semester reflections versus university-issued course evaluations that are shared with school administrators. Just as we noted in our earlier discussions of *giving* feedback, carving out space for ongoing, formative feedback can help us learn from the widest variety of voices and ideas over time, and can even help us better prepare for more summative evaluations.

While we know that surveys can take many shapes and forms, and that you likely know best what kinds of questions would feel most helpful to explore with colleagues in your own contexts, in exhibit 10.1 we offer a sample of general, open-ended questions that we have found to be powerful and enlightening when gathering feedback about our work and teaching. We hope that you find these—and your adaptations of them—helpful in your own leadership, teaching, collaborating, and learning.

Of course, and as you now know well, adults with different ways of knowing may orient differently to the experience of inviting and receiving feedback through surveys. Instrumental knowers, for instance, will likely gravitate toward any concrete suggestions for improvement that arise, while socializing knowers may mine the data with an eye toward understanding how others are feeling about them and their work. Self-authoring knowers will likely appreciate the opportunity to directly solicit feedback on their practice, but may need to make a conscious effort to remain open to ideas or suggestions that fall beyond the bounds of what they were looking for or hoping to learn. Self-transforming knowers, too, may eagerly embrace the opportunity to learn how others are thinking and feeling, but may need gentle encouragement to let go of some of the feedback, especially if it reflects more of an outlying perspective than a common concern. In all cases, however, one of the most promising aspects

EXHIBIT 10.1

### Informal Survey Questions for Seeking Out Feedback

- What are some aspects of _____ (e.g., our work together, my coaching, our professional development initiative, my teaching, my leadership, our feedback processes) that are working well for you?
- What, if anything, are some aspects of _____ that feel less helpful to you?
- Is there anything you suggest, wish for, wonder about, or recommend that could make _____ more meaningful for and/or supportive to you?
- Do you have any additional comments or suggestions that you think would be helpful for me to understand?

*Thank you so much for sharing your thoughts and feelings with me.*

of employing informal surveys to enhance your practice is that they involve *solicited* feedback—and thus presuppose a certain openness to learning and growth on the part of the initiator.

*Geoff's example: Seeking out feedback in the transition from an instrumental to socializing way of knowing*

While adults with any way of knowing and any professional role can request, benefit, and learn from an informal survey to gather feedback, we next share Geoff's powerful story of seeking out feedback to grow and improve as a curriculum team leader. A mid-career high school social studies teacher, Geoff was passionate about "making a difference," and volunteered to lead the curriculum team because he felt confident that he had the knowledge and skills to put his money where his mouth was. While Geoff was well aware of the new curriculum mandates coming down the pipeline in his district (e.g., aligning the pace and sequence of history instruction to the Common Core), he held very strong views about the "right" way to meet these objectives, and described himself as a "traditional, old-school teacher" who was good at "getting things done." Developmentally, Geoff displayed many characteristics of an instrumental knower, as he firmly believed that there were "right" and "best" practices for teaching that required strict fidelity, and had trouble taking in colleagues' perspectives when they offered contrary ideas. He'd found some success with his teaching methods in the classroom, and—since he was generally well regarded by his peers and administrators—he felt empowered to foreground these approaches in the curriculum planning. As he often said to his colleagues during team discussions and debates, "It works for me, so it can work for you!"

After a few weeks in his lead role, however, Geoff found himself increasingly frustrated by colleagues' "critical feedback." In particular, two teachers on the team were aggressively pushing him to adopt a more "flexible, progressive" approach they felt would better reflect the school's core philosophy. While in truth, Geoff had been cataloguing such challenging experiences for some time (even outside of the team context), things really came to a head one afternoon when Thomas, one of the teachers Geoff considered to be an "ally" on the curriculum team, "accused" Geoff of humiliating him and walked out of the meeting. In the moment just before, Geoff had told Thomas that one of his ideas "wasn't applicable" since he brought it up outside of the agreed-upon agenda. But, seeing the genuine pain and embarrassment in Thomas's expression, he felt unsettled and confused. Needless to say, this was *not* the outcome Geoff had intended.

So while Geoff had genuinely been trying to do the right thing by Thomas, the team, and the students they were working to serve, it suddenly seemed clear to him that the "right" thing wasn't quite working. Admittedly, Geoff was a little worried that Thomas might report him to the assistant principal or that he might lose his title as team leader, but he found himself even more concerned about how to make things right with Thomas—and with all of his team members—so that he could be a better leader with and for them. While he wasn't sure what this would look or feel like, he knew intuitively that something had to change.

For adults like Geoff who are grappling with moments of uncertainty or questioning, gathering more information through an informal survey can be a powerful strategy for crafting a path forward and a plan for growth, regardless of one's way of knowing. In Geoff's case, sharing with his colleagues that he "needed their help," and that he genuinely "wanted to get better" so that he could be even better *for them*, was a powerful framing for the informal survey he then asked them to complete. The survey, which was based on some of the questions in exhibit 10.1, helped Geoff to understand more clearly what he was doing well, as well as what kinds of things might further help his team reach their goals. Perhaps even more importantly, the survey helped him to understand that how others *felt* about his leadership mattered just as much as—if not more than—his sense of what was "right" and "wrong" for the curriculum. As one teacher on the team powerfully (and anonymously) explained, "I know you really care about this work, but it doesn't always feel like you care about *us*—the people on the team. You need to get better at acknowledging our value and contributions."

Seeking out and hearing feedback in this way helped Geoff to more genuinely appreciate and grow from what his colleagues had to say, and to consider next steps toward improving his team leadership. More specifically, Geoff began to recognize the importance of being less "run by" his own needs, and deliberately carved out multiple opportunities during meetings for *everyone* to share. Simultaneously, through his earnest efforts and openness to feedback, he found himself developing new internal capacities to more sensitively orient to others' needs and feelings.

## Strategy 2: Mini-Convenings

In our work with educational leaders of all kinds, we strive to help adults learn about and experience the power of collegial inquiry in action. As we have described, collegial inquiry is a form of reflective practice that helps us to push our deep thinking and self-growth by exploring our own and others' ideas, assumptions, beliefs, and values about practice and problems of practice with trusted colleagues.[4] While collegial inquiry can and does take many different forms, we often facilitate a special kind of case-based discussion that we call *convening*.[5] This pedagogical strategy—which can be a powerful support to adults with any way of knowing—was designed to create a holding environment for the safe exploration of problematic or puzzling dilemmas of practice.[6] More specifically, after establishing safe, participatory norms, conveners compose, share, and discuss written descriptions of complex challenges in order to take broader and bigger perspectives on the issues at hand, and to learn and grow together as they see things anew. For more about the developmental process of convening, please see *Leading Adult Learning*.[7]

While the collaborative consultation process inherent in convening is a powerful tool for growth and development, it can sometimes be helpful when seeking out feedback to engage in a more abbreviated form of collegial inquiry, which we introduce and refer to here as a *mini-convening*. Mini-convening—which does not require a written case—can be employed in triads, teams, and professional learning communities, and, like its "big sister" namesake, can help support and challenge adults who make meaning at any place along the developmental continuum.[8] The big idea behind mini-convenings is that, in growth-oriented teams, PLCs, and other safe contexts, we can actually *ask* our colleagues for feedback about a particular problem, goal, or challenge; and we can "convene" the group to receive feedback that is intentionally normed and structured to help us (and the entire group) gently push our thinking and meaning making. For example, in teams or PLCs, individuals can present something to the group that they would like to get better at, grow about themselves, or otherwise get help with via focused collegial consultation—including behavior management challenges, leadership conundrums, interpersonal dynamics, and other problems of practice.

Importantly, when you are convening a group in this new "mini" way (just as when full convenings are implemented), the goal is not necessarily to solve a problem or answer a question immediately. Rather, the objective—for the convener—is to carefully consider and open up to alternative perspectives and differing interpretations that may shed new light on actions, assumptions, and sense making (both one's own and others').[9] For this reason, after the convener verbally presents the focus of the mini-convening to the group, he or she *listens* (i.e., does not respond) and quietly processes information (takes notes, jots down questions and insights, etc.) as the other group members discuss the selected topic, problem of practice, or dilemma and refer to the convener in the third person.

While we know it can sometimes be hard to hold back our reflexive responses as others discuss something very important to us, we have learned that this kind of taking in and holding back from speaking can help us listen more deeply and in different ways (i.e., instead of preparing a response). It can also create a more open space for group members to safely introduce their thinking, questions, and insights in relation to our questions and requests. While the time allotted for different adaptations of mini-convenings can vary, we recommend twenty-five minutes at a minimum and forty at a maximum since we have found these timeframes to be most effective. To be of best help and to further illuminate the process, we offer a sample protocol for mini-convening in exhibit 10.2.

Once a group or team agrees that they would like to try this new process as a way of giving and receiving feedback, it will be important for members to agree upon "living norms" and confidentiality agreements, which need to be revisited before the start of each mini-convening.[10] In addition, the group or team will want to:

- agree on how much time will be invested into each mini-convening;
- decide how many mini-convenings will occur in each group or team meeting;
- create a list of who will be the convener during each session and who will serve as facilitator/timekeeper;
- build in at least five minutes between mini-convenings for a "step back" to check in on norms and refocus for the next mini-convening; and[11]
- build in at least five minutes up front for checking in and five minutes at the end for checking out as a team.

EXHIBIT 10.2

## A Protocol for Mini-convening

*The following protocol can be used to convene a group of colleagues (e.g., team, PLC, leadership cabinet, or district leadership team) around a self-identified question, dilemma, problem of practice, or goal for professional growth and improvement.*

1. **5 minutes:** The convener introduces the context and his or her dilemma, challenge, or way in which he or she hopes to grow, as well as one or two questions that she or he would like to guide the feedback discussion during the mini-convening.
2. **15 minutes:** The rest of the group/team/PLC reflects together on the questions posed by the convener. The group refers to the person being consulted to (e.g., the convener) in the third person. The convener listens but does not participate in this discussion.
3. **1 minute:** During this time, the convener and the group pause silently to reflect on and synthesize feedback. When the convener feels ready, he or she then moves the group to step 4.
4. **4 minutes:** The convener responds to the group, reflects out loud, and generates one next step that she or he will plan to take from that point. Depending upon group norms, conveners can check back in with the group about progress in later sessions.

*Note:* Adapted from Drago-Severson, *Leading Adult Learning*, 93.

As you might imagine, it is also important for individuals who will convene the group to carefully prepare for their mini-convenings. In other words, prior to the designated meeting time, the person being consulted to (i.e., the convener) will want to reflect on what he or she would like help with (i.e., a pressing problem, dilemma, or struggle in terms of how he or she would like to grow from group feedback), as well as the particular question(s) that will be posed to the group. In this way, this new model of small-group consultation can facilitate self-growth and, importantly, can be a powerful support for *all* participants as they work together to explore new ideas and perspectives. After all, we learn so much from one another, whether we are a convener or a participant in any kind of convening group.

*Naomi's example: Seeking out feedback in the transition from*
*a socializing to self-authoring way of knowing*

Like the informal surveys we discussed earlier, mini-convenings can be a powerful support for adults with any way of knowing. Nevertheless, to help ground this promising practice in a real-life example, we next describe the experiences of Naomi, a teacher leader who was working to grow her practice in the transition from socializing to self-authoring.

Naomi, who was the lead teacher in her high school's English department, met regularly with the four other department heads on campus to collectively discuss schoolwide processes (e.g., examining student data, professional development, and their school's new teacher observation and evaluation cycles). As they discussed these important matters, Naomi came to think and feel, based on her observations and conversations, that many of her teacher-leader colleagues felt more comfortable than she did delivering critical feedback to the teachers they were supporting. While recognizing this gap was an early move on Naomi's part toward a more self-authoring way of knowing (i.e., she was beginning to hold this part of her experience and sense making out as "object"), she was eager to learn more about how her colleagues were able to offer constructive feedback so well, and how she could too.

As she explained to her colleagues during one monthly meeting, she really wanted their help because she was coming to see that, too often, she "hid" behind her "sunny and bright" persona when interacting with the teachers in the English department. "I *really* want to be authentic and honest," she shared, "and to stop hiding—but I can see that expressing appreciation feels delicious to me, while using words with a more negative hue makes me feel like a dark cloud is gathering within and outside of me."

In response to Naomi's courageous request for help with getting better at offering more direct feedback and sharing what she was "truly thinking and feeling" (a challenge for many socializing knowers), the group agreed to meet the following week for a mini-convening with Naomi. Importantly, because Naomi was asking for help that implicated her internal capacities (not just particular skills or solutions), the team strove to help Naomi with next steps *while also* providing gentle developmental "wonderings" that could support and challenge her thinking. For example, Naomi's team members helped her to more deeply probe the feelings and anxieties that bubbled up for her when she was tasked with conveying challenging feedback. "I wonder what's *really* at stake for Naomi in these moments?" one colleague asked. "I wonder if there are colleagues with whom she might feel more comfortable testing out authentic feedback?" another chimed in. As Naomi listened to and reflected on these important questions, the group was careful to reassure her that feeling comfortable with offering difficult feedback was actually "a capacity she could grow within herself over time and with practice."

While the team offered many important insights and wonderings during Naomi's mini-convening, she left feeling particularly appreciative of a quote from Rainer Maria Rilke that her colleague Stewart shared with the group: "Be patient toward all that is unsolved in your heart and try to love the questions themselves, like locked rooms and like books that are now written in a very foreign tongue. Do not now seek the answers, which cannot be given you because you would not be able to live them. And the point is, to live everything. Live the questions now. Perhaps you will then gradually, without noticing it, live along some distant day into the answer."[12] As Stewart explained during the mini-convening, "loving the questions" was "sometimes an infuriating part of growing oneself—but it was always a key part of development," as we need time to grow into our bigger, more complex selves. He continued, "The question can actually be your future in camouflage." For Naomi, this felt like a powerful and "peaceful" reminder, because she came to see—with her colleagues' support—that identifying her improvement goal was indeed the first step toward being able to offer the kinds of feedback that she wanted to. Moreover, her mini-convening also helped her to take a greater perspective on the fears and assumptions that kept her "hiding in the sunshine" of a more socializing approach to her leadership.

As we shared in chapter 3's discussion of constructive-developmental theory, the transition from being run by and *subject* to something to being able to hold it out more, be responsible for it, and control it as *object* is the balance on which our very meaning making hinges. For Naomi, recognizing her emerging transition was a powerful "a-ha" moment—and supported a slight and important developmental shift that left her with a bigger view of herself and how she could get better in her work. As she shared with her colleagues after her mini-convening, she now felt it was "okay to feel uncomfortable in those moments" of giving hard feedback since she knew it was something she could and would grow to manage with their continued support.

## Strategy 3: Hosting a "Dinner Party"

Finally, we are excited to share a third powerful strategy for self-growth, which we affectionately refer to as the "Dinner Party Exercise." Inspired and informed by Robert Kegan and Lisa Lahey's path-finding work on Immunity-to-Change (ITC) Coaching and the developmental underpinnings of constructive-developmental theory, this exercise—like other components of Kegan and Lahey's larger developmental coaching arc—invites us to understand and see more deeply into our own assumptions and self-systems as pathways to growth.[13] In the simplest terms, this final strategy—which fortunately (or unfortunately?) does not require the hosting of an actual dinner party—involves picking "one big thing" we'd like to get better at in our work or personal lives, and developing a plan and collegial supports to help us do just that. We use our version of this exercise, which is similar to the version for ITC coaching and adheres to its framing and purposes, in our work with aspiring and practicing teacher leaders, assistant principals, principals, superintendents, district leaders, coaches, and other educators as an invitation to help them grow themselves in general and by purposely and deliberately seeking out feedback.

While this strategy for self-growth and development does *not* require real-life cooking, we refer to it as the Dinner Party Exercise because the first step involves generating a list of people who know you really well, whom you trust, and who care deeply about you, and inviting them to attend an imaginary dinner party at your home. For this dinner party of the mind, guests shouldn't worry about bringing a dessert or a main course. Instead, they should arrive at the door prepared to share with you the "one big thing" that, from their perspective, would make a substantial difference for you if "you could get significantly better at" it in your work or personal life.[14] In other words, each of your guests tells you what he or she believes is the *single most important thing* you could do to improve in your work or personal life—whether it be your leadership, instructional practice, collaborations, communications, delegations, or any other area for growth.

Now, as we explain when facilitating this exercise with educators of all kinds, your invitees can be people you know personally or professionally, and the guest list can be as long or as short as you see fit (as you don't have to worry about space limitations, social groupings, or seating arrangements). However, everyone you invite should be someone who cares about you and knows you very well. They should also be people you trust, and who genuinely want you to succeed. They should, in other words, "have your back." With this in mind, we don't think it's a good idea to invite a colleague you think has it out for you (even if he or she might offer a different or valuable perspective). From our view, this just isn't that kind of dinner party.

Now, since this is usually a hypothetical exercise and people won't actually be showing up with gift-wrapped copies of their most thoughtfully generated feedback, it can be very helpful, once you've finalized your guest list, to make a note next to each person about what *you* think he or she would identify as your "one big thing." Very often, for instance, we know *just* what those closest to us would say. In some cases, they've been saying it for ages! In other cases, and especially when we facilitate this exercise over a couple of days during institutes and seminars, people move beyond hypothetical lists and actually ask individuals about their one big thing (some people worry, for instance, that they can "only know what they can know"). We've recently discovered that some educators even text people on their lists as we are facilitating one-day workshops. While reaching out to others can certainly be a very powerful supplement to this activity, we consider it an optional extension that you can employ at your discretion.[15]

Regardless of how they generate their lists, educators in workshops around the world comment on how valuable it is to put these ideas down on paper and to see them next to each other—how they intersect, overlap, and align (or don't). Moreover, it doesn't matter if the individuals at your dinner party agree with one another, or even if *you* agree with what they have to say. In fact, *you* should be the very last person on the list, and you should feel free to cast your own vote about the one big thing you need to get better at, regardless of how it aligns with the other suggestions on your list, as Kegan and Lahey suggest in their original version of ITC. Essentially, the intention of the dinner party invitation is just to get it all out there—to get a variety of possibilities and perspectives down on paper—so you can look at the list and think carefully about what would feel most meaningful and important to you as an improvement goal.

Once you've created your final list of guests and their caring feedback suggestions (including your own), the hope and challenge is to select *one* area of growth that you would like to focus on as an improvement goal. This can be the same as your initial response to the question, or it can be inspired by something that one of your guests shared (either literally or hypothetically). The most important thing here is that your goal feels deeply meaningful to you, and that it involves a behavior (or nonbehavior) that is in your own control (i.e., it is not about other people's reactions to or treatment of you).[16] Of course, our ways of knowing have been found to influence both our rationale for picking an improvement goal and the nature of the goal we've selected.[17] For example, are you picking a goal that will help with getting a reward? Maintaining or moving away from the need to receive others' approval? Getting better at expressing or acting on your own values or beliefs? Or more effectively building and growing professional connections? Does the goal you've selected prioritize achieving concrete deliverables, empathizing more deeply with others, taking a firmer stand for your own ideas, or expanding some of your more deeply favored ways of thinking and seeing? Regardless of these potentially diverse orientations to what's essentially a developmentally oriented dinner party, the fact of the matter is that we may *ourselves* be uniquely positioned to recognize the growth moves that seem just out of our comfort zone but still attainable. Moreover, an awareness of developmental theory can shed additional light on our growing edges and the potential threads running through the items on our lists, whether they are related to work or our personal lives.

After selecting your improvement goal, it can be very helpful to share your goal with a trusted colleague or group and to engage in collegial inquiry around the goal itself. Why, for instance, do you think this would be powerful and important for you? Why do you think it has been hard for you in the past? What, from your perspective, tends to get in the way for you when you try to achieve your goal? Sometimes, we've learned, just talking about your goal and any surrounding issues or questions can help surface hidden assumptions, and it can also help your goal to feel more real and actionable than if you had just reflected on it privately. Related to this, putting your goal out in the open can make it easier to seek out and benefit from collegial supports and additional feedback as you work to meet your goal.

Importantly, a next step in this process is to observe yourself over time as you try to translate your goal into action. In particular, it can be very powerful to take more of a researcher's stance *on yourself*, and to strategically notice and document those times when you are able to realize your goal, and those times when it's harder for you to enact.[18] Stepping back and observing yourself in this way and keeping track of what you learn from doing so can help you better recognize and learn from patterns in your behavior, and gain even deeper insight into your leadership, teaching, collaborations, meaning making, and professional development. In fact, research suggests that thoughtful and consistent self-work on a deeply meaningful goal can lead to noticeable and significant change in a relatively short amount of time (e.g., in about four to six months).[19] With time, and with the right kinds of supports and challenges, you may find that you've moved on to have a different relationship to your improvement goal—and this, from our perspective, is the gift of this foundationally important work.[20]

As we mentioned earlier, this is one very important part of a larger set of exercises that comprise the Immunity to Change Coaching Program.[21] For your reference, we summarize in exhibit 10.3 the key steps of the Dinner Party Exercise as we employ it.

*Magdalena's example: Seeking out feedback in the transition*
*from a self-authoring to self-transforming way of knowing*
Just as with the prior strategies for self-growth that we've described, hosting a "dinner party" can be a powerful support for adults who make meaning

EXHIBIT 10.3

## Key Steps for Hosting a Developmental Dinner Party for Your Self-growth and Improvement

1. Create a list of colleagues, friends, and/or family members to invite to a "dinner party of the mind." Invitees should be people who know you very well, whom you trust, and who care deeply about you and your success. You should also include your own name at the end of this list. Instead of bringing a food item to share, guests (including you) should "bring" an answer to the following question: *What do you think is the single most important thing I need to do to get better in my work or in my personal life?*

2. Next to the names on your dinner party list, please jot down what you would imagine as each guest's response. You should also mark down your own response at the end of the list.

   2b. *(Optional) You may find it helpful to follow up with individuals to actually ask about what they see as your "one big thing."*

3. After considering the generated list (and observing any patterns or trends), pick *one single thing* that you would like to focus on as an improvement goal (something you would really like to get better at). This can be your suggestion or a guest's, but it should feel meaningful and important to you.

4. Share your goal with a colleague or team to engage in collegial inquiry around the goal you've selected. Sometimes, just talking about your goal and related questions can help it feel more real and actionable than reflecting on it privately.

5. Observe yourself in action. This means, for example, taking a researcher's stance with the hope of recognizing and learning from patterns.

*Note*: Adapted from Kegan and Lahey, *ITC Facilitator's Workshop*, 55–57. For a fuller description of the ITC coaching process, see Kegan and Lahey, *Immunity to Change*; Kegan and Lahey, *ITC Facilitator's Workshop*; or www.mindsatwork.com.

with any way of knowing. However, we next share the example of Magdalena, a charter school principal who sought help with her improvement goal during an early stage of her transition from a self-authoring toward a self-transforming way of knowing.

After participating in a version of the Dinner Party Exercise as part of a longer-term developmental coaching experience, Magdalena, who was just beginning her fifth year as school principal, decided that she wanted to get better at "delegating in meaningful ways." For years, Magdalena held the reins of nearly every initiative in her school *very tightly* to ensure that things were done to *her* exacting specifications. While, at first, this kind of influence and control felt very comfortable and reassuring to Magdalena as a self-authoring knower, it also meant incredibly long hours that, increasingly, were coming to feel unsustainable as her school grew in size and complexity. It was also, she began to feel, directly connected to the diminished morale she was beginning to sense around the building.

"I guess I'm something of a micro-manager," she confided when first considering her "one big thing"—and indeed, in addition to being the lone point person for admissions, staff hiring, professional development, teacher evaluations, school culture, and student discipline, Magdalena took it upon herself to lead the data team, and she regularly sat in on extracurricular activities and departmental meetings. So, when she invited some of her most trusted teachers and supervisors to her growth-oriented dinner party and they confirmed her propensity for "over-influencing," she decided that "trusting her teachers, supervisors, and staff more by delegating more" was a meaningful goal for her personal and professional growth. While, on the one hand, Magdalena considered her passion and "presentness" important strengths of her leadership (and key benefits of her self-authoring capacities), she simultaneously recognized that "stretching herself to really empower others" could help her to become a more compassionate, effective leader, and could likewise support her hope of "bringing the school community—teachers, staff, parents, children, all of us—closer together."

In her mid-year self-evaluation, Magdalena courageously documented her new improvement goal, and discussed it at length with her district supervisor, Chrissy (a veteran leader who also made meaning somewhere between a self-authoring and self-transforming way of knowing). Because Magdalena knew that Chrissy's feedback reflected her deep investment in and respect for Magdalena as a principal and professional—as well as Chrissy's own rich experience as an educational leader—she asked Chrissy if she would be willing to meet regularly to engage in conversation about her improvement goal. Meeting once every three weeks or so, Magdalena felt, would be a powerful support and challenge for growth, so she was delighted when Chrissy agreed to help.

While Magdalena really appreciated Chrissy's generosity, time, and thoughtful expertise, Chrissy offered feedback on a few occasions that Magdalena "didn't understand or agree with." Sometimes, Chrissy's questions left her feeling exposed and uncertain, and sometimes her suggestions felt too far afield from what Magdalena wanted to do and be as the principal (e.g., when Chrissy suggested setting up a teacher committee to lead professional development). During these challenging moments, Magdalena (like many self-authoring knowers) had no trouble letting Chrissy know how she was feeling and what she was thinking. For example, Magdalena said things like, "I'm not saying that your feedback is flawed. I am saying that I need help understanding your feedback. Can you help me better understand where you're coming from on this one?"

Fortunately, Chrissy took Magdalena's questions and inquiries in the spirit of learning in which they were offered, and Magdalena ultimately felt that her ongoing, collaborative meetings with Chrissy were really helping her "let go of the reins" in ways that upheld high standards *and* built human capacity in her teachers and her school. For example, Magdalena invited a few of her most trusted colleagues (yes—those same teachers she invited to her dinner party) into a "gradual release mentoring plan" designed to help them take on increasing leadership in the school. Powerfully, Magdalena connected her emerging confidence to "rely on colleagues as supports and leaders" to her growing trust in and respect for Chrissy as a feedback partner. As Magdalena explained, "Having Chrissy, having her as a mirror to reflect back the best and the worst of me so clearly, is just such a gift. I want to be that person for my teachers—and I want to help more of my teachers be that person for each other." In this way, and representative of the larger developmental shift she was making in her thinking and work, Magdalena's experiences seeking out and learning from feedback helped her to grow and improve her leadership in meaningful and lasting ways.

## CHAPTER SUMMARY AND CONCLUSION

In this chapter, we illuminated the critical importance of *seeking out* feedback as a way to grow our leadership, our instructional practice, and ourselves. Since who we are as leaders, educators, and feedback givers matters so immensely in the many domains of our work and lives—and since, in other words, our capacities, perspectives, personalities, and developmental orientations will influence how well we hold our multiple roles and responsibilities—learning through and from feedback can fuel key parts of our continued growth, development, and effectiveness. It can also model our deep commitment to change and improvement for those in our care.

To be of best help as you seek to enhance your noble work in these important ways, this chapter highlighted three promising strategies for seeking out and growing from feedback—informal surveys, mini-convenings, and the Dinner Party Exercise—that can be employed by and with adults with each and any way of knowing. We truly, truly hope these ideas and practices are useful to you, and we wish you wings as you soar to new heights in all of your endeavors.

Before we invite you once again to consider a series of questions designed to help you extend and apply your learnings from this chapter, we want to preview an action planning opportunity that will follow in the epilogue. A tying together of the ideas and prompts you've considered throughout this book, this activity will help you solidify next steps for growing and authentically engaging in developmentally oriented feedback in your school or professional context.

## REFLECTIVE QUESTIONS

One last time, we'd like to invite you to consider a few reflective questions, which can be used for independent thinking and/or group conversation. As always, you may find it helpful to free-think or free-write privately in relation to these questions, and then engage in discussion with one or more colleagues.

+ What are one or two things you would like to do to enhance your practice of growth and self-development?
+ What is one strategy for seeking out feedback that you would like to employ or adapt?
+ After reading this chapter and this book, what do you see as one or two of your more important takeaways?

# The Promise and Power of Feedback for Growth

*That is what learning is. You suddenly understand something you've understood all your life, but in a new way.*

—DORIS LESSING

Throughout this book, we have argued that adding a developmental layer to the best of what we know about feedback can help us even more effectively offer supports and challenges for growth that can be heard, taken in, and acted upon by adults who make sense of their work and the world in qualitatively different ways. While deeply effective and actionable feedback is important for its own sake—to help us best serve our students and the adults in our care—current pressures have pushed feedback to the foreground of educational reform efforts and policies, and an understanding of *feedback for growth* has never been more necessary.

Again and again, leaders and educators of all kinds voice a desire to get better at feedback—to learn how to *do* feedback well in light of these imperatives—because they know how important it is and can be. As one school principal recently said, reflecting on the power of good feedback:

I really believe in the power of strong feedback not only to move practice, but to change minds, to change lives. I can name feedback conversations that have literally altered the course of my career: a pizza shop conversation in October 2009, a discussion about templates in the spring of 2010, a formal post-observation conference in September 2011, an e-mail from a friend of mine that same month. These feedback 'experiences' stand out as turning points—peaks and valleys—in my work. Feedback is a very real agent of change.

Much like good teaching and leading, we tend to know good feedback when we see, hear, or experience it, but it can still be hard to identify "that thing" that makes good feedback so meaningful and transformative to us and others. Often, it can be even harder to translate that thing convincingly into our own practice. While, inarguably, there are many components of effective, actionable feedback that are important to acknowledge (including its content, context, and style), we believe that a developmental understanding of and approach to feedback is *the* missing piece needed to expand our larger feedback conversations, and to make a real and lasting difference for educators and the students they serve with love and care.

While, of course, feedback for growth is neither a panacea nor an easy fix for the complex challenges we face in education today, it *is* a powerful, guiding philosophy that can help us more effectively invest in ourselves and each other, every day. This, ultimately, is an investment we need to make as we navigate new terrain and carve out new possibilities, and it is one that all of us deserve. Indeed, dedicating our time and hearts to nurturing genuine, developmental cultures of feedback is one powerful way to build human capacity, demonstrate faith in personal and organizational improvement, and model the importance of "never underestimating your teachers" or yourselves (as Robyn Jackson recently phrased it).[1] This, in the end, is the hope behind our conceptualization of feedback for growth, and the promise of putting it into practice together as we live and learn our way through the vital work ahead.

To help you step forward courageously in your feedback and leadership, we next invite you to engage in an action planning exercise that can help you to bring together and apply some of your key learnings from this book. As always, we hope you find it meaningful and helpful.

## EXTENDING YOUR LEARNINGS: DEVELOPING AN ACTION PLAN TO ENHANCE YOUR PRACTICE OF FEEDBACK FOR GROWTH

As we near the end of this part of our journey together, and as you look ahead to what's next in your practice and leadership, we hope that there is an aspect of feedback for growth, the giving and/or receiving of it, that you would like to develop and explore further in a personal action plan. Action planning in this way, we have found, can give you an opportunity to: (a) further develop your own ideas about how to even more effectively support improved performance and internal capacity building through feedback; (b) apply one or two theoretical ideas (e.g., ways of knowing, holding environments, the preconditions for feedback for growth) to intentionally grow yourself and advance your feedback practice; and (c) consult with and receive feedback from a colleague about your plan. Next, we present a process you can use to develop a plan and engage in collegial consultation.

## Selecting Your Focus

Thinking over all we've explored in this book, and also looking back at your responses to the reflective questions at the end of each chapter, please select *one* aspect of your feedback practice that you would like to get better at as a next step (i.e., an aspect of your practice you find particularly challenging, or an idea for improvement you consider especially compelling). While we realize and hope that you will continue down multiple avenues of exploration as you grow yourself and your practice of giving feedback for growth, we want to emphasize here that the *most important* part of selecting a focus for this round of action planning is that it feels personally meaningful to you. The following are a few example feedback goals and objectives that educators and leaders of all kinds have voiced to guide their action planning:

- Offer more developmentally oriented feedback during formal observation cycles.
- Share more challenging or difficult feedback with team members after intervisitations.
- Follow up on feedback—in developmental ways—to offer supports and challenges to teachers with different ways of knowing.
- Develop a culture more supportive of feedback for growth on a team or PLC.
- Teach colleagues about key principles and practices of feedback for growth.
- Refine goal-setting processes with supervisees before and after formal evaluations.
- Help teachers feel safe in considering and sharing their ways of knowing as a support to goal setting, feedback, and collaboration.
- Differentiate feedback more effectively to align with recipients' general or dominant ways of knowing.
- Seek out feedback to grow as a principal, assistant principal, teacher leader, and/or practitioner of any kind.
- Be more present for teachers who are struggling or in crisis (i.e., balance caring supports with challenges for growth during difficult times).
- Overcome obstacles—those that are self-generated and those that are externally mandated—that get in the way of more effective practice.

- Support colleagues' growing capacities to *give* feedback to the adults in their care.
- Learn how to be honest in offering feedback to supervisors and create conditions where it's okay to do this.
- Discern when to offer feedback/advice versus allowing people to discover solutions on their own.
- Learn how to ask for feedback from a supervisor and/or leadership cabinet.
- Balance a constructive with an inquiry-oriented approach in feedback.

## Developing Your Plan

To help you as you develop a written action plan (which can be in narrative or bullet form), we have included a series of steps and question prompts to guide your writing in exhibit E.1. These are offered to give you a starting place for exploring your ideas in greater depth.

## Consulting with a Partner: Timing and Process

After you've completed your written outline or sketch of the practice you'd like to implement, please find a partner and exchange plans for review. In exhibit E.2, we offer a suggested protocol for engaging in collegial inquiry with your partner about both of your plans for growth. We recommend allocating twelve minutes of reflection for each partner (as this timing often works well), but, of course, you can adapt the duration and process to best fit your needs and circumstances.

EXHIBIT E.1

### Guiding Steps for Action Planning

1. Please select *one* way you'd like to advance your practice of feedback for growth. This can be "one next step" that you would like to implement to further support your efforts to improve your own instructional capacity or that of adults you supervise, coach, and/or collaborate with.
2. Please consider how one or more of the ideas presented in this book might inform your thinking about advancing your practice for growing yourself or helping others grow from feedback. It may be helpful to consider specific connections between theory and your practice.
3. What questions/challenges/dilemmas seem especially important for you to consider in terms of advancing your practice of feedback for growth? What kinds of help and support would you like to receive during consultation?

EXHIBIT E.2

### A Protocol for Consulting with Your Action Planning Partner

**SUGGESTED TIMING:**
- Author #1 **(12 minutes)**
- 1-minute transition/stretch/free space
- Author #2 **(12 minutes)**
- 1-minute reflections on process

**SUGGESTED PROCESS:**
1. Author #1 explains plan and indicates requests for help. **(2 minutes)**
2. Colleague consults to Author #1. **(8 minutes)**
3. Author #1 reflects on experience and shares next action step. **(2 minutes)**
4. Colleagues switch roles (and repeat timing).

We truly hope that these action planning practices and processes will be useful to you in your incredibly important work. Before signing off (at least for now), with genuine appreciation, confidence in you, and best, best wishes, we would like to share a few final reflections about the beauties, complexities, and possibilities of feedback for growth. Thank you, as always, for thinking and aspiring with us.

### FEEDING BACK WITH DEVELOPMENTAL INTENTION: ON WINGS AND METAMORPHOSES

*We are all butterflies. Earth is our chrysalis.*

—LEEANN TAYLOR

An article posted on the *Scientific American* website in August 2012 reminded us that in biology, *metamorphosis* refers to a profound change in form and being that takes place as an organism transitions from one stage of life to the next—such as from the caterpillar to the pupa, or from the pupa to the adult butterfly.[2] So too can we, as human adults, transform our ways of seeing and making meaning of the world as we grow, learn, and develop our internal capacities, capabilities, and competencies over time. Yet, just like caterpillars, we need appropriate conditions and *forms of holding* to nurture metamorphosis in others and ourselves.

In order for the slow-moving caterpillar to transform into a butterfly capable of astounding feats of flight, important changes must take place within the pupa that allow the creature's nascent wings to grow and develop. These signals activate and create conditions for remarkable and externally invisible changes within the chrysalis. Yet one fact that astounds us about the caterpillar-to-butterfly metamorphosis is that "some caterpillars walk around with rudimentary wings tucked inside their bodies, though you would never know it by looking at them."[3]

Those of us who choose to lead with developmental intention, either on occasion or more consistently, can be helped in this important and vital work by choosing to think about the wings of development that are tucked inside each and every one of us, though we might otherwise miss them in our work with one another day after day. When thinking about giving and receiving feedback, then, it can be helpful to pause and remember the different leaders, mentors, and teachers in our lives who sensed our invisible wings and acknowledged our promise for growth. What was it that these helpful guides did or didn't do that felt to us like a support to our growth? To the development of our rudimentary wings? And, alternately, of the many adults in our care and in our lives, whose soon-to-be wings might we ourselves intuit, perhaps even before their bearers notice, feel, or sense them for themselves?

As we have discussed throughout this book, a developmental perspective can help us to offer feedback in ways that support improved performance and internal growth, for both others and ourselves. Attention—of the deepest and most genuine kind—is indeed a powerful tool that we can call upon when we're privileged to offer feedback for growth. Promisingly, *amazingly*, the things one pays attention to have a tendency to grow. There is a great power and hope in noticing the wings of promise in people with whom we interact each and every day, and in offering and being offered feedback for growth. We hope that this book assists you in stepping forward in your path finding and needed work. We wish you well as you search for wings to develop in others, and as you continue to nourish the special wings others may have searched for and found tucked deep inside you. In these ways, feedback for growth can help *lift us up*—all of us—as we extend our wings and transform our practice, our schools, our coaching, our teams, our systems, ourselves, and each other.

In a final but related example, we'd like to share an image of a noble, great egret that lifts our spirits and inspires us to imagine all the possibilities for *launching* implicit in a developmental approach to feedback. Among the many egrets living in or near the wetlands of the American Sun Belt, David Severson, our trusted thought partner and Ellie's dear husband, recently came across a particularly large and regal great egret right at the moment of takeoff. With an elegance nearing perfection, the impressive bird simply stepped forward into the air, just like that, and David was blessed enough to capture that precious instant on his iPhone. Looking at the picture, which we've shared with you in figure E.1, and imagining this magnificent bird gaining a bigger and greater perspective as she soared higher and higher overhead, we couldn't help but smile at the thought that—somewhere and somehow, way back in this great egret's earliest days of learning and life— she must have achieved this astounding capacity through some natural form of learning through feedback.

Like the experiences and fellow creatures that fortuitously transformed our egret's early self into a strikingly magnificent symbol of avian beauty, each of us has the power to help those around us grow and *lift off from the ground* with our feedback and thoughtful care. Moreover, like the beautiful, inspiring egret herself, each of us deserves to be nurtured, strengthened, and *well held* by feedback as we strive in our bodies, hearts, and minds for new and ever-unfolding heights.

We thank you, tremendously, for accompanying us on this feedback journey, and for the many flights of growth we know you will inspire—and take—in your vital work.

**FIGURE E.1**

## A great egret, or great white heron, takes flight in Bonita Springs, Florida

# Notes

## Chapter 1

1. Eleanor Drago-Severson, *Becoming Adult Learners: Principles and Practices for Effective Development* (New York: Teachers College Press, 2004a), 1–36; Eleanor Drago-Severson, *Helping Teachers Learn: Principal Leadership for Adult Growth and Development* (Thousand Oaks, CA: Corwin Press, 2004b), 1–35; Eleanor Drago-Severson, *Leading Adult Learning: Supporting Adult Development in Our Schools* (Thousand Oaks, CA: Corwin and Learning Forward, 2009), 1–60; Eleanor Drago-Severson, *Helping Educators Grow: Strategies and Practices for Leadership Development* (Cambridge, MA: Harvard Education Press, 2012), 1–58; Robert Kegan, *The Evolving Self: Problems and Process in Human Development* (Cambridge, MA: Harvard University Press, 1982), 23–113; Robert Kegan, *In Over Our Heads: The Mental Demands of Modern Life* (Cambridge, MA: Harvard University Press, 1994), 15–334; Robert Kegan, "What 'Form' Transforms?: A Constructive-Developmental Approach to Transformative Learning," in *Learning as Transformation*, eds. Jack Mezirow and Associates (San Francisco: Jossey-Bass, 2000), 35–70.

2. Drago-Severson, *Helping Teachers Learn*, 1–20, 69–148; Drago-Severson, *Leading Adult Learning*, 69–250; Drago-Severson, *Helping Educators Grow*, 127–165; Eleanor Drago-Severson, Jessica Blum-DeStefano, and Anila Asghar, *Learning for Leadership; Developmental Strategies for Building Capacity in Our Schools* (Thousand Oaks, CA: Corwin Press, 2013), 23–49, 77–107.

3. Matthew Burns and Cullen Browder, "House, Senate Take Bites from Common Core Apple," *WRAL*, June 4, 2014, http://www.wral.com/house-senate-take-bites-from-common-core-apple/13701482/; "Race to the Top," Wikipedia, http://en.wikipedia.org/wiki/Race_to_the_Top.

4. William A. Firestone, "Teacher Evaluation Policy and Conflicting Theories of Motivation," *Educational Researcher* (2014), doi: 10.3102/0013189X14521864; Bill Gates, "Annual Letter from Bill Gates," *Gates Foundation* (2013), http://www.gatesfoundation.org/who-we-are/resources-and-media/annual-letters-list/annual-letter-2013; Douglas N. Harris, William K. Ingle, and Stacey A. Rutledge, "How Teacher Evaluation Methods Matter for Accountability: A Comparative Analysis of Teacher Effectiveness Ratings by Principals and Teacher Value-Added Measures," *American Educational Research Journal* 51, no. 1 (2014): 73–109; Ian Davis, "The New Normal," *McKinsey Quarterly* (2009), http://www.mckinsey.com/insights/strategy/the_new_normal.

5. Charlotte Danielson, "Evaluations That Help Teachers Learn," *Educational Leadership* 68, no. 4 (2011): 35–39; Robert J. Garmston and Bruce M. Wellman,

*The Adaptive School: A Sourcebook for Developing Collaborative Groups* (Rowman & Littlefield Publishers, 2013), 13–25; Kathryn P. Boudett, Elizabeth A. City, and Richard J. Murnane (eds.). *Data Wise: A Step-by-Step Guide to Using Assessment Data Results to Improve Teaching and Learning* (Cambridge, MA: Harvard Education Press, 2005), 11–28, 97–115.

6. Rich Ginsberg and Neal Kingston, "Caught in a Vise: The Challenges Facing Teacher Preparation in an Era of Accountability," *Teachers College Record* 116, no.1 (2014): 1–48, http://www.tcrecord.org/Content.asp?ContentId=17295.

7. Philip Hallinger, Ronald H. Heck, and Joseph Murphy, "Teacher Evaluation and School Improvement: An Analysis of the Evidence," *Educational Assessment, Evaluation and Accountability* 26, no.1 (2014): 5–23.

8. Ibid.,18.

9. Alyson L. Lavigne and Thomas L. Good, *Evaluating Teachers and Students: Moving Beyond the Failure of School Reform* (New York: Routledge, 2013), 92–116; Kim Marshall, *Rethinking Teacher Supervision and Evaluation: How to Work Smart, Build Collaboration, and Close the Achievement Gap* (San Francisco: Jossey-Bass, 2013), 20–63.

10. Krissia Martinez, "An Approach to Productive Feedback for Teachers," Carnegie Foundation, 2013, http://commons.carnegiefoundation.org/what-we-are -learning/2013/an-approach-to-productive-teaching-feedback/; Jeannie Myung and Krissia Martinez, "An Approach to Productive Feedback for Teachers," Carnegie Foundation, 2013, http://commons.carnegiefoundation.org/what -we-are-learning/2013/an-approach-to-productive-teaching-feedback/.

11. Daniel Weisberg et al., *The Widget Effect: Our National Failure to Acknowledge and Act on Differences in Teacher Effectiveness* (New York: New Teacher Project, 2009), 1–35.

12. Harris, Ingle, and Rutledge, "Teacher Evaluation Methods," 73–105; Lauren Sartain, Sara Ray Stoelinga, and Eric R. Brown, *Rethinking Teacher Evaluation in Chicago: Lessons Learned from Classroom Observations, Principal-Teacher Confer- ences, and District Implementation* (Chicago: Consortium on Chicago School Research, 2011), 21–41; Claire Sinnema and Viviane Robinson, "The Leaderhsip of Teaching and Learning: Implications for Teacher Evaluation," *Leadership and Policy in Schools* 6, no. 4 (2007): 319–335.

13. Charles T. Clotfelter, Helen F. Ladd, and Jacob L. Vigdor, "Teacher Credentials and Student Achievement: Longitudinal Analysis with Student Fixed Effects," *Economics of Education Review* 26, no.6 (2007): 673–679; Herbert Marsh and John Hattie, "The Relation Between Research Productivity and Teaching Effectiveness," *Journal of Higher Education* 73, no. 5 (2002): 606–608; Marshall, *Rethinking Teacher Supervision and Evaluation*, 7–17; Jennifer K. Rice, *Teacher Quality: Understanding the Effectiveness of Teacher Attributes* (Washington, DC: Economic Policy Institute, 2003), 1–50.

14. Harvard Business School Publishing Corporation, *Giving Feedback: Expert Solutions to Everyday Challenges* (Boston: Harvard Business Press, 2006), 1–23.

15. Drago-Severson, *Becoming Adult Learners*, 2–36; Drago-Severson, *Helping Teachers Learn*, 3–35; Drago-Severson, *Leading Adult Learning*, 31–60; Drago-Severson, *Helping Educators Grow*, 19–58; Drago-Severson, Blum-DeStefano, and Asghar, *Learning for Leadership*, 23–49; Kegan, "What 'Form' Transforms," 35–60.

16. Ibid.
17. Ronald Heifetz, *Leadership Without Easy Answers* (Cambridge, MA: Harvard University Press, 1994), 1–17.
18. Ronald Heifetz and Martin Linksy, *Leadership on the Line: Staying Alive Through the Dangers of Leading*, vol. 465 (Cambridge, MA: Harvard Business Press, 2002), 9.
19. Ronald Heifetz, Alexander Grashow, and Martin Linsky, *The Practice of Adaptive Leadership: Tools and Tactics for Changing Your Organization and the World* (Cambridge, MA: Harvard Business Press, 2009), 8–12.
20. Heifetz, *Leadership Without Easy Answers*, 1–15; Heifetz and Linsky, *Leadership on the Line*, 1–35; Heifetz, Grashow, and Linsky, *The Practice of Adaptive Leadership*, 1–48.
21. Tony Wagner et al., *Change Leadership* (San Francisco: Jossey-Bass, 2006), 10.
22. Drago-Severson, *Leading Adult Learning*, 39–45; Drago-Severson, *Helping Educators Grow*, 19–53; Drago-Severson, Blum-DeStefano, and Asghar, *Learning for Leadership*, 51–72; Kegan, *In Over Our Heads*, 137–334; Robert Kegan and Lisa L. Lahey, *Immunity to Change: How to Overcome It and Unlock Potential in Yourself and Your Organization* (Boston: Harvard Business Press, 2009), 1–86.
23. Linda Darling-Hammond et al., "Evaluating Teacher Evaluation," *Phi Delta Kappan* 93, no.6 (2012): 8–15; Bill Gates, "Measures of Effective Teaching," *Gates Foundation* (2012), http://www.gatesfoundation.org/media-center/press releases/2013/01/measures-of-effective-teaching-project-releases-final-research-report.
24. Kegan, *The Evolving Self*, 23–296; Kegan, *In Over Our Heads*, 15–352; Kegan, "What 'Form' Transforms?," 35–70.
25. Drago-Severson, Blum-DeStefano, and Asghar, *Learning for Leadership*, 116–123.

## Chapter 2

1. Douglas Stone and Sheila Heen, *Thanks for the Feedback: The Science and Art of Receiving Feedback Well* (New York: Viking Penguin, 2014), 4–6.
2. http://www.businessdictionary.com/definition/feedback.html.
3. Stone and Heen, *Thanks for the Feedback*, 4.
4. John W. Fleenor, Sylvester Taylor, and Craig Chappelow, *Leveraging the Impact of 360-Degree Feedback* (San Francisco: Pfeiffer, 2008), 1.
5. Grant Wiggins, "Seven Keys to Effective Feedback," *Educational Leadership* 70, no.1 (2012): 10.
6. Eleanor Drago-Severson, *Becoming Adult Learners: Principles and Practices for Effective Development* (New York: Teachers College Press, 2004a), 17–33; Eleanor Drago-Severson, *Helping Teachers Learn: Principal Leadership for Adult Growth and Development* (Thousand Oaks, CA: Corwin Press, 2004b), 1–35; Eleanor Drago-Severson, *Leading Adult Learning: Supporting Adult Development in Our Schools* (Thousand Oaks, CA: Corwin and Learning Forward, 2009), 1–60; Eleanor Drago-Severson, *Helping Educators Grow: Strategies and Practices for Leadership Development* (Cambridge, MA: Harvard Education Press, 2012), 1–58; Eleanor Drago-Severson, Jessica Blum-DeStefano, and Anila Asghar, *Learning for Leadership: Developmental Strategies for Building Capacity in Our Schools* (Thousand Oaks, CA: Corwin Press, 2013), 51–71; Eleanor Drago-Severson, Patricia Roy, and Valeria

von Frank, *Reach the Highest Standard in Professional Learning: Learning Designs* (Thousand Oaks, CA: Corwin Press and Learning Forward, 2015), 1–33; Robert Kegan, *The Evolving Self: Problems and Process in Human Development* (Cambridge, MA: Harvard University Press, 1982), 73–221; Robert Kegan, *In Over Our Heads: The Mental Demands of Modern Life* (Cambridge, MA: Harvard University Press, 1994), 74–330; Robert Kegan, "What 'Form' Transforms: A Constructive-Developmental Approach to Transformative Learning," in *Learning as Transformation: Critical Perspectives on a Theory in Progress*, eds. Jack Mezirow and Associates (San Francisco: Jossey-Bass, 2000), 37–69.

7. Gordon A. Donaldson Jr., *How Leaders Learn: Cultivating Capacities for School Improvement* (New York: Teachers College Press, 2008), 1–25; Thomas R. Guskey, "New Perspectives on Evaluating Professional Development" (paper presented at the Annual Meeting of the American Educational Research Association, Montreal, Quebec, Canada, April 19–23, 1999), 1–12; Thomas R. Guskey, *Evaluating Professional Development* (Thousand Oaks, CA: Corwin Press, 2000), 1–33; Jessica Blum-DeStefano, "Teaching and Learning with Self: Student Perspectives on Authenticity in Alternative Education" (PhD dissertation, Teachers College, Columbia University, 2014), 129–200, 225–260.

8. Elisa MacDonald, "When Nice Won't Suffice," *Journal of Staff Development* 32, no. 3 (2011): 45.

9. Richard DuFour and Robert Marzano, "High-Leverage Strategies for Principal Leadership," *Educational Leadership* 66, no. 5 (2009): 62.

10. Jenny Anderson, "States Try to Fix Quirks in Teacher Evaluation," *New York Times* (2012): A1, http://www.nytimes.com/2012/02/20/education/states-address -problems-with-teacher-evaluations.html?_r=2&hpw&; Douglas N. Harris, William K. Ingle, and Stacey A. Rutledge, "How Teacher Evaluation Methods Matter for Accountability: A Comparative Analysis of Teacher Effectiveness Ratings by Principals and Teacher Value-Added Measures," *American Educational Research Journal* 51, no. 1 (2014): 75–108; Kim Marshall, *Rethinking Teacher Supervision and Evaluation: How to Work Smart, Build Collaboration, and Close the Achievement Gap*, 2nd ed. (San Francisco: John Wiley & Sons, 2013), 19–85.

11. Marshall, *Rethinking Teacher Supervision and Evaluation*, 1.

12. Alyson L. Lavigne and Thomas L. Good, *Improving Teaching Through Observation and Feedback: Beyond State and Federal Mandates* (New York: Routledge, 2015).

13. Jenny Anderson, "States Try to Fix Quirks in Teacher Evaluations," *New York Times*, February 19, 2012, http://www.nytimes.com/2012/02/20/education /states-address-problems-with-teacher-evaluations.html.

14. Janet Looney, "Developing High-Quality Teachers: Teacher Evaluation for Improvement," *European Journal of Education* 46, no. 4 (2011): 440–450.

15. Harris, Ingle, and Rutledge, "How Teacher Evaluation Methods Matter," 75–108; Heather C. Hill and Pam Grossman, "Learning from Teacher Observations: Challenges and Opportunities Posed by New Teacher Evaluation Systems," *Harvard Educational Review* 83, no. 2 (2013): 371–380.

16. Charlotte Danielson, "Evaluations That Help Teachers Learn," *Educational Leadership* 68, no. 4 (2011): 38–39.

17. Ibid.

18. Ibid., 38.

19. MacDonald, "When Nice Won't Suffice," 45.
20. Ibid., 45.
21. Ibid.
22. Betty Achinstein, "Conflict Amid Community: The Micropolitics of Teacher Collaboration," *Teachers College Record* 104, no. 3 (2002): 421–425; Sandra Crespo, "Elementary Teacher Talk in Mathematics Study Groups," *Educational Studies in Mathematics* 63, no. 1 (2006): 29–48; Marnie Curry, "Critical Friends Groups: The Possibilities and Limitations Embedded in Teacher Professional Communities Aimed at Instructional Improvement and School Reform," *Teachers College Record* 110, no. 4 (2008): 733–768; MacDonald, "When Nice Won't Suffice," 45–47; Lorraine M. Males, Samuel Otten, and Beth A. Herbel-Eisenmann, "Challenges of Critical Colleagueship: Examining and Reflecting on Mathematics Teacher Study Group Study Interactions," *Journal of Mathematics Teacher Education* 13, no. 6 (2010): 459–465; David Slavit and Tamara H. Nelson, "Collaborative Teacher Inquiry as a Tool for Building Theory on the Development and Use of Rich Mathematical Tasks," *Journal of Mathematics Teacher Education* 13, no. 3 (2010): 201–217; Stephen Sawchuck, "Teachers' Ratings Still High Despite New Measures: Changes to Evaluation Systems Yield Only Subtle Differences," *Education Week* 32, no. 20 (2013), http://www.edweek.org/ew/articles/2013/02/06/20evaluate_ep.h32.html
23. Stone and Heen, *Thanks for the Feedback*, 5.
24. Kegan, *In Over Our Heads*, 307–333; Kegan, "What 'Form' Transforms," 40–62; Robert Kegan and Lisa L. Lahey, *Immunity to Change: How to Overcome It and Unlock Potential in Yourself and Your Organization* (Boston: Harvard Business Press, 2009), 11–59.
25. Stone and Heen, *Thanks for the Feedback*, 15–28.
26. Carol Dweck, *Mindset: The New Psychology of Success* (New York: Random House, 2006), 3–44.
27. Stone and Heen, *Thanks for the Feedback*, 192.
28. Susan M. Brookhart, *How to Give Effective Feedback to Your Students* (Alexandria, VA: ASCD, 2008), 1–57; Raoul J. Buron and Dana McDonald-Mann, *Giving Feedback to Subordinates* (Center for Creative Leadership, 1999), 1–23; Linda G. Cheliotes and Marceta F. Reilly, *Coaching Conversations: Transforming Your School One Conversation at a Time* (Thousand Oaks, CA: Corwin Press, 2010), 63–77; Linda G. Cheliotes and Marceta A. Reilly, *Opening the Doors to Coaching Conversations* (Thousand Oaks, CA: Corwin Press, 2012), 75–88.
29. Brookhart, *How to Give Effective Feedback to Your Students*.
30. Buron and McDonald-Mann, *Giving Feedback to Subordinates*, 2–22; "Communication Skills Training," *Mind Tools*, http://www.mindtools.com/page8.html; Jane Ellison and Carolee Hayes, *Effective School Leadership: Developing Principals Through Cognitive Coaching* (Lanham, MD: Rowman & Littlefield, 2013), 1–24; Stone and Heen, *Thanks for the Feedback*, 29–102; Sloan R. Weitzel, *Feedback That Works: How to Build and Deliver Your Message*, vol. 88 (Greensboro, NC: Center for Creative Leadership, 2007).
31. Bill Gates, "Measures of Effective Teaching," *Bill and Melinda Gates Foundation*, 2012, http://www.gatesfoundation.org/media-center/press-releases/2013/01/measures-of-effective-teaching-project-releases-final-research-report; Harris,

Ingle, and Rutledge, "How Teacher Evaluation Methods Matter," 75–108; Weitzel, *Feedback That Works*, 2–15.

32. Stone and Heen, *Thanks for the Feedback*, 70.

33. Arnold B. Bakker and Wilmar B. Schaufeli, "Positive Organizational Behavior: Engaged Employees in Flourishing Organizations," *Journal of Organizational Behavior* 29, no. 2 (2008): 147–151; Buron and McDonald-Mann, *Giving Feedback to Subordinates*, 10–19; "Communication Skills Training," http://www .mindtools.com/page8.html; Barbara L. Fredrickson and Marcial F. Losada, "Positive Affect and the Complex Dynamics of Human Flourishing," *American Psychologist* 60, no. 7 (2005): 687; Jacoba M. Lilius et al., "The Contours and Consequences of Compassion at Work," *Journal of Organizational Behavior* 29, no. 2 (2008): 193–213.

34. David A. Sousa, "Brain-Friendly Learning for Teachers," *Educational Leadership* 66, no. 9 (2009), http://www.ascd.org/publications/educational_leadership /summer09/vol66/num09/Brain-Friendly_Learning_for_Teachers.aspx.

35. Bakker and Schaufeli, "Positive Organizational Behavior," 149.

36. "Communication Skills Training," http://www.mindtools.com/page8.html; Marshall, *Rethinking Teacher Supervision and Evaluation*, 19–85; Jeannie Myung and Krissia Martinez, "An Approach to Productive Feedback for Teachers," *Carnegie Foundation*, 2013, http://commons.carnegiefoundation.org/what-we -are-learning/2013/an-approach-to-productive-teaching-feedback/; David Perkins, *King Arthur's Round Table: How Collaborative Conversations Create Smart Organizations* (Hoboken, NJ: John Wiley & Sons, 2003), 5–38; Weitzel, *Feedback That Works*, 16–19.

37. Drago-Severson, Blum-DeStefano, and Asghar, *Learning for Leadership*, 159–165.

38. Buron and McDonald-Mann, *Giving Feedback to Subordinates*, 4–9; "Communication Skills Training," http://www.mindtools.com/page8.html; Paul Hershey and Kenneth H. Blanchard, "Life Cycle Theory of Leadership," *Training & Developmental Journal* 23, no. 2 (1969): 26–30; Paul Hershey and Kenneth H. Blanchard, *Management of Organizational Behavior: Utilizing Human Resources* 4th ed. (Englewood Cliffs, NJ: Prentice Hall, Inc., 2012), 10–16; Grant Wiggins, "Seven Keys to Effective Feedback," *Feedback* 70, no. 1 (2012), 10–16.

39. Grant, "Seven Keys to Effective Feedback," 10–15.

40. Danielson, "Evaluations That Help Teachers Learn," 35–38.

41. Marshall, *Rethinking Teacher Supervision and Evaluation: How to Work Smart, Build Collaboration, and Close the Achievement Gap*, 36–48; Weitzel, *Feedback That Works: How to Build and Deliver Your Message*, 5–13; Wiggins, "Seven Keys to Effective Feedback," 10–14.

42. Danielson, "Evaluations That Help Teachers Learn," 35–38; Richard F. Elmore, *Agency, Reciprocity, and Accountability in Democratic Education* (New York: Oxford University Press, 2005), 277–299; Richard F. Elmore, "Leadership as the Practice of Improvement," *Improving School Leadership* 2 (2008): 37–55; Marshall, *Rethinking Teacher Supervision and Evaluation*, 43–85.

43. Peter R. Garber, *Giving and Receiving Performance Feedback* (Amherst, MA: HRD Press, 2004), 5–11; Perkins, *King Arthur's Round Table*, 25–38; Robert Ryshke, "Teachers Crave Meaningful Feedback and Want to Learn," *Southern Education Desk* (2012), http://www.southerneddesk.org/?p=2284.

44. Drago-Severson, *Helping Teachers Learn*, 1–35; Drago-Severson, *Leading Adult Learning*, 5–60; Drago-Severson, *Helping Educators Grow*, 1–58; Drago-Severson, Blum-DeStefano, Asghar, *Learning for Leadership*, 51–70; Kegan, *The Evolving Self*, 25–113; Kegan, *In Over Our Heads*, 15–335; Kegan, "What 'Form' Transforms," 37–59.

## Chapter 3

1. Eleanor Drago-Severson, *Becoming Adult Learners: Principles and Practices for Effective Development* (New York: Teachers College Press, 2004a), 17–36; Eleanor Drago-Severson, *Learning Adult Learning: Supporting Adult Development in Our Schools* (Thousand Oaks, CA: Corwin/Sage Inc., 2009), 31–62; Eleanor Drago-Severson, *Helping Educators Grow: Strategies and Practices for Supporting Leadership Development* (Cambridge, MA: Harvard Education Press, 2012), 19–59; Robert Kegan, *The Evolving Self: Problems and Process in Human Development* (Cambridge, MA: Harvard University Press, 1982), 73–111; Robert Kegan, *In Over Our Heads: The Mental Demands of Modern Life* (Cambridge, MA: Harvard University Press, 1994), 136–305; Robert Kegan, "What 'Form' Transforms?: A Constructive-Developmental Approach to Transformative Learning," in *Learning as Transformation*, eds. Jack Mezirow and Associates (San Francisco: Jossey-Bass, 2000), 58–69.
2. Robert Kegan and Lisa L. Lahey, *Immunity to Change: How to Overcome It and Unlock the Potential in Yourself and Your Organization* (Boston: Harvard Business School Press, 2009), 11–84.
3. Michael Basseches, *Dialectical Thinking and Adult Development* (Norwood: NJ, Ablex, 1984), 2–36; Marcia B. Baxter-Magolda, *Knowing and Reasoning in College: Gender-Related Patterns in Students' Intellectual Development* (San Francisco: Jossey-Bass, 1992), 17–34; Marcia B. Baxter-Magolda, *Authoring Your Life: Developing an Internal Voice to Navigate Life's Challenges* (Sterling, VA: Stylus Publishing, 2009), 6—11; Mary Belenky et al., *Women's Ways of Knowing* (New York: Basic Books, 1986), 2–24; Kegan, *The Evolving Self*, 25–73; Kegan, *In Over our Heads* (Cambridge, MA: Harvard University Press, 1994), 5–67; Kegan, "What 'Form' Transforms," 35–70; Kegan and Lahey, *Immunity to Change*, 11–59; Lee L. Knefelkamp and Timothy David-Lang, "Encountering Diversity on Campus and in the Classroom: Advancing Intellectual and Ethical Development," *Diversity Digest* 3, no.2 (2000): 10; Lawrence Kohlberg, "Stage and Sequence: The Cognitive-Developmental Approach to Socialization," in *Handbook of Socialization Theory and Research*, ed. David A. Goslin (New York: Rand McNally, 1969), 347–380; Lawrence Kohlberg, *Stage and Sequence: The Cognitive Developmental Approach to Socialization: The Psychology of Moral Development* (San Francisco: Harper & Row, 1984), 5–23; William G. Perry Jr., *Forms of Intellectual and Ethical Development in the College Years* (New York: Holt, Rinehart and Winston, 1970), 3–12; Jean Piaget, *The Origins of Intelligence in Children* (New York: International Universities Press, 1952), 10–323.
4. Piaget, *The Origins of Intelligence in Children*, 1–20; Jean Piaget, *The Moral Judgment of the Child*, M. Gabain trans. (New York: Free Press, 1965, original work published in 1932), 1–102.
5. Carol Dweck, *Mindset: The New Psychology of Success* (New York, Ballantine Books, 2006), 15–18.

6. Dweck, *Mindset*, 15–22.

7. Drago-Severson, *Becoming Adult Learners*, 3–51.

8. Maria A. Broderick, "A Certain Doubleness: Reflexive Thought and Mindful Experience as Tools for Transformative Learning in the Stress Reduction Clinic" (unpublished doctoral dissertation, Harvard University Graduate School of Education, Cambridge, MA, 1996); Robert Goodman, "A Developmental and Systems Analysis of Marital and Family Communication in Clinic and Non-Clinic Families" (unpublished doctoral dissertation, Harvard University, Cambridge, MA, 1983); Kegan, *The Evolving Self*, 15–73; Kegan, *In Over Our Heads*, 3–37; Kegan "What 'Form' Transforms," 35–70; Robert Kegan et al., *Executive Summary: Toward a "New Pluralism" in the ABE/ESOL Classroom; Teaching to Multiple "Cultures of Mind"* (NCSALL Monograph #19a) (Boston: World Education, 2001a), 48–65; Robert Kegan et al., *Executive Summary: Toward a "New Pluralism" in the ABE/ESOL Classroom; Teaching to Multiple "Cultures of Mind"* (NCSALL Monograph #19) (Boston: World Education, 2001b), 1–26; Kegan and Lahey, *Immunity to Change*, 1–75; Lisa Lahey, *Males and Females Construction of Conflicts in Work and Love* (unpublished doctoral dissertation, Harvard Graduate School of Education, Cambridge, MA, 1986), 10–17.

9. Laurent A. Daloz, *Effective Teaching and Mentoring: Realizing the Transformational Power of Adult Learning Experiences* (San Francisco: Jossey Bass, 1986), 11–28; Carol Gilligan, Robert Kegan, and Theodore Sizer, "Memorial Minute: William Graves Perry Jr." *Harvard Gazette Archives*, http://www.news.harvard.edu/gazette/1999/05.27/mm.perry.html.

10. Drago-Severson, *Helping Teachers Learn*, 21–34; Drago-Severson, *Leading Adult Learning*, 36–57; Drago-Severson, *Helping Educators Grow*, 19–48; Kegan, *The Evolving Self*, 26–69; Kegan, *In Over Our Heads*, 3–37.

11. Kegan, *In Over Our Heads*, 10.

12. Kegan, "What 'Form' Transforms," 52–64; Drago-Severson, *Helping Educators Grow*, 35.

13. Kegan and Lahey, *Immunity to Change*, 1–24.

14. Kegan, *In Over Our Heads*, 188–197.

15. Drago-Severson, *Helping Educators Grow*, 44–45; Kegan and Lahey, *Immunity to Change*, 1–29.

16. Drago-Severson, *Leading Adult Learning*, 31–58; Drago-Severson, *Helping Educators Grow*, 28–46; Eleanor Drago-Severson, Jessica Blum-DeStefano, and Anila Asghar, *Learning for Leadership: Developmental Strategies for Building Capacity in Our Schools* (Thousand Oaks, CA: Corwin Press, 2013), 57–68; Kegan, *The Evolving Self*, 161–253; Kegan, *In Over Our Heads*, 73–335; Kegan, What 'Form' Transforms," 52–64.

17. Robert Kegan, "22nd Annual Conflict Resolution Symposium Keynote Address" (speech, Ottawa, Canada), January 31, 2013.

18. Lisa Lahey et al., *A Guide to the Subject-Object Interview: Its Administration and Interpretation* (unpublished manuscript, 1988), 3–125.

19. Kegan, *The Evolving Self*, 115.

20. Drago-Severson, *Helping Teachers Learn*, 22, 169, 184; Drago-Severson, *Leading Adult Learning*, 56–58, 12–13, 57, 310; Drago-Severson, *Helping Educators Grow*, 2–3, 20, 55–56; Drago-Severson, Blum-DeStefano, and Asghar, *Learning for*

*Leadership*, 34–35, 92–94, 128–129, 161; Kegan, *In Over Our Heads*, 62–63, 343, 347; Kegan, "What "Form" Transforms," 58–69.

21. Kegan, *The Evolving Self*, 115–132, 162–163.
22. Ibid., 116.
23. D. W. Winnicott, *The Maturation Processes and the Facilitating Environment* (New York: International Universities Press, 1965), 5–15.
24. Kegan, *The Evolving Self*, 116.

## Chapter 4

1. L. S. Vygotsky, *Mind in Society: The Development of Higher Psychological Processes* (Cambridge, MA: Harvard University Press, 1978), 86.
2. Eleanor Drago-Severson, Jessica Blum-DeStefano, and Anila Asghar, *Learning for Leadership: Developmental Strategies for Building Capacity in Our Schools* (Thousand Oaks, CA: Corwin Press, 2013), 91.

## Chapter 5

1. Robert Kegan and Lisa L. Lahey, *Immunity to Change: How to Overcome It and Unlock the Potential in Yourself and Your Organization* (Boston: Harvard Business School Press, 2009), 307–310, 318–323.
2. Jed Lippard, *Adult Developmentally Oriented Instructional Leadership: An Exploratory Qualitative Study of Two Principals' Efforts to Support Instructional Improvement Among Teachers Whose "Ways of Knowing" Differ* (unpublished doctoral dissertation, Cambridge, MA, Harvard Graduate School of Education, 151–153).
3. Karen F. Osterman and Robert B. Kottkamp, *Reflective Practice for Educators: Improving Schooling Through Professional Development*, 2nd ed. (Thousand Oaks, CA: Corwin, 1993), 1.
4. Kegan and Lahey, *Immunity to Change*, 308.
5. Ibid.

## Chapter 6

1. Eleanor Drago-Severson, Jessica Blum-DeStefano, and Anila Asghar, *Learning for Leadership: Developmental Strategies for Building Capacity in Our Schools* (Thousand Oaks, CA: Corwin Press/Sage Inc., 2013), 116–123.
2. Ibid.
3. Eleanor Drago-Severson, *Helping Educators Grow: Strategies and Practices for Leadership Development* (Cambridge, MA: Harvard Education Press, 2012), 12.
4. Carol Dweck, *Mindset: The New Psychology of Success* (New York: Random House, 2006), 15–22.
5. Robert Kegan, Lisa Lahey, Andy Fleming, Matthew Miller, and Inna Markus, "The Deliberately Developmental Organization" (extended whitepaper), *Way to Grow* (2014): 1–15.
6. Jessica Blum-DeStefano, "Teaching and Learning with Self: Student Perspectives on Authenticity in Alternative Education" (PhD dissertation, Teachers College, Columbia University, 2014), 47–48, 179–180.
7. Kegan et al., "The Deliberately Developmental Organization," 6.
8. Ibid., 1, 6.
9. Ibid., 1, 6.

10. Drago-Severson, *Helping Educators Grow*, 120–124; Drago-Severson, Blum-DeStefano, and Asghar, *Learning for Leadership*, 100–101, 120–122; Blum-DeStefano, "Teaching and Learning with Self," 180–188, 213–215.
11. Kegan et al., "The Deliberately Developmental Organization," 7.
12. Ibid., 10.
13. Drago-Severson, *Helping Educators Grow*, 86–88.
14. Elisa MacDonald, "When Nice Won't Suffice: Honest Discourse Is Key to Shifting School Culture," *Journal of Staff Development* 32, no. 3 (2011): 45.
15. Lisa Lahey et al., *A Guide to the Subject-Object Interview: Its Administration and Interpretation* (unpublished manuscript, 1988), 3–125.
16. Kenneth Leithwood and Doris Jantzi, "Collective Leadership: The Reality of Leadership Distribution Within the School Community," in *Linking Leadership to Student Learning*, eds. Kenneth Leithwood and Karen S. Louis (San Francisco: Jossey-Bass, 2012), 11–24; Anne Lieberman, Roy Patricia, and Valerie von Frank, *Reach the Highest Standard in Professional Learning: Learning Communities* (Thousand Oaks, CA: Corwin Press/Sage Inc., 2014), 15–38; Vivian Troen and Katherine Boles, *The Power of Teacher Teams: With Cases, Analyses, and Strategies for Success* (Thousand Oaks, CA: Corwin Press/Sage Inc., 2011), 5–20.
17. Eleanor Drago-Severson, *Helping Teachers Learn: Principal Leadership for Adult Growth and Development* (Thousand Oaks, CA: Corwin Press, 2004b), 69–136; Eleanor Drago-Severson, *Leading Adult Learning: Supporting Adult Development in Our Schools* (Thousand Oaks, CA: Corwin Press and Learning Forward, 2009), 71–148; Drago-Severson, *Helping Educators Grow*, 156–162; Drago-Severson, Blum-DeStefano, and Asghar, *Learning for Leadership*, 23–48.
18. Drago-Severson, *Helping Teachers Learn*, 1–19; Drago-Severson, *Leading Adult Learning*, 3–30.
19. Drago-Severson, Blum-DeStefano, and Asghar, *Learning for Leadership*, 77–216.
20. Kegan et al., "The Deliberately Developmental Organization," 13.

### Chapter 7

1. Robert Kegan and Lisa Lahey, *How the Way We Talk Can Change the Way We Work: Seven Languages for Transformation* (San Francisco: Jossey-Bass, 2001), 126–128.
2. Ibid., 126–127.
3. Ibid., 128.
4. Ronald A. Heifetz, *Leadership Without Easy Answers*, vol. 465 (Cambridge, MA: Belknap Press of Harvard University Press, 1994). 1–11; Ronald A. Heifetz, Alexander Grashow, and Martin Linsky, *The Practice of Adaptive Leadership: Tools and Tactics for Changing Your Organization and the World* (Cambridge, MA: Harvard Business Press, 2009), 8–12.
5. *Google*, s.v. "inquiry," https://www.google.com/webhp?sourceid=chrome-instant&ion=1&espv=2&ie=UTF-8#q=definition+of+inquiry.
6. Kegan and Lahey, *How the Way We Talk Can Change the Way We Work*, 133.
7. Ibid., 132–133.
8. Ibid., 133.

9. Carl Rogers, "Experiences in Communication," *Listening Way*, 2014, http://www.listeningway.com/rogers2-eng.html.

## Chapter 8

1. Center for Transformative Teacher Training, "Overview of the Real Time Teacher Coaching® Model," http://transformativeteachertraining.com/coaching_model.php.
2. Richard DuFour and Robert Marzano, *Leaders of Learning: How District, School and Classroom Leaders Improve Student Achievement* (Bloomington, IN: Solution Tree Press, 2011), 14–15.
3. Robert Kegan, "On the Hidden Power of Paid Attention: The Need to Know," *Andover Review* (1978): 24–36.
4. Ellen Goodman, "In Praise of a Snail's Pace," *Washington Post*, August 13, 2005, http://www.washingtonpost.com/wp-dyn/content/article/2005/08/12/AR2005081201386.html.
5. Eleanor Duckworth, *The Having of Wonderful Ideas and Other Essays on Teaching and Learning* (New York: Teachers College Press, 2001), 15–30; Eleanor Duckworth, *"Tell Me More": Listening to Learners Explain* (New York: Teachers College Press, 2001), 1–38.
6. Eleanor Drago-Severson, *Helping Educators Grow: Strategies and Practices for Leadership Development* (Cambridge, MA: Harvard Education Press, 2012), 100–104.
7. Alan Briskin, Sheryl Erickson, Tom Callanan, and John Ott, *The Power of Collective Wisdom and the Trap of Collective Folly* (San Francisco: Berrett-Koehler, 2009), 9.
8. Robert Kegan, "Empathic Listening" (lecture, Minds at Work [MAW] Coach Certification Program [CCP] Residency, Cambridge, MA, October 15, 2014).

## Chapter 9

1. David A. Garvin and Joshua D. Margolis, "The Art of Giving and Receiving Advice," *Harvard Business Review*, January–February 2015, https://hbr.org/2015/01/the-art-of-giving-and-receiving-advice.
2. Ibid.
3. James L. Roussin and Diane P. Zimmerman, "Inspire Learning, Not Dread: Create a Feedback Culture That Leads to Improved Practice," *Journal of Staff Development* 35, no. 6 (2014): 37.

## Chapter 10

1. Ronald A. Heifetz, *Leadership Without Easy Answers* (Cambridge, MA: Harvard University Press, 1994), 2–17; Ronald A. Heifetz and Martin Linsky, *Leadership on the Line: Staying Alive Through the Dangers of Leading* (Boston: Harvard Business Review Press, 2002), 1–31; Ronald A. Heifetz, Alexander Grashow, and Martin Linsky, *The Practice of Adaptive Leadership: Tools and Tactics for Changing Your Organization and the World* (Boston: Harvard Business School Press, 2009), 10–38.
2. Eleanor Drago-Severson, *Becoming Adult Learners: Principles and Practices for Effective Development* (New York: Teachers College Press, 2004a), 17–33; Eleanor

Drago-Severson, *Helping Teachers Learn: Principal Leadership for Adult Growth and Development* (Thousand Oaks, CA: Corwin Press, 2004b), 1–35; Eleanor Drago-Severson, *Leading Adult Learning: Supporting Adult Development in Our Schools* (Thousand Oaks, CA: Corwin Press and Learning Forward, 2009), 1–60; Eleanor Drago-Severson, *Helping Educators Grow: Strategies and Practices for Leadership Development* (Cambridge, MA: Harvard Education Press, 2012), 1–58; Eleanor Drago-Severson, Jessica Blum-DeStefano, and Anila Asghar, *Learning for Leadership: Developmental Strategies for Building Capacity in Our Schools* (Thousand Oaks, CA: Corwin Press, 2013), 51–71; Eleanor Drago-Severson, Patricia Roy, and Valerie von Frank, *Reach the Highest Standard in Professional Learning: Learning Designs* (Thousand Oaks, CA: Corwin Press and Learning Forward, 2015), 1–33; Robert Kegan, *The Evolving Self: Problems and Process in Human Development* (Cambridge, MA: Harvard University Press, 1982), 73–221; Robert Kegan, *In Over Our Heads: The Mental Demands of Modern Life* (Cambridge, MA: Harvard University Press, 1994), 74–330; Robert Kegan, "What 'Form' Transforms?: A Constructive-Developmental Approach to Transformative Learning," in *Learning as Transformation,* eds. Jack Mezirow and Associates (San Francisco: Jossey-Bass, 2000), 37–68.

3. Drago-Severson, *Helping Educators Grow*, 192–193.
4. Drago-Severson, *Helping Teachers Learn*, 103–120; Drago-Severson, *Leading Adult Learning*, 153–210; Drago-Severson, *Helping Educators Grow*, 152–160; Drago-Severson, Blum-DeStefano, and Asghar, *Learning for Leadership*, 34–40.
5. Drago-Severson, *Leading Adult Learning*, 93, 199–205; Eleanor Drago-Severson, Jennifer Roloff-Welch, and Anne Jones, "Learning and Growing from Convening: A Context for Reflecting on Teacher Practice," in *Uncovering Teacher Leadership: Essays and Voices from the Field*, eds. Richard Ackerman and Sarah McKenzie (Thousand Oaks, CA: Corwin Press, 2007), 333–350; Drago-Severson, Blum-DeStefano, and Asghar, *Learning for Leadership*, 45–47.
6. Drago-Severson, *Leading Adult Learning*, 93.
7. Drago-Severson, *Leading Adult Learning*, 199–205; Drago-Severson, Blum-DeStefano, and Asghar, *Learning for Leadership*, 45–47; Drago-Severson, Roloff-Welch, and Jones, "Learning and Growing from Convening," 333–350.
8. Drago-Severson, *Leading Adult Learning*, 93.
9. Ibid., 201.
10. Drago-Severson, *Leading Adult Learning*, 93; Drago-Severson, *Helping Educators Grow*, 130–132; Drago-Severson, Blum-DeStefano, and Asghar, *Learning for Leadership*, 97–98.
11. Ibid.
12. Rainer Maria Rilke, *Briefe an einen jungen Dichter [Letters to a Young Poet]* (Leipzig, Germany: Insel Verlag, 1929).
13. Robert Kegan and Lisa L. Lahey, *How the Way We Talk Can Change the Way We Work: Seven Languages for Transformation* (San Francisco: Jossey-Bass, 2001), 11–87; Robert Kegan and Lisa L. Lahey, *Immunity to Change: How to Overcome It and Unlock Potential in Yourself and Your Organization* (Boston: Harvard Business Press, 2009), 11–120; Robert Kegan and Lisa L. Lahey, *ITC Facilitator's Workshop: Guide to Immunity-to-Change Exercise* (Cambridge, MA: Minds at Work, 2011), 55–56.

14. Kegan and Lahey, *ITC Facilitator's Workshop*, 55.

15. In the purest form of ITC coaching, coachees actually survey those on their list of invitees to learn whether or not they feel the improvement goal the coachee has selected is meaningful.

16. Kegan and Lahey, *How the Way We Talk Can Change the Way We Work*, 11–32; Kegan and Lahey, *Immunity to Change*, 31–60.

17. Ibid.

18. Kegan and Lahey, *How the Way We Talk Can Change the Way We Work*, 47–65; Kegan and Lahey, *Immunity to Change*, 31–58.

19. Kegan and Lahey, *How the Way We Talk Can Change the Way We Work*, 67–84; Kegan and Lahey, *Immunity to Change*, 47–51.

20. Kegan and Lahey, *Immunity to Change*, 11–75; Kegan and Lahey, *ITC Facilitator's Workshop*, 6–59.

21. Kegan and Lahey, *Immunity to Change*, 11–75; Kegan and Lahey, *ITC Facilitator's Workshop*, 6–59.

## Epilogue

1. Robyn R. Jackson, *Never Underestimate Your Teachers: Instructional Leadership for Excellence in Every Classroom* (Alexandria, VA: ASCD, 2013).

2. Ferris Jabr, "How Does a Caterpillar Turn into a Butterfly?" *Scientific American*, August 10, 2012, http://www.scientificamerican.com/article/caterpillar-butterfly -metamorphosis-explainer/.

3. Ibid.

# Acknowledgments

_Gratitude is the memory of the heart._

—JEAN BAPTISTE MASSIEU

We think it a fitting end to a book about feedback to shine a bright light on the many giving individuals—friends, colleagues, family members, students, mentors, educators, and thought partners—whose wisdom, insight, and courageous sharings have shaped this book (and us) in important and meaningful ways. We hope you have known and felt our deep gratitude long before reading about it here, and we thank you—tremendously—for the gift of you in our lives. This book is a tribute to you, and an expression of our deep admiration for all that you have taught us and helped us to learn.

To begin, we are indebted to the many dedicated educators who have generously shared their thinking and experiences with us in workshops, institutes, university courses, coaching relationships, research endeavors, and professional learning initiatives in schools, districts, and other organizations. Learning with, alongside, and from you continues to be a privilege. We thank you from our hearts for the heroic work that you do every day to make schools better places for children, youth, and adults. We also express our special appreciation to and for the many teachers, leaders, and professionals who have participated in our longitudinal research, including and especially those who completed the feedback questionnaires that enriched our thinking and writing for this project. We thank you for sharing your wisdom with us; it infuses these pages.

We would also, as authors, like to express our deep gratitude to Professor Robert Kegan of the Harvard Graduate School of Education for creating his constructive-developmental theory and for all of the many ways it continues to inform and inspire our work, collaborations, teaching, and lives. Thank you, Bob, for all that you give to the world.

Together, we voice special appreciation and tremendous gratitude to Dr. David Severson, for his great and enduring company in thought; his

203

generosity of heart, mind, and soul; his tireless support of us and this work...and his stunning photography. Thank you for teaching us and for sharing your wisdom with us. You, David, are an artist and philosopher, and we are so grateful for the lifting wings you share so generously with both of us. You are beautiful.

We trust, too, that the following individuals and groups know why we mention them here, with heartfelt thanks and admiration: Matt Aborn, Dan Alpert, Mary Anton-Oldenburg, Anila Asghar, David Chojnacki, Robb Clouse, Kara Coffino, Tracy Crow, Claudia Engal, Howard Gardner, Bernard Gassaway, Anne Jones, India Koopman, Shana Lindsey-Morgan, Andy Malone, Kim Marshall, Pat Maslin-Ostrowski, Blessing Nuga, Christy O'Connor, Chelsey Saunders, Mike Scott, Josh Stager, TC Turtles, Len Wards, Bob Weintraub—and the inspiring students and faculty at Teachers College, Columbia University, at the Harvard Graduate School of Education, and at Bank Street College of Education.

Next, we express our deepest appreciation to Caroline Chauncey, Editor-in-Chief and Associate Director of Harvard Education Press. Thank you, Caroline, for your gracious and brilliant help, your enduring trust and support, and the many, many contributions you have made to this book. Your feedback is world-class, and we feel so very fortunate to have you as a trusted guide. We also express our deep appreciation for the entire Harvard Education Press team for their thoughtful communications, leadership, and expert support during all stages of bringing this work to readers.

In terms of additional acknowledgments, I, Jessica, would like first to express my enduring gratitude to my teacher, mentor, and cherished partner in this work, Ellie Drago-Severson. Thank you from all of me for everything you are and do, and for the honor of accompanying you in this most exciting work and writing. You *are* adult development, and I am grateful every day for the great fortune of our collaboration and connection.

I would also like to thank my family—my incomparable network of support and love—who have given me the roots, tools, and time to pursue my dreams. I know how very, very lucky I am to have my ever-loving and much-loved parents, Deborah and Richard Blum; my absolutely amazing parents-in-law, Linda and George DeStefano; and my dear sister and friend for life, Allison Blum-Kamalakaran. I hope, one day, to adequately express how much each of you means to me.

And finally, my acknowledgments could never be complete without special mention of my husband, George DeStefano, and our sons, Orin and Perry DeStefano. Thank you for being you, my true loves. May we always share and speak our hearts with courage and tenderness.

I, Ellie, would like to also express my heartfelt appreciation for my family, friends, colleagues, and partners in thought for their care and support, which have strengthened me in ways that are difficult to put into words. These individuals have strongly influenced the contributions I can make, and they influenced this work in powerful and inspiring ways.

I begin my private expressions of gratitude by voicing heartfelt appreciation for a few additional friends, colleagues, and partners in thought who have contributed to this book in meaningful and different ways because of their influence and presence in my life. I trust you know in your heart why I mention you here: Richard Ackerman, Janet Aravena, Bill Baldwin, Ira Bogotch, Judith Brady, Maria Broderick, Deb Brooks-Lawrence, Tom Buffett, Deanna Burney, Kirsten Busch, Chuck Cahn, Bud Drago, Carl Drago, Joe Drago, John Drago, Paul Drago, Eleanor Duckworth, David Eddy Spicer, Jane Ellison, Katie Embree, Susan Fuhrman, Sue Steubner, Monica George-Fields, Deb Helsing, Stephanie Hirsch, Tom James, Julia Ji, Susan Moore Johnson, Lisa Lahey, Daphne Layton, Sarah Levine, Jed Lippard, Andrew Mandel, Neville Marks, Victoria Marsick, David McCallum, Kathleen McCartney, Elizabeth Neale, Peter Neaman, Aliki Nicolaides, Lisa Pilaski, Julie Porter, Barbara Rapaport, Kate Scott, Hannah Sevian, and Steve Silverman.

I have had the privilege of longer-term relationships with many practicing educators from different organizations. I am thankful for all that they have taught me and continue to teach me as we strive together to create conditions supportive of adult growth and leadership development. I offer warm gratitude for the following organizations and the people behind and within them who have enabled my learning, including: the NYC CFN 108 principal and assistant principal teams as well as the assistant principals from CFN 107; Minds at Work; Teach for America and its SSLF program; Summit Public Schools; New Visions Charter Schools of New York; the Cahn Fellows Program at Teachers College; the School Leaders Network; the Executive Leadership Institute of New York (ELI), and especially the leaders affiliated with the Advanced Leadership Program for Assistant Principals (ALPAP); the Summer Principals Academy and Urban Education Leaders Program at Teachers College; the Near East South Asian Council of Overseas Schools (NESA); Learning Forward; the Bowman School; Prospect Hill Academy Charter School; and the network, district, and school leaders in New York State.

I also offer special and deep gratitude for two of my many teachers and mentors.

For more than twenty-five years, I have benefited enormously from the modeling, teachings, and cherished friendship of Professor Howard

Gardner of the Harvard Graduate School of Education. I consider myself blessed to enjoy the precious gift of learning from and with you, Howard. Thank you for so selflessly sharing your wisdom and your light with the world and with me. Thank you for your indescribable forms of support and for your presence in my life. Your teaching, modeling, and theories inspire my life, my teaching, and my commitments. You model goodness and inspire all who are blessed to know you. I am very grateful for your friendship and brilliance, and for the gift that is you. I hope you know how very much you and your presence mean to me. Thank you so very much from my heart.

Also for more than twenty-five years, I have been blessed with the precious gift of learning from and with Professor Robert Kegan of the Harvard Graduate School of Education. During these years, I have been the beneficiary of Bob's extraordinary gifts as caring teacher, trusted advisor, wise mentor, thought partner and collaborator in research, cherished friend, and treasured colleague. I have also benefited from experiencing firsthand how you, Bob, truly and ingeniously create holding environments. No words could ever truly express how grateful I am for your friendship, for your modeling, for your brilliant teachings, and for the gift that you are to this world and to me. I thank you, Bob, dear teacher, colleague, and cherished friend, for developing your theory, for the ways it and you have altered my life, and for teaching and modeling how to support adult development. You help me to understand better how to hold others, how to help them grow, and how to create conditions that support growth. I thank you for sharing your light, commitments, and ways with me. I hope you feel my deepest gratitude and admiration as I work to share light with others. Thank you from deep in my soul for all that you are, for all that you teach, nourish, and model, and for sharing your gifts. You are inspiration and light.

It is so very important for me to acknowledge and offer love and gratitude for my own beginnings. I pause here to voice my deepest expressions of love to those who most shaped my life and what I am able to offer in support to others—my family. My late father, Dr. Rosario Drago, and my late mother, Mrs. Betty Drago, have been my guides and finest teachers. While they have passed from this world, they live each and every day in my life and work. They guide me in spirit. With tender and extraordinary love, wisdom, joy, exemplary hard work, and care, my parents modeled loving, giving, learning, and leadership that continue to inspire and to hold me. It is on their shoulders that I continue to stand, so that I might see a little farther. Their love, their courage, their care, and their presence strengthen and live in me.

I thank all of my six siblings and their families for their love, for their presence, and for their support over many years. Thank you for all that you teach me.

And then, there's Jessica Blum-DeStefano, thought partner, cherished collaborator, and cocreator of this book. Thank you for being you, and for joining in *leading with love* and *care*. Thank you for the gift of learning with, alongside, and from you, Jess. In addition to being enormously grateful for our collaboration in bringing this book and its ideas to life for readers, I am equally grateful for our colleagueship, for our partnership, and for your presence in my life. Our collaboration—fueled by deep respect, reciprocal giving, and love—is testament to the power of learning and working together. Two turtles.

Words can help with capturing the gifts others have given toward helping to make a difference in this world, but I find myself writing and rewriting this final part of the acknowledgments. My final acknowledgment is one gigantic, tender, and enormous appreciation to you, David Severson, my North Star, partner, soul mate, and teacher. I could share more pages and many chapters of gratitude for you, and for your influence and for your selfless and tremendous forms of love, support, and care. Here, I offer a summary of greatest gratitude, David-Love. Please feel deeply appreciated for holding, supporting, and sustaining my life with your tender and attentive love. You and your love enliven me. You and I share the enduring commitment to building a better world. How does a person thank the sun for its warmth, nurturing light, and support to and for growth? No words could adequately capture the depths of my love for you and the breadth of my gratitude, respect, and care for you. Somehow and some way, I hope that you feel showered with gratitude of loving kind. Thank you for your faith in me and for belaying me each step of the way. Thank you for the impossible-to-describe love, gifts, sacrifices, and compromises that you so easily give each and every day. Thank you for the gift of you, the gift you are, your loving companionship, and your friendship every step—every day. David, thank you for your enduring love, for all that you teach me, for the many ways in which you help me to grow. YOU are light in my life. You are cherished love, angel, and touchstone. I love you and I thank you from all of me.

# About the Authors

ELEANOR DRAGO-SEVERSON is Professor of Education Leadership and Adult Learning & Leadership at Teachers College, Columbia University. A developmental psychologist, Ellie teaches, conducts research, and consults to school and district leaders, teacher leaders, and organizations on professional and personal growth and learning; leadership that supports principal, teacher, school, and leadership development; and coaching and mentoring in K–12 schools, university settings, and other adult education contexts. She is also an internationally certified developmental coach who works with leaders to build internal capacity and achieve goals. Her work is inspired by the idea that schools must be places where adults and children can grow, and she is dedicated to creating the conditions to achieve this and to helping leaders and educators of all kinds to do the same on behalf of supporting adults and youth. At Teachers College, Ellie is director of the PhD Program in Education Leadership, teaches aspiring and practicing principals in Columbia University's Summer Principal Academy and aspiring superintendents in the Urban Education Leaders Program, and also coaches principals, assistant principals, and teacher leaders in the Cahn Fellows Program for Distinguished Leaders. Teachers College has recognized her teaching with three awards. She earned her BA from C.W. Post, Long Island University, and her masters and doctorate from the Harvard Graduate School of Education, where she was awarded a postdoctoral fellowship from 1998 to 2001. Prior to her work at Teachers College, she served on the faculty at the Harvard Graduate School of Education (1998–2005), where she was awarded the Morningstar Award for excellence in teaching (2005).

Ellie is author of the best-selling books *Helping Teachers Learn: Principal Leadership for Adult Growth and Development* (Corwin, 2004) and *Leading Adult Learning: Supporting Adult Development in Our Schools* (Corwin/The National Staff Development Council, 2009), as well as *Becoming Adult Learners: Principles and Practices for Effective Development* (Teachers College Press, 2004) and *Helping Educators Grow: Practices and Strategies for Supporting*

*Leadership Development* (Harvard Education Press, 2012). She is also a coauthor of *Learning for Leadership: Developmental Strategies for Building Capacity in Our Schools* (Corwin, 2013) and *Learning Designs: Reach the Highest Standard of Professional Learning* (Corwin, 2015).

JESSICA BLUM-DeSTEFANO earned her PhD in Education Leadership from Teachers College, Columbia University, after nine rewarding years as a teacher and school leader in alternative education settings. Her research is situated at the intersection of adult development and student voice, and highlights the foundational role of individual identity, authenticity, and relationships for both students and teachers. Jessica is an adjunct instructor at Bank Street College of Education and, for the past seven years, has co-taught adult development with Ellie in the Summer Principals Academy at Teachers College. She is also a coauthor of *Learning for Leadership: Developmental Strategies for Building Capacity in Our Schools* (Corwin, 2013). Jessica holds additional degrees from Emory University (BA), Hofstra University (MA), and Teachers College (M.Phil.).

ELLIE AND JESSICA are cofacilitators of the Developmental Leadership Institute for School Change at Teachers College, Columbia University. They work closely together on numerous research, writing, teaching, and professional development projects.

# Index